PLAY INTERACTIONS

Summary Publications in the Johnson & Johnson Baby
Products Company Pediatric Round Table Series:

1. *Maternal Attachment and Mothering Disorders:
   A Round Table*
   Edited by Marshall H. Klaus, M.D.
   Treville Leger and
   Mary Anne Trause, Ph.D.

2. *Social Responsiveness of Infants*
   Edited by Evelyn B. Thoman, Ph.D. and
   Sharland Trotter

3. *Learning Through Play*
   By Paul Chance, Ph.D.

4. *The Communication Game*
   Edited by Abigail Peterson Reilly, Ph.D.

5. *Infants At Risk: Assessment and Intervention*
   Edited by Catherine Caldwell Brown

6. *Birth, Interaction and Attachment*
   Edited by Marshall Klaus, M.D. and
   Martha Oschrin Robertson

7. *Minimizing High-Risk Parenting*
   Edited by Valerie Sasserath, Ph.D. and
   Robert A. Hoekelman, M.D.

8. *Child Health Care Communications*
   Edited by Susan M. Thornton, M.S. and
   William K. Frankenburg, M.D.

9. *Childhood Learning Disabilities and Prenatal Risk*
   Edited by Catherine Caldwell Brown

10. *The Many Facets of Touch*
    Edited by Catherine Caldwell Brown

11. *Play Interactions: The Role of Toys and Parental
    Involvement in Children's Development*
    Edited by Catherine Caldwell Brown and
    Allen W. Gottfried, Ph.D.

PLAY INTERACTIONS:

The Role of Toys
and Parental Involvement
in Children's Development

Edited by
Catherine Caldwell Brown
and
Allen W. Gottfried, Ph.D.

Introduction by
Allen W. Gottfried, Ph.D.

Sponsored by

Johnson & Johnson
BABY PRODUCTS COMPANY

Library of Congress Cataloging in Publication Data
Main entry under title:

Play interactions.

(Johnson & Johnson Baby Products Company pediatric round table series; 11)

Bibliography: p.
1. Play — Psychological aspects. 2. Toys — Psychological aspects. 3. Child development. 4. Parent and child. I. Brown, Catherine Caldwell. II. Gottfried, Allen W. III. Johnson & Johnson Baby Products Company. IV. Series. [DNLM: 1. Child development. 2. Parent-child relations. 3. Play and playthings. WS 105.5.P5 P7215]

BF717.P5766 1985   155.4'18   85-7580

ISBN 0-931562-13-9 (pbk.)

Copyright ©1985 by Johnson & Johnson Baby Products Company.

Printed in the United States of America. All rights reserved. Except as permitted under the Copyright Act of 1976, no part of this publication may be reproduced or distributed in any form or by any means or stored in a data base or retrieval system, without the prior written permission of the publisher.

*To the many wonders and great joy play brings
to infants and young children throughout the world*

CONTENTS

List of Participants — ix

Preface
   Robert B. Rock, Jr., M.A., M.P.A. — xiii

Foreword
   T. Kerry McCarter, Director of Marketing, Child Development Products — xv

INTRODUCTION
   Allen W. Gottfried, Ph.D. — xvii

PART I — THE ORIGINS OF PLAY

Beyond the Ethology of Play — 3
   Brian Vandenberg, Ph.D.

**Child-Structured Play:
A Cross-Cultural Perspective** — 11
   Helen B. Schwartzman, Ph.D.

The Affective Psychology of Play — 19
   Greta G. Fein, Ph.D.

PART II — PLAY AND DEVELOPMENTAL PROCESSES

The Developmental Progression of Exploration and Play — 31
   ✓ Larry Fenson, Ph.D.

**Play-Language Relationships
and Symbolic Development** — 38
   Lorraine McCune, Ed.D.

Intrinsic Motivation for Play — 45
   Adele Eskeles Gottfried, Ph.D.

Computer Play — 53
   Daniel W. Kee, Ph.D.

Origins and Developmental Processes of Play — 61
   Brian Sutton-Smith, Ph.D., *Discussant*

PART III — THE SOCIAL SIGNIFICANCE OF PLAY

**Pretense: Practicing and Playing
with Social Understanding** — 69
   Inge Bretherton, Ph.D.

Pretend Play in the Family   79
   Judy Dunn, Ph.D.

Play, Peer Interaction, and Social Development   88
   Kenneth H. Rubin, Ph.D.

Social Class and Pretend Play   96
   Vonnie C. McLoyd, Ph.D.

PART IV — PARENT-CHILD INTERACTION IN DIFFERENT POPULATIONS

Caregiver-Infant Interaction: The Study of Maltreated Infants   107
   Dante Cicchetti, Ph.D.

Play in the Hospital   113
   Jerriann M. Wilson, M.Ed.

The Social Significance of Play   122
   Jay Belsky, Ph.D., *Discussant*

PART V — CONSEQUENCES OF PLAY MATERIALS AND PARENT-CHILD INTERACTION

Play Materials and Intellectual Development   129
   Robert H. Bradley, Ph.D.

Home Stimulation and Cognitive Development   142
   Theodore D. Wachs, Ph.D.

Parent-Child Interaction and Social-Emotional Development   152
   Leila Beckwith, Ph.D.

Mothers' Interactive Behavior in Play Sessions and Children's Educational Achievement   160
   Phyllis Levenstein, Ed.D.

Parent-Child Play: A Playful Evaluation   167
   Bettye M. Caldwell, Ph.D., *Discussant*

SUMMARY

The Relationship of Play Materials and Parental Involvement to Young Children's Development   181
   Allen W. Gottfried, Ph.D.

References   187

PARTICIPANTS

Leila Beckwith, Ph.D.
Associate Professor
Department of Pediatrics
University of California
Los Angeles, California 90024

Jay Belsky, Ph.D.
Associate Professor
Division of Individual and Family Studies
Pennsylvania State University
S-110 Henderson Human Development Building
University Park, Pennsylvania 16802

Paul S. Boorujy
Vice President and General Manager
Child Development Products Division
Johnson & Johnson Baby Products Company
Grandview Road
Skillman, New Jersey 08558

Robert H. Bradley, Ph.D.
Associate Professor and Research Director
Center for Child Development and Education
University of Arkansas
33rd and University Avenue
Little Rock, Arkansas 72204

Inge Bretherton, Ph.D.
Associate Professor
Human Development and Family Study
Gifford Building
Colorado State University
Fort Collins, Colorado 80523

Catherine Caldwell Brown
Science Writer
105 Somerville Road
Ridgewood, New Jersey 07450

Bettye M. Caldwell, Ph.D.
Conaghey Professor of Education
College of Education
University of Arkansas
Center for Child Development and Education
33rd and University Avenue
Little Rock, Arkansas 72204

Dante Cicchetti, Ph.D.
Associate Professor
Department of Psychology and Social Relations
Harvard University
1184 William James Hall
33 Kirkland Street
Cambridge, Massachusetts 02138

Richard L. Cook
Director, International Business Development
Johnson & Johnson Baby Products Company
Grandview Road
Skillman, New Jersey 08558

Judy Dunn, Ph.D.
Research Scientist
MRC Unit
University of Cambridge
Sub Department of Animal Behaviour
Madingley, Cambridge
England CB3 8AA

Greta G. Fein, Ph.D.
Professor of Education
University of Maryland
College of Education
Department of Curriculum and Instruction
Harold Benjamin Building, Room 2304
College Park, Maryland 20742

Larry Fenson, Ph.D.
Associate Professor
Department of Psychology
San Diego State University
San Diego, California 92120

Adele Eskeles Gottfried, Ph.D.
Professor
Department of Educational Psychology
California State University, Northridge
Northridge, California 91330

Allen W. Gottfried, Ph.D.
Associate Professor of Psychology and Pediatrics
Department of Psychology
California State University
State College Boulevard
Fullerton, California 92634

John D. Hall
Product Director, Direct Marketing
Child Development Products
Johnson & Johnson Baby Products
  Company
Grandview Road
Skillman, New Jersey 08558

Florence Helitzer
Science Writer
59 Harrison Street
Princeton, New Jersey 08540

Daniel W. Kee, Ph.D.
Associate Professor
Department of Psychology
California State University, Fullerton
Fullerton, California 92634

Phyllis Levenstein, Ed.D.
Adjunct Associate Professor
Social Sciences Interdisciplinary Program
State University of New York at
  Stony Brook
Executive Office, Verbal Interaction
  Project, Inc.
3268 Island Road
Wantagh, New York 11793

Carla G. Lounsbury
Sales Promotion Manager
Johnson & Johnson Baby Products
  Company
Grandview Road
Skillman, New Jersey 08558

T. Kerry McCarter
Director of Marketing
Child Development Products
Johnson & Johnson Baby Products
  Company
Grandview Road
Skillman, New Jersey 08558

Lorraine McCune, Ed.D.
Associate Professor
Education/Psychology Department
Rutgers University
Graduate School of Education
10 Seminary Place
New Brunswick, New Jersey 08903

Vonnie C. McLoyd, Ph.D.
Associate Professor of Psychology
Mason Hall
University of Michigan
Ann Arbor, Michigan 48109

Bonnie J. Petrauskas
Professional Relations
Johnson & Johnson Baby Products
  Company
Grandview Road
Skillman, New Jersey 08558

Robert B. Rock, Jr., M.A., M.P.A.
Director of Professional Relations
Johnson & Johnson Baby Products
  Company
Grandview Road
Skillman, New Jersey 08558

Nancy Rosenbower-Musco, R.N.
Senior Medical Services Associate
Johnson & Johnson Baby Products
  Company
Grandview Road
Skillman, New Jersey 08558

Kenneth H. Rubin, Ph.D.
Professor and Head
Graduate Program in Developmental
  Psychology
University of Waterloo
Waterloo, Ontario N2L 3G1
Canada

Helen B. Schwartzman, Ph.D.
Associate Professor
Department of Anthropology
Northwestern University
2006 Sheridan Road
Evanston, Illinois 60201

Brian Sutton-Smith, Ph.D.
Professor, Graduate School of
  Education Building
University of Pennsylvania
3700 Walnut Street
Philadelphia, Pennsylvania 19104

Brian Vandenberg, Ph.D.
Assistant Professor
Department of Psychology
University of Missouri
8001 Natural Bridge, Room 224
Stadler Hall
St. Louis, Missouri 63121

Theodore D. Wachs, Ph.D.
Professor, Department of
  Psychological Sciences
Purdue University
West Lafayette, Indiana 47907

Jerriann M. Wilson, M.Ed.
Director, Child Life Department
Johns Hopkins Hospital
Instructor in Pediatrics
Johns Hopkins University
School of Medicine
600 N. Wolfe Street
Baltimore, Maryland 21205

Preface

Now that Johnson & Johnson has established a significant presence in the field of children's toys and play materials, we at the Baby Products Company often hear expressions of surprise that the company did not do so long ago. We are the first to agree that the marketing of toys is a logical extension of the Baby Products line and the company's commitment to infant and child health development. This was obviously a major factor influencing our decision in 1974 to enter the toy and play materials field. However, we felt our commitment to marketing these products entailed some broader responsibilities to children, their parents, and the child health care professionals involved in their care and education.

These responsibilities led us to spend the better part of five years in research and careful study of the developmental needs of children before marketing our Child Development program toy line. We believed it was essential to create design protocols which would meet children's developmental needs in an age-appropriate way. This belief led to what we feel is a unique toy development technique. Our research and engineering has not only designed a line of children's age-appropriate toys—which can be used differently at different growth milestones—but it has also coupled toy use with an educational information system for parents. This scientific approach has helped generate truly developmental toys. Research has demonstrated that these toys are at the innovative edge of product development for toy usage in terms of how a child interacts with his/her environment.

Earlier in our program, Pediatric Round Table #3, *Learning Through Play,* provided an excellent analysis of the nature of play and how its quality could be enhanced for the benefit of children. It, in effect, offered guidelines for parents and health professionals. Now, in Pediatric Round Table #11, *Play Interactions,* we have a state-of-the-science update by twenty leading child development authorities which rewardingly supports our basic beliefs. It underlines our emphasis on the contribution of play materials specifically designed to meet children's environmental and emotional needs, coupled with an educational system which tells parents and professionals how they can make a positive, age-appropriate contribution to children's development.

We hope that you will share our interest in and enthusiasm for this publication. It offers a comprehensive insight into the science behind what makes the quality of play interactions so important to a child's developmental environment.

Robert B. Rock, Jr., M.A., M.P.A.
Director of Professional Relations

Foreword

I am often asked, "Why is Johnson & Johnson, a child-*care* company, entering the *toy* business?" My answer is that our products *look* like toys and *play* like toys, but they are actually skill-enhancing implements! This statement generally requires more explanation — but not today. As experts in child development, you already know the importance of well-designed play materials to a child's development and how closely linked care and development are to the overall well-being of the child.

That's why Johnson & Johnson is pleased to sponsor this Round Table. As a company committed to children's well-being, we have a critical interest in the progress of child development research. We look to your work to give caregivers the guidance they need to ensure that every child has the opportunity to reach his full potential. And, practically speaking, we will look to your research to guide our efforts in providing effective supporting products.

Child development is a vital, exciting new field. By offering each child an improved chance to reach her full potential, a scientific understanding of child development offers us nothing less than a better world.

Yet this *is* a new field, born in the twentieth century. It is difficult to see where current child development research will lead. It is possible that thirty years from now we will look back and see the work discussed here as the vacuum tube of child development. It may lead to unseen frontiers, analogous to personal computers and satellite communications. Certainly, if anyone can provide breakthroughs, it is the group assembled here.

T. Kerry McCarter
Director of Marketing
Child Development Products

INTRODUCTION

Allen W. Gottfried, Ph.D.

Play is an intriguing, ubiquitous, and developmentally significant phenomenon. The nature of play, its determinants and consequences, have received scholarly explanation for a number of centuries. Over the years, scientists from various disciplines have asked questions about play ranging from the reasons for its existence and its meaning in phylogeny to what it tells us about the cognitive and social development in humans. Play is by no means a trivial and simple set of behaviors. It is a complex multidimensional sequence of behaviors that changes considerably in process and morphology, particularly during infancy and the early childhood years.

Like many other psychological constructs, play is easier to recognize and observe than to define. One of the major obstacles to deriving an established or acceptable definition is that no single behavior or set of behaviors encompasses the many forms of play. There is exploratory play, in which the infant or young child examines via manipulation the characteristics of objects. Functional play involves sensorimotor practice or what may be called playful repetition. In constructive play, the young child attempts to create something, such as pictures, forms, or objects. There is play that does not include objects and play that is object oriented. Object-oriented play may involve a single object, multiple objects, and combinatory object play. Play activities may be unstructured (free play) or under the organization of another person such as a parent or teacher — structured play. There is solitary play, parallel play, and social play. Pretense or imaginative play itself comes in a variety of forms. It can be verbal or nonverbal, solitary or social. There is also a mature form of play, common in older children and adults, called games-with-rules.

Although a definition of play is difficult to derive, there is consensus on the common characteristics of play behaviors (Rubin, Fein, & Vandenberg, 1983). First, play is intrinsically motivated rather than extrinsically motivated. Play behaviors occur for their own sake rather than as a result of external demands or reinforcements. Second, the focus of play is on the activity itself and not on the outcome or consequence of the activity. Third, object-oriented play is not simply exploratory behavior but involves what the young child can do with an object. Fourth, play involves the derivation or imposing of novel meaning on objects and events. Fifth, there is the freedom in play to be nonrule based, particularly in the case of pretend play. Sixth, in play, the young child is actively involved in the activity. There is a seventh characteristic I would like to add to this list, and that is the obvious affective component of pleasure. Pleasure is both inherent in the play activity itself and a result of play activities. This is evident in the satisfaction, laughter, and joy seen in children during and immediately after play. Hence, the young child is not only the director and performer of play activities but also a spectator who provides positive or pleasurable self-feedback.

Culture and family clearly influence the content and style of play. Toys, which are integral and important vehicles of play, and technological changes in society and education, have a substantial impact on children's play interests and activities. Within and across varying environments, however, researchers have delineated developmental progressions of play during the early years. These progressions can be briefly summarized: (1) from simple object manipulation to engaging in object relationships, (2) from actions with real objects to actions with imaginary objects, (3) from sensorimotor to abstract forms of play (e.g., pretend), (4) from self-centered play to play that includes others, and (5) from solitary to social interactive play and social pretense. In the progression of object play, initially the infant will reach for and manipulate a single object. Subsequently, the child will play with multiple objects simultaneously, for example, banging blocks together or using one to maneuver another. At a more advanced level, the child will display combinatory play with different objects in a spontaneous and appropriate way, such as feeding a doll with a bottle or shoveling sand into a dump truck.

Another transition, related to object play, takes the child from functioning with actual objects to activities in which the child employs substitute objects and then imaginary objects. This is known as decontextualization. Within the social realm of pretense, the child's play is egocentric or focused only toward the self, and gradually comes to include others. Upon young children's entry into toddler and nursery groups, there is another social progression that is so obvious. Initially, children's play is solitary and individualistic. In the process of socialization, children will engage in similar parallel play and gradually will participate in intense social interactive and sociodramatic play. It is noteworthy that progressions in children's play are not mutually exclusive from each other. They are integrated and to some degree confluent developments.

Play is a special interaction with the environment for young children. It is a unique way to learn about the world and a creative way to express their knowledge, enact their representations of experiences, and display psychological advances in many domains. The various forms of play and their progressions are highly informative in terms of what they tell us about developmental maturity as well as emerging functions. Evidence indicates that play is related to children's social and emotional development. It is an important indicator of children's language and symbol systems, and of the meanings children give to persons, places, and events. It is also an index of children's imagination, curiosity, motivation, preferences, interests, and persistence.

Since play contributes to and reflects so many aspects of psychological development, it is not surprising that play has numerous practical implications. Curricula in early childhood education programs throughout the world are built around play. Whether in structured, semistructured, or unstructured settings, play provides ways of evaluating parent-child and peer relationships, and of examining children's perceptual skills and motor dexterity. For a number of years, play has been a valuable tool in clinical assessment and treatment. Play is a rich organizing construct that has furnished a wealth of knowledge about young children's development.

This Johnson & Johnson Pediatric Round Table was devoted to play and how toys or play materials and parental involvement in the process of play interactions contribute to young children's development. Here, scholars had the opportunity to present current theorizing, speculations, and empirical findings on play. The Round Table was conceptualized into five sections: (1) origins of play, (2) play and developmental processes, (3) social significance of play, (4) parent-child interactions in different populations, and (5) consequences of play materials and parent-child interaction.

Papers in Part I address issues concerning the adaptive value of play and humans as myth-makers, the emotional basis of and affective template representation in pretend play, and the search for universal play behaviors across diverse cultures. Presentations in Part II deal with cognitive, linguistic, and motivational processes of play. The papers describe developmental progressions from infancy through the early childhood years; relationships between play and language with implications for symbolic development; cognitive discrepancy, competence, and attribution approaches to intrinsic motivational aspects of play; and the exciting new phenomenon of computer play. Papers in Part III elaborate the construct of play by examining the role of social processes. These papers focus specifically on social representation in symbolic play, play within the family context, peer play interactions in preschool settings, and socioeconomic correlates of pretend play. The papers in Part IV concern parent-child interactions and the applications of play and toys in clinical populations. Part V deals with interactions within the home environment. Extensive research programs on the cognitive, social, emotional, and educational outcomes of home stimulation and parent-child interactions are presented. Finally, the Round Table summary paper puts forth an integrative analysis of current longitudinal investigations in North America demonstrating that play materials and parental involvement are two of the most potent and pervasive home environmental factors related to young children's developmental status. This Round Table provides a comprehensive and insightful analysis of young children's play interactions.

PART I
THE ORIGINS OF PLAY

BEYOND THE ETHOLOGY OF PLAY

Brian Vandenberg, Ph.D.

When I first became interested in studying play, I felt that it was essential to explore the ethological and comparative research, whose main objective is to identify the adaptive functions of play. I discovered that the adaptive benefits of play are not obvious. No primary drives such as hunger, thirst, or sex are satisfied, and play seems to be the antithesis of goal-directed, problem-solving abilities that are so clearly essential to the survival of any species (e.g., Vandenberg, 1978).

This has led to speculation that the adaptive functions of play are more indirect. Perhaps, through play, important cognitive and social skills are stimulated that enhance the probability of species survival. Much of the research on play in nonhuman animals, and with humans as well, has investigated this indirect link, but the strength of supporting data is open to debate (Smith, 1982).

We confront a conundrum. We can assert that play has adaptive value because it exists — a circularity that is disquieting. Or we can argue about its indirect contribution to more obviously adaptive functions — a position that *begins* with the assumption that play is, at best, a biological epiphenomenon.

However, this conundrum may be the result of the way we have conceptualized the problem. Perhaps it points out the limitations of using a biological approach for understanding behavioral and psychological phenomena. Evolutionary theory, with its emphasis on adaptation, is the premise upon which ethological and comparative approaches are built. But what if we began our investigation of humans by asking, "What are the features of a being that is capable of creating a theory of evolution and interpreting the world almost exclusively from this vantage point?" This turns the process of investigation on end: Evolutionary theory, instead of providing the assumptive framework for gathering data, becomes an important datum in itself. The answer to the question, "What are the characteristics of a being that would create evolutionary theory?" entails a different approach to human life than does an ethological perspective. It also has very different implications for our understanding of play.

Myth and Reality

The datum of evolutionary theory suggests that humans are myth-making beings who create reality through belief in stories they have constructed about it. By *myth,* I do not mean "mistake," as the word is sometimes used in modern terminology, but myth in the sense of a lived-in belief system that orders and gives meaning to life. Perhaps the most pervasive myth of our culture is the myth of Science, of which evolutionary theory is a part.

We cannot easily gain insight into our own myth systems, and it is only when we come into contact with another foreign myth system that we can begin to see the relativity of our own. Unfortunately, we are prone to relegate the myth systems of others to the realm of fantasy, and to reify our own as Reality. This explains why it is difficult to take science or evolutionary theory as a datum to be explained rather than as a system for explaining.

Hypnosis and the placebo effect are two phenomena that give empirical support to the idea of humans as myth-makers. These phenomena have several important features in common. Consider the process of hypnosis: One individual, sometimes a stranger, frequently holding a position of status or power, skillfully tells another person a story about reality. The narrative is different from what is commonly considered reality: "Your hand is anesthetized," or "You feel no pain in your tooth." A similar process occurs in the placebo effect: A person of status or power leads the subject to believe that the administered treatment is a potentially powerful curing agent, when in "reality" it is not. In both cases, if subjects come to believe the stories, they respond as if the stories were true and thereby create the reality they believe in. I think this reveals a fundamental epistemological axiom of human functioning: that through belief in stories about reality, we create our reality.

Considerable research has been undertaken to identify the critical factors that differentiate those who can be hypnotized from those who cannot. The only factor that has been consistently found is the ability to become engrossed in fantasy (Bowers, 1976). Stated in a different way, those capable of investing belief in another reality are more hypnotically suggestible. In the placebo effect, as well, the treatment can be of benefit only when the person believes it can help.

Thus, the individual must not only possess the cognitive and symbolic abilities necessary to create and understand complex myths but also make the emotional commitment of belief. When all these aspects are brought together, a story has *meaning* for the individual. Through belief, a myth becomes reified, becomes ours, and gives meaning to our lives.

Meaning is related to hope. Hope is the forward-looking component to living meaningfully within a life myth that links past, present, and future. To lose hope, to lose the basis for emotional commitment to life, is to lose life itself. Indeed, the loss of hope has been cited as a cause of death among concentration camp victims (Frankl, 1959), for those grieving and loss of a loved one (Epstein et al., 1975), and for those suffering from a life-threatening illness (Kubler-Ross, 1969).

Children as Myth-Makers

The existing data indicate that hypnotic susceptibility is inversely correlated with age (Gardner & Olness, 1981). This suggests that as children grow into adulthood, the boundaries between reality and fantasy become more entrenched, and it becomes increasingly difficult to entertain, in a believing way, alternative myths. To function as mature adults, we need our myths. Children's reality, on the other hand, is much more labile. They can more quickly reinvest belief in alternative realities. While this makes for good hypnotic subjects, the permeability of the boundary between fantasy and reality makes confident action in the world difficult. The process of development could be construed, in this framework, as the process of becoming rooted in the various myths of the culture.

What might be some of the factors that affect this development? Increasing cognitive and symbolic sophistication enable the child to comprehend and use the complex myths of the culture. The other essential component, the investment of emotional belief in a myth, is facilitated by *trust* in the caregivers, which enables the child to invest confidently in the cultural myths that parents transmit. A strong sense of self and self-esteem comes from confidence in one's own efficacy within a trusted cultural myth system about reality.

Human Play

The view of humans as myth-making and believing beings suggests that reality, for humans, is a trusted fantasy. To be human, and to live in a meaningful way within a culture, requires that we live in and through a very sophisticated, abstract system that is largely imaginary. To be incapable of fantasy is to be barred from human culture. Thus, in fantasy play, children are displaying their human capacity as myth-making beings who create imaginary worlds that structure, energize, and give meaning to experience. The myths and fantasies of childhood are not eroded by the onset of logic and reason; rather they are replaced with more sophisticated adult myths about the importance of logic and reason. Ironically, the mythical belief in logic and reason by adults has led to the myth that adults have no myths. This perspective suggests that fantasy, not logic, is the fundamental adaptive attribute in humans.

Myth-making and believing, of course, necessarily entail cognitive, symbolic, and social abilities. But what is crucial is where ontological priority is placed. A biological framework of adaptation is likely to stress the primary importance of these cognitive, social, or symbolic abilities, which are enhanced through play. The perspective I am offering assumes that play is a manifestation of the fundamental properties of myth, and that cognitive, social, and symbolic abilities are concomitant aspects of myth-making. Put another way, the importance of play and fantasy are not to be found in their indirect stimulation of cognitive skills and problem solving. Rather, play and fantasy are central features of what it means to be human, and problem-solving skills are a spin-off of the ability to imagine.

The ethological perspective also has led to the term *practice play*, derived from watching young animals playfully perform actions that will later be used in serious contexts as adults. A kitten stalking and attacking a ball of yarn would be an example; its human counterpart can be found in children playing house.

However, the tense excitement that accompanies much of children's play implies that it is more than mere practice. For example, a four-year-old friend of mine frequently pretends that she is a cheerleader. She dances, jumps, and twirls in youthful imitation of her older heroines. Although we might be tempted to speculate that she is practicing a role that she may later adopt, it is unclear why she has picked this particular role to practice and why she plays it with so much gusto. A clue to a more complete explanation is that her mother was a cheerleader and has talked to her daughter about it. Thus, her daughter is attempting to construct a possible future for herself as she plays with a myth about maturity and adulthood that has been presented to her by her mother. In its meaning, its immediacy, and its emotional richness, her play is closer to hope than to rehearsal.

Many ethologists would be skeptical about using the term *hope* to describe practice play. Does it make sense to say that a kitten playing with a ball of yarn is involved in hope? But this criticism raises the question that is the focus of my discussion: What starting point should be used for understanding play in humans? The ethological approach is basically reductionistic, since understanding of human functioning is derived from an analysis of the lowest common factors among species. Such an approach, in my view, is likely to hinder our understanding of the unique features of human play. The approach I am advocating begins with an analysis of uniquely human features. This approach places ontological priority on the existence of hope, myth, and meaning, and makes these starting points for understanding humans.

Trust and Power

Trust is an important element in children's play. When infants play with their caregivers, considerable trust is involved. Adults are likely to toss the infant into the air, make ghoulish faces and emit strange sounds and shrieks, and play with parts of the infant's body. This is playful for the infant because it is incongruent *and* because it is done with a trusted caregiver. If such activities were performed by a stranger, the infant would become extremely frightened. This type of play brings the infant to the edge of terror. It introduces new realities that can be safely embraced because of the trust between the adult and the infant. Such play reinforces the link between child and parent, thereby strengthening the child's grounding in the parents' myth world. At the same time, it encourages the exploration of new alternatives outside the usual rituals of action. In this way, it also gives tacit support to the growth of the child as a unique individual who will create his or her own personal version of the cultural myths.

Most of children's social play, however, is conducted with peers, not adults. Unlike play with adults, peer play involves a power relationship among equals. This can be both liberating and threatening. Brian Sutton-Smith (1984) has pointed out that the usual psychological theories of play present a middle-class, sanitized view of children's play. The darker, more hostile and aggressive side of peer play has been generally ignored. One reason we have overlooked it is that it does not fit our model of play as a stimulant for the cognitive, social, and symbolic abilities that are necessary to succeed in school. However, if peer play is seen as the siren call of individuality, as a place for negotiating one's identity with equals, then a different picture emerges. The sense of efficacy that peer play affords is sometimes purchased at the expense of adult norms. Indeed, it is the opposition to adult norms that gives some peer play its thrill.

Cultural Myths and Toys

Our culture is a materialistic one that places a great deal of emphasis on ownership. Status and identity are closely linked to one's ability to possess scarce, expensive, and coveted objects. Children do not escape this myth. Indeed, it could be argued that one's developmental status is, in part, defined by ownership of objects. A tricycle is a must for a preschooler; one's first two-wheeler is a major rite of passage; to be a teenager without a stereo is to suffer developmental arrest; cars are a prerequisite of the late teens; and entrance into adulthood is not complete until one owns a house. Within this framework, toys sometimes take on greater importance than mere playthings; they can also be objects of status, as the "Cabbage Patch Kids" craze has demonstrated.

To summarize, our understanding of play is very closely tied to the theory we adopt about humans. Ethological approaches, with their emphasis on biology, focus on identifying the adaptive features of play. The approach I have sketched suggests that myth, meaning, and hope are fundamental aspects of human life and that play is an important manifestation of these phenomena. At a more basic level, my intent has been to playfully examine some myths about play, and it is in this spirit that I welcome your comments and suggestions.

DISCUSSION

Greta Fein: I enjoyed your paper very much, but I'm dialectician enough to feel that hope by itself is like a dangling participle. Would you say that in order to talk about hope, one needs to talk about dread, or perhaps fear? I think they're inextricably intertwined.

Brian Vandenberg: I agree. Both of them come from the uncertainty of the future, at least in part.

Vonnie McLoyd: Brian, can you be more specific about the methodological implications of your argument? What are we as psychologists doing that we should or should not be doing as we study play?

Brian Vandenberg: For starters, I think we should shift play from an independent to a dependent variable. The frequent use of play as an independent variable reflects the underlying belief that it is a stimulant for other, more important behaviors such as problem solving and social skills.

Lorraine McCune: Whether we think of play as a dependent or an independent variable is a very interesting question. Personally, I think that we should be thinking of play as both a dependent and independent variable. In my own work, I think of play as an independent variable because I'm interested in seeing what it predicts, but I think of it even more as a dependent variable because my major interest is in how it reflects the underlying symbolic development of a child.

Judy Dunn: Do you really mean to reject all adaptive explanations of play, Brian?

Brian Vandenberg: Not exactly. I just don't think we have to justify play's existence by trying to find its adaptive function, because that forces us into a paradox and potentially gets us into trouble. We start our behavioral analysis of what's going on from the perspective of other species, which causes us to miss some things and misinterpret others.

Inge Bretherton: What you're saying, basically, is that it's a mistake to use animals as our models instead of human beings. But I think you could fit what you've said, as another layer, onto an ethological framework.

Brian Vandenberg: My point is that we don't have to justify the study of human play biologically. The theory of evolution is a very powerful myth, but there are other ways of looking at things. We can look at them spiritually, for example.

Helen Schwartzman: An adaptive approach to play may be partly an attempt to legitimize the subject matter. If we can tie play to this central myth, we can make it and ourselves seem legitimate and real.

Brian Vandenberg: The evolutionary myth is very pervasive in our culture. Corporate law, for instance, is based on the survival of the fittest.

Leila Beckwith: In your scheme, Brian, are there better myths and myths that are less good? Would you say that play, compared with other ways of becoming human, perhaps includes more hope and less dread?

Brian Vandenberg: I'm not sure about that, but I do think certain myths work better in our culture than others. In the United States we judge our myths in terms of science, as I've said, and also in terms of utility and pay-off. That's why we try so hard to find adaptive functions — an evolutionary purpose — for play.

Kenneth Rubin: Are there normal children who don't engage in fantasy play?

Brian Vandenberg: Probably there are some who are not vigorous fantasy players. I don't believe that pretend play is a necessary condition for normal development, if that's what you're asking. But imagination is, and to invest in a cultural myth requires an individual to be able to engage in fantasy, even though what we call it is reality.

Theodore Wachs: What I got out of what you were saying, Brian, is that one of the things that produces individual differences in play is the tension between cultural demands for socialization and the child's own need for personal control. This suggests that, in a sense, if you could measure the child's need for personal control, you could make predictions about individual differences in play. The question is, where would they emerge? Would they emerge in the absence of pretend play, for example, or in the intensity of play?

Brian Vandenberg: I don't know. I do clinical work with autistic or schizophrenic children, and their fantasies are very bizarre. They also engage in a lot of rituals, which may suggest that control is very important. It's a good question.

CHILD-STRUCTURED PLAY: A CROSS-CULTURAL PERSPECTIVE

Helen B. Schwartzman, Ph.D.

The study of unfamiliar cultures throws into relief aspects of one's own culture that are familiar and probably taken for granted. Anthropology is based on the premise summarized in the proverb, "It is hardly a fish that can discover the existence of water" (Kluckhohn, 1949). In this paper, cross-cultural studies of child-structured play are used to examine a number of ideas about children's play that are usually taken for granted by American researchers.

Child-Structured Play

I define child-structured play as the play (and toys) that children create on their own, often out of sight of adults. Team sports, board games, and other highly structured games, which adults introduce to children and which may require adult supervision, are referred to as adult-structured play. One of the most important differences between these two play forms is that adult-structured play has been greatly studied in laboratories, schools, and playgrounds while child-structured play has been investigated only infrequently.

The most extensive study of the child-structured play of Western children is Iona and Peter Opies' (1969) collection of English children's street games. The Opies collected and catalogued over 150 games that demonstrate what children can do using themselves as the major "implements" in a game or using very simple materials (cans, sticks, stones) and structures (walls, streets, fields).

The Opies also performed an analysis of games diminishing or growing in popularity over the last 50 years in Britain. This analysis revealed that the games undergoing pronounced decline were those best known to adults and most likely to be promoted by them. The games that were flourishing or increasing in popularity were those that adults did not feel comfortable in encouraging (such as knife-throwing, chasing in the dark) or those in which adults were least proficient (such as ball bouncing, long-rope skipping).

The Opies are particularly critical of the view that contemporary children can no longer entertain themselves and that traditional games have been extinguished or are in the process of dying out. They argue (and their collection substantiates this) that this is not happening but that it may become a reality, because

> nothing extinguishes self-organized play more effectively than does action to promote it. It is not only natural but beneficial that there should be a gulf between the generations in their choice of recreation. (p. 16)

In most non-Western cultures the opportunities for children to engage in self-organized play are greater because they are considered competent at an earlier age than Western children and therefore there are fewer watchful eyes on their behavior. Such cultures often see play as "just natural," as a behavior that does not need to be strictly supervised, organized, or promoted by adults. Though it may be actively discouraged in some societies (Feitelson, 1954; 1977), play is more generally tolerated or ignored.

Questioning Current Assumptions

When reports and examples of child-structured play in a variety of cultural settings are examined in detail (Schwartzman, 1978), they force us to question a number of assumptions about play made by Western researchers and educators:

1. *That play does not occur (or occurs less frequently) when children must assume childcare and other economic responsibilities at an early age.* The basic assumption here is that children must have "legitimate time" (Singer, 1973) or relatively long undisturbed periods of time for play, especially imaginative play, to develop. The ethnographic literature suggests, however, that children develop ingenious ways to combine work with play. For example, Harkness and Super (1983), in their investigation of a rural Kipsigis community in Kenya, found that "children's playing often takes place in the context of work." Kipsigis children might initiate a game of tag while watching the family cows, for instance, or climb a tree while looking after a younger sibling. Such

reports suggest that children who are required to work by their parents do not give up play but merely restructure it to suit the context.

2. *That children from "disadvantaged" families and/or less "economically complex" societies play less frequently and less imaginatively than children from economically advantaged families in complex societies.* This argument has been advanced by a number of psychologists and educators (Feitelson & Ross, 1973; Feitelson, 1977; Smilansky, 1968). However, studies made in contexts that are familiar and not threatening to the children (in neighborhoods as opposed to schools or laboratories) frequently do not reveal deficiencies, although they may show differences in play style and content (Schwartzman, 1984; Labov, 1972). These children's self-structured play is often highly imaginative and creative, unlike the stilted and nonimaginative behavior that they apparently produce when tested in artificial contexts. The design and creation of ingenious toys by lower income children and by non-Western children also demonstrate this point.

3. *That peer groups are natural and important socialization experiences for all children.* The research of Konner (1975) with the !Kung Bushmen suggests that peer groups, as we think of them, are not universal social experiences of children; they may even be maladaptive. Because of the practice of long birth spacing and the small group size of the Bushmen, children interact in multi-age as opposed to same-age peer groups. Konner argues that multi-age groups may be the more common experience for children over the history of humankind. Western researchers' ideas about peer relations in infancy and early childhood, he says,

> are almost entirely an artifact of laboratory investigations of childcare conditions in advanced industrial states. In this context we can begin to understand the bizarrely inept form of social behavior which we know in the laboratory and nursery as "parallel play" and "collective monologue." (p. 122)

4. *That children must have sufficient and appropriate space and toys allotted to them by adults to engage in particular types of play.* Play space, "toy ownership," and the presence of manufactured toys in a culture are assumed to provide the proper stimuli for play, particularly imaginative play (Feitelson, 1977). Early play reformers believed that there was an absence of play among urban immigrant and lower-working-class children in large American cities because they lacked privacy and space to store play objects. The playground movement developed as an effort to encourage proper play, discourage "rowdy" behavior, and "teach children leadership and cooperation, develop skills

and health, and encourage imagination and creativity" (Mergen, 1980). Play leaders who knew how and when to organize and structure children's activities on the playground were believed to be particularly important in achieving these ends.

In most societies children do not have their own private space (at least not interior space) or an assemblage of their own ready-made toys, as most middle-class American children do, and yet they are able to construct active play lives for themselves. Urban children in cities as different as Lusaka, New York, and Port-au-Prince transform various environments into play areas of their own design, employing apparently useless and even dangerous space and material (trash heaps, abandoned buildings) in very creative ways.

Child-Designed Toys

Children are able to use whatever materials are available to create a variety of child-designed play materials. The majority of descriptions of such child-designed toys are brief reports included in anthropologists' monographs. For example, Cora DuBois (1944) reports the following in her study of Alorese children:

> Children play a great deal. Girls emphasize food-gathering activities and cooking; boys emphasize hunting. It is noteworthy that the children have many games and toys, some of which are very ingenious — for example, a pressure squirt gun that is fashioned of bamboo. (p. 59)

Maretzki and Maretzki (1963) report that the children of Taira in Okinawa meet the "minimum of equipment" with a "maximum of inventiveness and enthusiasm" in their play. Stones, peas, or seeds may be used as marbles; empty cartons are trucks and boats; cabbage leaves become helmets; and bamboo pieces are daggers.

The fact that Western children also use natural materials as well as their own toys in creative and imaginative ways is documented to some extent in fiction and biographies as well as in psychologists' reports of their own children's activities. Though there is no systematic research tradition here, a variety of studies have been done on relationships between particular types of toys and on play environments (usually adult-designed) and specific types of behavior. In general, these studies reflect American researchers' and parents' interest in improving the behavior of children by manipulating the external environment.

The most interesting recent research on toys and their influence on behavior attempts to answer such questions as: Do minimally structured, highly ambiguous toys or objects produce more imaginative play? Do children seem to prefer toys that are minimally structured or highly structured? In a study by Pulaski (1970) it was found that children measured as "high in fantasy" preferred minimally structured toys (such as clay and blocks), whereas children measured as "low in fantasy" preferred highly structured toys (such as dolls and trucks). Pulaski also reported that children aged five to eight produced more pretend or imaginative stories when toys were minimally structured. My own research also suggests that preschool children prefer less structured materials during imaginative play. However, studies of young children (two-year-olds) suggest that more structured toys (highly prototypical or realistic) increase instances of pretending at this age (Fein, 1975).

Designs for Children's Play

Cross-cultural research on child-structured play has several implications for design (material designs and interactional designs). It is important to ask in formulating any type of design for play:

1. What type of play do the children for whom this design is intended naturally engage in most frequently? What type of play will this particular design support? Child-structured play? Adult-structured play? How does it do this?

2. Does the design promote resourcefulness, self-sufficiency, and self-organization? Does it encourage reliance on adults or highly structured toys, equipment, and space for organizing action? Does the environment reward or frustrate a creative and inventive use of materials?

3. Does the design promote peer or multi-age group play? Which experience do we wish to promote?

4. Is the design premised on any unexamined beliefs about what types of play specific groups (children from various cultures, classes, etc.) can or cannot engage in? How do these beliefs express themselves in the design? What will this design teach children, teachers, and parents?

5. Is the design premised on the idea that play should occur in a separate time and space from all other activities? Does such a design support a dichotomy between play and work, or between play and everything else? Do we want children to learn to divide activities in this

fashion, or would it be more sensible to integrate play and work? How can (or can) play materials and environments "teach" this view?

Paradox is itself intrinsic to play and I think that everyone who works with children's play experiences a type of "be spontaneous" paradox (see Bateson, 1972). How can we study, plan, or design for a type of behavior that is, in part, characterized by spontaneity and which resists deliberate plans, design, or organization? How do we encourage playfulness without preempting it? How can we "understand" play without missing the point?

DISCUSSION

Allen Gottfried: Some of the likenesses found in cross-cultural studies seem to be saying there are universals about play — a pleasure component, an imaginary-constructive component, a pretense component, and so on. I'm wondering whether anthropologists, who try to seek out universals, have also found any culturally specific or nonuniversal components of play.

Helen Schwartzman: For some of the reasons Brian Vandenberg talked about, I think it's most interesting to build our understanding of play on imaginative play which, as I read the ethnographic literature, is one of the more universal experiences you can find. Competitive games are a type of play that is not universal, though many of us in this society think that they are. As you say, anthropologists are particularly interested in developing models that are applicable around the world, and it might be a mistake to base them on a conception of play or way of playing that is not universal.

Jay Belsky: Have you found any consistent sex differences across cultures? Both the slides you've shown and personal experience in my household suggest it's the boys with the trucks and the guns.

Helen Schwartzman: When you look at an anthropologist's slides or photographs, you have to ask who's taking the picture and what kind of play and players does this photographer pay attention to? Based on the literature, it certainly seems to be the case that little boys are engaged in, or at least that anthropologists take pictures of and talk about boys engaged in, that kind of play more frequently than girls.

Dante Cicchetti: During research I was doing last summer on the development of peer relationships, I noted that some of our maltreated boys were playing "female" games, dressing up like women getting ready for work, for example, but they were also playing with guns. They'd be all decked out in female regalia and want to run with guns at the same time. The females also did "male" things, but far less frequently. It was striking how many more boys than girls displayed these behavior patterns. I'm reporting this because, if there are universals, one way to find out how universal they are, and how impervious to experience they may be, is to study pathological populations as well as other cultures, other social classes, and so on.

Helen Schwartzman: Yes. One of the values of doing that kind of research is that it changes your perspective, just as studying non-Western societies does.

Inge Bretherton: Can you tell us something about other cultures' theories on play? We've talked about the Western idea, although our ideas may be much less unified than we think, but have anthropologists studied other theories of play? One way of getting around our own myth-making and making it a little more complete is to find out what other people's myths are.

Brian Sutton-Smith: The terms they use for games and play are quite different in some places. They look at a thing which looks like the thing we've got, but their explanations of them are not the kind of explanations we give.

Helen Schwartzman: There have been studies of folk theories of play and children's theories of play in Mexico, in South Africa, and also here with American fifth graders.

Vonnie McLoyd: Helen, you mentioned in your paper that some researchers have reported instances in which parents of other cultures have discouraged children's play. Do the studies explain the parents' rationale? That should say something about what their theory of play and its role in development is.

Helen Schwartzman: The research that I had most in mind was Feitelson's. As you know, her work has been used to support the idea that non-Western or nonmiddle-class kids somehow engage in lesser forms of play, or don't know how to imagine or pretend.

Judy Dunn: In my own work and in other research done in England, it's been found that a small minority of working-class and lower-class mothers very actively discourage pretend play. The rationale is that they are agitated about the connection between lying and deceit and fantasy. It's very, very important to them that their children should not end up dishonest. They follow through on this as the children grow up, too. In seven-year-olds, pretend play is regarded as real deceit. But the children seem remarkably resilient to the parental attitude — they just go off and play with friends.

Helen Schwartzman: That's the point to emphasize: There is a difference between parental attitudes and what, in fact, the kids are doing.

Inge Bretherton: I think some middle-class parents have the same worries. I talked to a group of parents the other day, and they expressed many concerns that are usually attributed to lower-class mothers: the lying idea, the question of what should you do when boys start dressing up as girls and putting on lipstick and parading around the neighborhood, what should you do if your children pretend to shoot each other, and so on. These were upper-middle-class mothers, and they were very upset about some of these issues.

Brian Sutton-Smith: In some cultures, play takes place in almost a religious context. It's a sacral event, in contrast to the profane, the industrial, the obligatory event.

Helen Schwartzman: A work-play dichotomy, which is something I'd like to get away from, is found in some cultures but not found in others. In some societies, children learn that play and work are integrated as opposed to separate kinds of activities. In fact, in this society, if you go and look in work settings where play isn't supposed to occur, you find that it does occur.

Jay Belsky: Would you say something about what you're observing by watching adults play in their work and how that informs your understanding of children's play? In a nutshell, what does that perspective afford you?

Helen Schwartzman: When I was working for the Illinois Department of Mental Health, I had to attend lots and lots of meetings about a whole variety of subjects. I found myself noticing that the people in the meetings were engaging in playful activities that seemed very similar to those shown by children I had studied. That is, some of the things I saw in work settings were the same things that we had called play when children were doing them. Although no one in the setting would have called these activities play or recognized them as play, some people did talk about some of what they did as "dancing," so I picked up on that metaphor. I became very intrigued with how certain social forms that we typically identify as work settings, such as meetings, provide individuals with all sorts of opportunities to engage in pretense and play and deception, to say one thing and mean something else, and so on. A meeting can provide people with a setting for play. It's like a sandbox for adults, if you will. That's the approach that I'm trying to follow right now, in a nutshell.

Lorraine McCune: Can you give us an example of play in a work setting, Helen?

Helen Schwartzman: What intrigued me most was that people used the meeting form, which we think of as promoting instrumental behavior, for all sorts of expressive interactions. They used the content of the meeting, whatever it was, to tell stories about themselves, just as children tell stories about themselves when acting out play themes and routines.

Adele Gottfried: Any activity can be put on a dimension of playfulness and workfulness, as I see it, whether it is a child's play activity or an adult's work activity. What I see as most important is how much self-determination and interest value an activity has, which defines the playfulness end, versus how much somebody feels that he or she is being forced to do an activity, which defines the workfulness end. Just as work can be playful for adults, play can be workful for children, depending on the contingencies that are attached to the particular behavior or activity.

Helen Schwartzman: It's important not to define play and work solely on the basis of the kind of activity being engaged in. The orientation or approach that individuals take to the activity has to be included, too, and I'm happy to see that idea emphasized in your paper, Adele.

THE AFFECTIVE PSYCHOLOGY OF PLAY

Greta G. Fein, Ph.D.

It is difficult to find a notable developmental theorist who has not offered some observations about pretend play at least in passing. For the most part, however, these theorists were preoccupied with other aspects of development—such as the growth of convergent thought (Piaget), the socialization of mind (Vygotsky), symbolic action (Mead, 1934), or psychosexual development (Freud, Erikson). Play was not of central interest in these theories. Rather, a conceptual framework for one aspect of development was extended to another, which the theory was not initially designed to consider (Sutton-Smith, 1979).

Unfortunately, with the exception of Piaget (1962), these theoretical extensions were not based on intensive study of pretend play as it develops in normal children. Rather, these theorists used prototypical exemplars, often invented, to support their analyses. In a recent study, my students and I examined the pretend play of master players: children who, in the judgment of their teachers and trained observers, engaged frequently in extended pretense with their peers (Fein, 1985). In that study, we identified five characteristics or properties of pretend play that need to be considered in theorizing about the behavior.

1. *Referential freedom:* the pretending child's fluid relation to persons, objects, or other aspects of the immediate environment

2. *Denotative license:* the loose and uncertain relation between actual pretend episodes and the child's own past experiences

3. *Affective relationships:* the centrality of emotionally consequential aspects of living expressed in pretend themes

4. *Sequential uncertainty:* unexpected moment-to-moment shifts of action, affect, and scene

5. *Self-mirroring:* a reflection of the self in relation to other selves

The purpose of the present paper is twofold. First, I will examine previous theoretical accounts of these aspects of pretense. Second, I will outline some theoretical notions that might integrate current knowledge and pose problems for future research.

Pretense as Referential Freedom

A pretending child might treat a stick as a horse, a shell as a cup, or a doll as a real baby. A two-and-a-half-year-old might treat a mop as a fishing pole and then as an oar, the carpet as sea water, and a chair as a boat. How can this behavior be explained? One explanation holds that pretense simply reflects the child's confusion about the nature of things in the real world (Stern, 1924). In this view, the child who treats a mop as if it were a fishing pole or an oar is overextending the fuzzy and only partially formed concepts of fishing pole and oar.

Representational theorists take a different view. Vygotsky (1967), for example, maintained that the child who treats the mop as if it were a fishing pole or an oar, far from being confused, is acquiring the ability to differentiate meaning from object. The action of rowing expresses the child's meaning of an oar as "something to move a boat," and the mop serves as a substitute for the object while referring to it. The extant evidence supports the substitution hypothesis rather than the confusion hypothesis (Elder & Pederson, 1978; Jackowitz & Watson, 1980; Pederson, Rook-Green, & Elder, 1981; Watson & Fischer, 1977; Fein & Robertson, 1975; Kagan, 1981).

Children who engage in high levels of pretense relative to their agemates are more competent and creative (Fein, 1981; Rubin, Fein, & Vandenberg, 1983). Referential freedom seems to mark children's representational competence rather than incompetence. One might even describe pretense as an orientation in which the immediate environment is deliberately treated in a divergent manner. Pretense neither reflects the child's confusion nor leads to confusion.

Pretense as Denotative License

Referential freedom refers to the pretending child's divergent relation to the immediate environment. By denotative license, I mean to suggest that the playing child also adopts a divergent stance with respect to actual experience. The pretend events generated by master players are inventions rather than documentaries of real-world occurrences, a read-out of what the child feels might be (some of which may have been) rather than an accurate account of the child's knowledge of what is.

A recent version of correspondence theory (proposed by Sears, 1947) holds that pretense represents children's knowledge of everyday events organized as "scripts." Several important implications of this idea are discussed by Bretherton (1984). A pretend statement referring to a restaurant, for example, would be understood by the players as meaning "This is a restaurant, and everything we know of restaurants applies to the actions we are about to perform." According to script theorists, pretend statements can be understood as statements "of" real-world events based on children's everyday experiencing of these events. Thus, pretend scenarios can illuminate children's real-world knowledge.

Consider, however, the following episode.

Sally (to Alison): Why don't you go and do your homework? You got any homework? You want to play with your teddy bear?

Ellen: No, she's being a bad girl today.

Alison: No I didn't.

Sally (to Ellen): What did she do?

Ellen: She picked up a knife. Was trying to kill her dad.

Alison (frowning): No, I didn't! I just maked a play one.

Ellen (warmly hugs and kisses Alison): That's O.K., then.

It may be helpful to note that Ellen's mother and father are divorced, that her mother remarried a few weeks before this scene occurred, and that Ellen's visits to her father in a distant city are unhappy occasions. But even though Ellen's past encounters with father or mother may have been the real-life materials from which this episode was constructed, the relation between past event and pretend episode is not one of literal correspondence.

In pretend episodes, children sometimes portray events they are unlikely to have experienced and persons, families, and family relationships that are unlikely to exist. Because of the apparent arbitrariness of the blend of real-life knowledge and imagination, pretend episodes cannot be viewed as literal representations of familiar routinized life events. Contrary to expectations of script theory, familiar event sequences appear either elliptically or in altered form. Further, children appear to exercise considerable denotative license in the meanings expressed in pretend episodes (Genishi, 1983).

Metacommunication theory offers an interesting alternative to the correspondence theories described above. Bateson (1956), commenting on the denotative peculiarity of pretend play, noted that "the playful nip denotes the bite, but it does not denote what would be denoted by the bite." He has suggested the idea of pretense as framed behavior. The play frame represents a kind of understanding by the players that their pretend behavior consists of statements *about* behavior, not statements *of* behavior. In this view, the players arrive at a mutual understanding that play episodes do *not* denote actual life events.

Pretense as Affective Relations

Divergent thinking is characterized by associations that are novel and original but not bizarre or inappropriate. In pretend play, however, there is often ludicrous distortion, exaggeration, and extravagance. Cognitive theorists have all but ignored the affective side of pretense expressed in the distortion, exaggeration, and extravagance.

Psychoanalytic theorists generally agree that pretend play is a response to internal or external emotional demands. However, they disagree on whether these demands come from specific past experiences and deprivations or whether they reflect more contemporary and generic sources of anxiety. For example, Waelder (1933) is responsible for the traumatic theory of pretense in which "excessive experiences are divided into small quantities, reattempted and assimilated in play." These excessive experiences are specific, disturbing events (e.g., a painful visit to the dentist) that are repeated and thereby mastered in play. The traumatic theory of play thus offers a special case of correspondence theory in which emotionally distressing, but actually experienced, events are rendered in play.

Other psychoanalytic theorists (Peller, 1954; Erikson, 1977) contend that play expresses the focal anxieties of a particular phase of libidinal development rather than particular life events. In Peller's view, these anxieties change with age. Early concerns about the body are expressed in play themes that deal with skill and mastery; these are followed by themes that deal with the pre-Oedipal mother (for example, the all-powerful mother who nurtures and restricts, leaves and returns); next come play themes that reflect the child's Oedipal anxieties; and so on.

Even though vivid life experiences may find their way into pretend episodes, Peller would argue that these experiences are converted into symbols conveying deeper emotional meanings. These meanings reflect general, age-appropriate anxieties that transcend particular life events. For instance, the child's anxiety about maternal separation might be rendered in a pretend episode about the mother's death, as well as in episodes about babysitters or going to school.

Unfortunately, attempts to examine psychoanalytic views have tended to dwell on the traumatic experience view (Gilmore, 1966). Some of the episodes generated by master players in our study were about specific unpleasant experiences (such as illness). Others were about happy occasions (weddings, dances, picnics, family cookouts). Most of the episodes were thematically fluid. Often, outer forms seemed to frame more basic affective issues similar to those discussed by Peller. Little systematic attention has been given to the notion that these affective issues reflect children's changing emotional preoccupations or to the possibility that pretense is associated with the regulation of emotion with regard to these preoccupations.

Pretense as Sequential Uncertainty

Garvey (1977) noted that children seem to have a repertoire of action plans that they use in pretend episodes. An action plan consists of a sequence of events or actions associated with particular roles in characteristic settings. One type of action plan might be "treating-healing"; another might be "averting threat." Once a plan is initiated, a fixed sequence of events unfolds. Because this sequence is fixed, other players know what their actions should be.

The following episode, produced by four six-year-olds, calls Garvey's notion of action plans into question. Rosa, the patient, has received medical attention from Cara, the doctor, and nurses Marla and Terry, for about ten minutes. Quite unexpectedly, Cara makes an announcement:

Cara (dramatically): My patient is dying.... Yes, I can see it. Nothing is getting warm in the body and she's not moving. (Rosa lies still with eyes closed.) She's not jerking. She's not breathing. What shall we say to her parents, and they're waiting outside.

Terry: Shhhhh. Let's keep quiet and pray to God. (She clasps her hands and on bended knees whispers) Please, please God, save my friend. She's a good friend. Please, God, help us.

(Terry tells Cara and Marla to close their eyes. She then mouths the numbers 1 to 10. At 10 she looks at the patient with an expression of joy on her face. Jubilantly, she tells the others to open their eyes.)

Terry: See, the chest is S-L-O-W-L-Y going up-up-down. God helped her to live again because we were all praying hard and we all worked hard. My mommy always says that God loves little children, you know.

In what sense does this episode illustrate an action plan? The theme of illness and treatment seems to call for a plan in which the patient either gets well, dies, or stays the same. During the ten minutes preceding the quoted episode, the patient stayed the same. Then Cara, without warning or negotiation, introduced the drama of death. Terry's marvelous response to the emergency is also spontaneous, a case of healing considerably beyond the medical situation prevailing until that point. In this example, all possible variations of the action plan occurred. The patient stayed the same, died, and was cured.

Rather than a general action plan such as "treating-healing," as proposed by Garvey, the previous episode was characterized by moment-to-moment improvisations. In an earlier article (Fein, 1985), I argued that in pretense, sequences do not occur in a fixed order and new themes can replace old ones without disturbing the play. The notion is that play is joyfully disorderly.

Pretense as Self-Mirroring

According to Mead (1934), the pretending child adopts a special stance toward the self. When children assume play roles, the events that unfold are essentially self-mirroring. The individual looks at a transformed self while retaining the core structure of a nontransformed self. That is, pretend play provides a vehicle in which the self, slipping outside the self, looks at the self. Mead believed that a self-mirroring system of this type implies the beginnings of conscious self-awareness.

The development of pretense as a self-mirroring system is the important issue addressed in studies of the transition from self-directed pretense to other-directed pretense (Fein, 1981). When pretense first appears, it is self-directed: Children feed themselves out of an empty cup or put themselves to sleep. It is only later that they perform these actions with a doll or a human partner. If these behaviors mark the beginning of self-awareness, they would be expected to coincide with the emergence of other behaviors thought to reflect this awareness, such as self-recognition (Amsterdam, 1972).

A Theoretical Proposal

Let us suppose that the pretending child is aware that the meanings given to objects in the immediate environment are counterconventional and that the experiences being rendered may be counterfactual, that is, may never have happened. Let us also suppose that pretense is essentially an affective, expressive activity, different from other affective, expressive activities because it is *about* affective states, not a direct expression *of* these states. These suppositions have implications for the kind of representational system needed to account for pretense and for the way this system functions.

I would like to endow the playing child with a representational system keyed to detect, pick up, and hold vivid life experiences. These experiences may be real, imagined, or derived from fantasies found on television or in books. Whatever the source or content, the experiences soaked up by this system are marked by intense feeling. Within this system, a separate template is reserved as a symbol of the self. This symbol, which mirrors the self as a pretend participant, conveys a consciousness of pretending.

The system I am talking about is designed to represent affective relationships such as "anger at," "fear of," "love for," "approval of," and also more subtle feelings about power and helplessness, safety and danger. It records subjective rather than objective information. Thus, pretend play provides clues about the child's inner world, but it does not reveal what the child's actual, observable world is like, what the child knows about this world, or what the child can do with it.

Because this affective symbol system represents real or imagined experience at a fairly general level, it permits children considerable latitude as to particulars. Although play partners may have had little real experience with each other's particulars, they are able to understand general affective meanings and improvise the details as they go along. In fact, the details do not matter so long as they fit reasonably well with the affective meaning being expressed.

Affective representational templates differ qualitatively and structurally from those associated with declarative and procedural knowledge (Mandler, 1983). Moreover, these templates play no direct role in the acquisition or application of convergent knowledge. Rather, affective templates permit children to think about emotionally important things—pleasant things and nasty things, satisfying things and confusing things. In pretend play, children are thinking out loud and sometimes together about experiences that have emotional meaning for them.

In effect, I am proposing a double-layered system of representation, one for practical knowledge and another for affective knowledge. This double-layered system emerges during the third year of life as pretend sequences become increasingly marked by nonstereotyped, personal, counterfactual inventions. I am also suggesting that this affective system is essential for an individual to become conscious of an inner life and to gain control over its expression. Pretense is about emotion, decontextualized from immediate, authentic, gut responses and, importantly, uncoupled from the actual experiences and settings in which these gut responses are likely to occur.

The theoretical framework summarized here integrates several research areas, generates testable hypotheses, and identifies new areas of inquiry. While the particular theoretical fictions proposed may need to be revised, refined, or abandoned in response to future research, attention to the affective power of pretense is long overdue.

DISCUSSION

Inge Bretherton: I'd like to know a little more about the idea of affective symbols, which is very interesting.

Greta Fein: The distinction between decontextualizing and uncoupling is very important theoretically. Decontextualizing alters the playing child's relation to the immediate environment; uncoupling alters the child's relation to actual experience. This distinction pertains to the affective symbol system. Positing such a system permits us to integrate pretend play research with psychoanalytic theory. Peller has given us suggestive clues about universal affective themes that may very well not be culture-specific. These themes reflect emotional-affective issues that children face in growing up no matter where they live. I think we can take Peller's suggestions and translate them into observables. We can also generate hypotheses, as I tried to do in the paper, about the *origins* of pretend play, and we can make those hypotheses fairly theory-specific. In our field I'm not sure we can ever talk about grand theory, but I think we can develop useful constructs that are a bit better than heuristics, and this is what I'm proposing.

Inge Bretherton: You described some very highly charged affective stories by your master players. Perhaps it's the feelings, the affect in the stories that children play out, that really relate to the myths we talked about earlier.

Greta Fein: Pretend play involves highly charged affect, but I'm not sure play episodes should be seen as either "action plans" or a story. Pretend play can be given story form, but I think that's an operation on the feeling. In other words, I think we're talking about bottom-up processing, not top-down processing.

Brian Sutton-Smith: It depends on what you mean by a story. In an adult story you need a hero, a tale, and so on, but little children just need a climax, a separation, say, to make a story.

Greta Fein: At this point I would like not to impose too much structure on the product of pretending. I think that if we begin to treat it as a structured product — a "story" — we'll move away from emphasis on the freedom, the license, that children exercise. If you want to define a story as anything that links one concept with another, I'll say sure. But I don't want to compare pretend in any way to a formal narrative that has logic and coherence.

Brian Sutton-Smith: That doesn't have to be implied in the story metaphor. For example, highly exciting minimal units are still a part of narrative theory about stories, and they're the kind that little children produce. Other kinds are produced, say, in Indian folktales: very bizarre units, not logical or rational.

Lorraine McCune: I think what your paper addresses, and also what some of Inge Bretherton's paper addresses, is the question of how children construct the knowledge base from which they operate in pretense and, secondly, how they draw on that knowledge base in constructing their pretend games. The background here is script theory, which has had such a strong influence on the way people have looked at play during the last few years. The way I read Inge as looking at script theory is that there is something children know about situations that they construct through a lot of experience. When they draw on it, do they play it out as a story? No, not necessarily, as your examples document very nicely. Even with the two-year-olds that I observe, a 20- or 30-part play scene between a mother and a child might include only seven play acts. They just keep cycling through them, in varying orders.

What we come back to is, does script theory help us at all with respect to this? I mean, we have the question of how they construct the knowledge and how they draw on it, and people have been putting script theory in the middle and saying, okay, this will help us out, and once we've said this, we know something. But I don't really know if we do or we don't.

Greta Fein: I'm increasingly beginning to feel that not only will it not help us out, it is going to hinder us. It's going to pull us towards imposing upon pretend play a convergent model of thinking. And I think that is a deprivation, a failure to get from pretend the kind of thing that we're missing, which is a deeper understanding of children's affective life. What makes pretend exciting is that it provides us with access to this affective life — to vivid, extraordinary, important, emotional experiences. We tend to convert everything we touch into logical formalisms, and so script theory becomes very appealing. It's got this nice computer model, and it seems that by using it we can solve all our problems. But I don't think we will solve them at all. I think we'll simply delay the reckoning, and it's a pity to do that with pretend play.

Kenneth Rubin: The scripts that I've seen in children's play are not based on "reality" at all. The roles are determined by dominant status in the group, by friendship, by social factors. The scripts are determined by familiarity of the participants with the themes, and the episode that we labeled play is framed by these social-relational factors. What is scripted are the roles that the children are playing, based on the relations that they have with peers.

PART II
PLAY AND DEVELOPMENTAL PROCESSES

THE DEVELOPMENTAL PROGRESSION OF EXPLORATION AND PLAY

Larry Fenson, Ph.D.

Newborn babies enter the world with a range of reflexive behaviors, such as orienting, sucking, and startle responses, but they have no knowledge of the world they encounter. Largely through their playful transactions with people and objects, they gain information about physical and social aspects of their environment. At first, these transactions are mainly visual, but at about five months of age manipulative investigation begins to combine with visual exploration, vastly enhancing the range of sensorimotor experiences. By the end of the first year of life, pretend play is added to visual exploration and manipulative investigation.

Researchers have found it convenient to look at these three types of play in relative isolation, and I respect these distinctions in the present paper. Thus, I consider, in turn, developmental changes in visual exploration, manipulative investigation, and pretend play. The reader should remember, however, that these behaviors generally occur together in the playing child.

Visual Exploration

Infants are visually responsive to their environment from the moment of birth. Newborn babies are most likely to be visually attracted to stimuli showing high rates of change, such as moving objects and pulsating lights. Infants' visual interest increases markedly at about two months of age, with a corresponding improvement in scanning and tracking abilities. These new skills enable infants to notice and inspect more subtle aspects of visual events, such as the complexity or detail in a pattern.

Older infants respond to visual events not only in terms of their perceptual characteristics but in terms of their meaning. Photographs of human faces, for example, hold special interest for the child by four months of age. With further visual experience, infants begin to construct a variety of fundamental schemes or concepts. Increasing memory ability enables them to notice and study departures from the normal arrangement of features in a pattern and, by about 12 months, to notice departures from a previously experienced sequence of events (Kagan, Kearsley, & Zelazo, 1978).

Manipulative Exploration

Physical contact with objects enables the infant to acquire many types of information not available by visual inspection alone: information about weight, flexibility, temperature, and other properties of objects. When infants handle things, they also experience new forms of visual input. They see objects move and change position as a result of their own actions. This combination of visual and manual exploration makes an inestimable contribution to infants' developing conceptions of the world.

During the first few months of life, manipulative exploration is quite limited. Babies do watch their own hand movements, but they cannot coordinate their hands and eyes and are unable to reach out and retrieve things. From five months of age on, with mastery of visually guided manual activity, manipulative exploration expands rapidly. Paralleling visual exploration, novel objects are selected and explored to a greater extent than familiar ones, at least by nine months (Rubenstein, 1976).

Unlike visual exploration, object manipulation offers the possibility of various kinds of feedback. Infants are most likely to play with objects that are reactive in some way, such as those with plasticity or sound potential (McCall, 1974). Variations in configural complexity alone, McCall found, exercised little influence on the infants' manipulative interest.

Toward the end of the first year, young children also begin to show an interest in how things work, as evidenced by their growing fascination with light switches, push buttons, and hinged lids on boxes (Piaget, 1952; Fenson et al., 1976). This interest centers less on cause-and-effect relations (such as the connection between a light switch and a lamp) than on the action of the device itself (such as the up and down positions of the light switch) and may account for the allure of "busy boxes" to young children around the first birthday.

Two new developments near the beginning of the second year of life alter infants' play in profound ways. First, infants begin to show awareness of the function or meaning of objects, that is, to accommodate their actions to culturally prescribed properties of objects. For example, American infants might push a toy car, insert a key in a lock, and throw a ball. Second, infants near the one-year mark develop the capacity to jointly consider two or more objects or events (Fenson et al., 1976). This new capacity sets the stage for the child's exploration of a wide range of interrelations among objects and events: functional relations, spatial relations, causal relations, and categorical relations.

Attention to *functional relations* may be seen, for example, in young children's play with a tea set, when they place a cup on a saucer or a lid on a pot. Constructions with building blocks require attention to a variety of *spatial relationships.* Children's developing appreciation of *causal relations* is illustrated when a child asks mother's help in removing the top to a tin containing blocks, showing recognition of the relation between a means (mother's help) and a goal (access to the blocks). *Categorical relations* between objects are explored when young children, during free play, physically combine objects that are alike in some way, such as size, color, function, or meaning.

Like visual exploration, then, manipulative exploration reflects the steady growth of cognition. As children develop an awareness of the functional-meaningful properties of objects and gain the ability to consider relationships, they become increasingly resourceful, thoughtful, and planful. As a consequence, they begin to control and regulate their play environment rather than behaving as captives of the play setting.

As children move into the preschool years, their manipulative exploration expands into a variety of forms of sensory and motor play: drawing and painting, construction activities with blocks and clay, sensory activities with water and sand, and motor activities with vehicles and climbing equipment. These activities give young children an opportunity to explore the properties of materials, to test and develop the capabilities of their own bodies, and to gain increasing mastery of their world.

Pretend Play

With the cognitive advances which usher in the second year of life, children begin to show another kind of play behavior that, at first glance, might seem at odds with the goal of mastery play. They begin to pretend, sometimes simulating and sometimes distorting reality. As we will see, however, these pretend activities are invaluable in helping infants and young children understand physical and especially social features of the world.

In the earliest form of pretense, at about one year, young children simulate their own daily routines, such as eating, bathing, and sleeping. Over the next few years, these early pretend behaviors expand into the elaborate and whimsical make-believe play that seems the very essence of childhood. Three trends characterize the way pretend play develops in young children from the second year of life into the preschool years: decentration, decontextualization, and integration.

1. *Decentration* (Piaget, 1962) refers to the young child's increasing tendency to incorporate other participants into pretend activities. The child's earliest pretend acts, at about 12 months of age, are directed toward the self, in the form of familiar schemes like eating and drinking from empty containers. The first decentered acts follow a few months later, in the form of actions directed toward animate and inanimate recipients (Fenson & Ramsay, 1980). The child, for example, might comb a doll's hair or pretend to feed a doll with an empty spoon. In these early instances of decentration, the child serves as the initiator or agent. Around 24 months, however, "animate" participants (e.g., dolls, stuffed toys) are regarded as agents in their own right rather than as mere passive recipients of the child's actions (Corrigan, 1982; Lowe, 1975). Thus, a child might seat a doll in front of a table setting and place a spoon in the doll's hand rather than feed the doll directly.

The emergence of sociodramatic play, that is, pretend play with other children, both reflects and contributes to the continuing decentering process in the preschool years. In dramatic play with one or more partners, children must learn to take turns, to respond reciprocally to the social initiations of other children, and to assume a variety of roles. They must also learn to communicate about the ongoing play drama. That is, they must engage in what Bateson (1972) terms metacommunication. They need to signal when they are moving in and out of the play frame, when they are changing roles, and the like (Bretherton, 1984).

2. *Decontextualization* (Werner & Kaplan, 1963) refers to the child's increasing ability to symbolically transform objects and other aspects of the environment in the service of pretense. The first instances of

decontextualization occur when the child substitutes a realistic replica for a real object, as by pretending to drink from a doll-sized baby bottle.

During the third year, children become capable of using highly nonprototypic substitute objects in their pretend play (Pederson, Rook-Green, & Elder, 1981). At this time they also begin to create imaginary objects to support their play activities. Substitution, invention, and other transformations of reality (e.g., adoption of fantasy roles such as Superman) become increasingly common in the preschool years (Matthews, 1977; McLoyd, 1980). It is typically in the child's fourth or fifth year that one of the most dramatic forms of symbolic invention takes place, the creation of an imaginary playmate.

3. *Integration* refers to the child's increasing ability to combine individual actions into coordinated behavior sequences. For most of the first two years of life, exploratory play has a piecemeal quality. The child appears to drift from one object or activity to another, as if "controlled by" rather than "in control of" the objects or activities in the immediate environment. However, between 18 and 24 months of age, two types of integration appear in the child's play.

The simplest type, termed *single scheme combinations* by Nicolich (1977) and first seen in spontaneous play at about 18 months, involves variations on a single theme. For example, a child stirs a spoon in a pot and then in a cup, or feeds two different dolls in succession. Within six months, a more complex type of action sequence, termed *multischeme combinations* by Nicolich, appears. For example, a child places a doll in a bed, then covers it with a blanket.

Although the first multischemes to appear in children's play are usually limited to no more than two acts in succession, they parallel in time, and perhaps in importance, the transition from one- to two-word utterances in the child's speech. There is, in fact, some evidence that the emergence of combinatorial speech and combinatorial play reflect expression in different modes of the same underlying symbolic competencies (McCune-Nicolich, 1981; O'Connell & Gerard, in press; Shore, O'Connell, & Bates, 1984).

As a result of the expansion of sequential combinations in the third year, the child's play is less often a collage of unrelated actions and more likely to include series of interconnected actions or minithemes. Recently, I studied the appearance of this new continuity in play by modeling small pretend skits for children 20, 26, and 31 months of age (Fenson, 1984). Children in their third year not only incorporated more elements of the skits into their play than did younger children but exhibited longer strings of interconnected actions, thereby reflecting a considerable degree of organization in their pretend play.

As children enter the preschool years, they begin to engage in more elaborate and integrated play episodes. These sustained play episodes are often organized around familiar "scripts," that is, everyday routines such as mealtime, bedtime, or going shopping (Nelson & Gruendel, 1981). These familiar routines enable children to act on the basis of shared knowledge, facilitating cooperative dramatic play (Nelson & Seidman, 1984) as well as adding coherence to individual play.

In summary, the lively forms of sociodramatic play in which preschool children delight represent the culmination of a variety of advances in social cognition. Social pretend play requires that children be able to communicate and metacommunicate, that they be able to fantasize, and that they be able to play, take turns, and respond reciprocally to the actions of other children. The foundations for these abilities are established in the first two to three years of life, through children's exploratory activities, through their individual pretend play, and through their social interchanges with others.

DISCUSSION

Jay Belsky: I know you agree, Larry, that it's important to distinguish between emergent and typical behaviors when discussing age ranges. When a higher level of behavior first emerges, it takes up only a small proportion of the ongoing stream of activity that the baby's engaged in. You really have to watch closely to see it, because most of the child's activities are at a much lower level of cognitive sophistication.

In the work we're doing on infant play, we're seeing earlier onsets of some behaviors, such as substitution and multischemes or sequences, than most of the literature suggests. In fact, one reason I've been looking forward to this paper, and to yours, Lorraine, is that the literature isn't clear on which comes first, substitution or sequencing.

Lorraine McCune: It depends on how you define your terms. If you take a Piagetian approach to substitution, he says very clearly that the substitution is constructed prior to the act. It's not that a child runs across something that reminds her of a phone and puts it to her ear. That wouldn't qualify as substitution. That would be sort of a mistake in assimilation. What's really required is either an announcement, which means you need a child who's verbal, or multiple uses of the same object. It's very problematical.

Allen Gottfried: Larry has clearly delineated the ordinality of various developments, but specifying ages is a real problem. For example, infants are said to favor novel objects at six to nine months, but we can demonstrate that in babies as early as two to three months. I think a lot of things will show up much earlier as we develop better conceptualizations and technology.

Larry Fenson: It seems to me that every investigator tends to find developments earlier than the investigators who preceded him or her. The first people who looked at Piaget's findings on play tended to find all these things occurring earlier than Piaget. That just happens. The time of emergence of a phenomenon is important for answering some questions, but when behavior becomes typical is an equally important issue. For example, in describing the playing child at a given age, you really want to look not at what may be the newest things but at what the typical behaviors are. Both kinds of information are useful and important, depending on what questions you're addressing.

Lorraine McCune: We need to know the context in which various behaviors would be elicited.

Judy Dunn: The child's social relationships are very important. We have a lot of observations of children early in the second year not being dependent upon objects for pretend exchanges — to echo Jay's point about behavior emerging earlier than is generally thought — but this takes place in the context of interaction with the mother or a sibling. In a way, it's boring to say infants can do these things three months earlier than someone else has said. I think it's more important to stress context.

Brian Vandenberg: Jay, do you observe the children individually or in groups?

Jay Belsky: Individually, except that the mother and the experimenter are there. We try to create an atmosphere that's very comfortable for the child, who sits on the floor with the toys. We ask our parents not to become involved in the play but to be affectively responsive. If the child looks up and smiles, the parent smiles back. If the child walks over to the parent, the experimenter might suggest a hug.

Brian Vandenberg: Especially in laboratory studies, it's very common to study individual children at play. Social interaction is considered almost a contamination of the "real" play, as if play were basically an asocial phenomenon. I agree with Judy Dunn that context is very important in studying play.

Jay Belsky: You can make a distinction between solitary play and group play. In this project, we're not studying groups. After the solitary free-play period, during which the mother behaves as I've just described, we go through an elicitation phase to see whether the child has capacities in his or her repertoire that weren't evident during solitary play. But if your point is that play should be studied in a variety of contexts, including social ones, I certainly agree.

Dante Cicchetti: In addition to studying children in a variety of contexts, we need to study various populations, both normal and atypical. For example, Judy Dunn mentioned earlier that some lower-class and working-class mothers in England discourage pretend play because they associate it with lying. Mothers of Down's syndrome infants and children also emphasize accurate real-world information during play, though for different reasons. For instance, they might tell a child who's playing "tea party" that babies don't drink coffee, they drink milk.

When we can see how affect, cognition, language, and symbolization go together, not only in "normals" but in a variety of atypical populations, I think we may find a different pattern of interrelationships for every atypical population that we look at.

PLAY-LANGUAGE RELATIONSHIPS AND SYMBOLIC DEVELOPMENT

Lorraine McCune, Ed.D.

Relationships between symbolic play and language in the past have customarily been framed in terms of "cognitive prerequisites" for language. However, recent theoretical analyses (e.g., Bates, 1979; Bates et al., 1977) suggest that linguistic and nonlinguistic abilities may reflect the same underlying cognitive structure; thus, they should be considered equal in sophistication and potentially equivalent in onset time. Rather than considering certain cognitive milestones as prerequisite to language milestones, then, one would attribute changes in both sets of abilities to a more abstract underlying base. Close correspondence in time of development is to be expected, with neither set of abilities necessarily preceding the other.

The shared cognitive basis for developments in language and symbolic play is the ability to symbolize. However, it is likely that more skills and experiences, beyond the shared cognitive base, are required for language production than for play. Thus, assessment of play can be used to judge the child's nonlinguistic symbolic ability. What additional capabilities characterize language skill? A model of language acquisition is needed which will include a number of dimensions, each of which can be assessed separately to yield predictions of language onset and development. Individual variation on such dimensions would increase our understanding of the phenomenon Piaget called *decalage:* an unevenness in development revealed by more sophisticated performance in one domain (such as symbolic play) than in another, closely related one (such as language).

A better understanding of decalage would be practically as well as theoretically useful. Many babies not speaking by 24 months are now seen by speech and language pathologists, but at present there is no clear way to distinguish the two-year-old who will experience a spurt in the next six months from the one who may be helped by intervention of some sort.

Theoretical Background

The theoretical background for my work on correspondences between play and language milestones, which I will describe shortly, combines Piaget's (1962) approach to play with Werner and Kaplan's (1963) approach to language. Despite major differences, these theorists attribute similar organizing activities to the child and offer similar structural descriptions of play (Piaget) and language (Werner and Kaplan), rendering their two approaches complementary rather than conflicting.

My hypotheses concerning play and language correspondences, and the underlying developments on which, theoretically, they are based, are summarized in Table 1.

On theoretical grounds, I consider a pretend action that shows an underlying knowledge of a corresponding real-life activity (Level 2) to be equivalent to the use of a word that shows knowledge of a real-life object or event. At this level, both the pretend action and the word refer to a symbolized internal event or entity which is only generally understood by the child, so that when the child pretends to drink from a cup or says the word *cup* this refers to the whole situation of drinking from a cup rather than only to the specific object itself. With development, objects and events are more fully analyzed. In pretend (Level 3), the child begins to differentiate actions from actors and is able to portray pretend actions using other actors than the self (e.g., feed doll rather than feed self). In language, the child shows a similar differentiation by speaking of the parts and attributes of objects and naming both objects and actions. The child might sometimes say "cup," sometimes "drink." The effect of this

Table 1. Sequences of Symbolic Development as Expressed in Play and Language

Underlying Development	Play	Language
Association of event with habitual action	1. Recognition of objects	Prelanguage communication
Representation of global event as a unit	2. Self-pretend	Single words, global reference
Analysis of represented object/event	3. Differentiated pretend Pretend with dolls Pretend at others' activities	Reference to broader range of entities, to parts of entities, to states
Juxtaposition of symbolic elements	4. Pretend combinations	Simple language combinations
Construction of relations among symbolic elements Store complete event while parts are organized	5. Planning Store symbolic goal while intervening steps are accomplished Keep dual meaning of substitute object (e.g., block = doll) while performing doll-appropriate activities	Developing language rules Store complete message while component parts are organized

development should be a sharp growth in vocabulary. Once events can be analyzed into components, it is a reasonable step for the child to juxtapose pretend actions to form play sequences (Level 4) and combine words to form short "sentences," such as "cup drink." Eventually, the child can symbolize prior to action and thus exhibits planning in play (Level 5) and the regularities of syntactic structure in language.

A Multidimensional Model of Language Acquisition

For the moment, we are assuming a process of cognitive development involving active construction on the part of the child in a manner described by Piaget's theory and a process of symbolic development which encompasses both cognitive processes and social interaction as proposed by Werner and Kaplan. A predictive model for language acquisition should therefore include both cognitive and social processes, and both internal consolidation and experience. In addition, biological developments would influence and interact with these dimensions. One can therefore consider biological developments, experiential activities, and cognitive construction as fundamental dimensions to be evaluated in understanding and eventually predicting essential aspects to language acquisition.

Each of the four transitions in symbolic development noted in Table 1 has biological, experiential, and cognitive (constructive) aspects. Cognitive construction can operate via experience only given certain biological readiness. For example, returning to the potential for decalage between onset of symbolic play and first words mentioned earlier, the following sequence of events can be suggested. Suppose different biological transitions are required for symbolization onset and for control of the vocal articulatory apparatus. Both transitions might occur early, along with appropriate experience, leading to correspondence in onset time of the two skills. Differences in timing of biological transition and/or experiential opportunities could lead to decalage. In an extreme case, articulatory capability might remain at a typical pre-12-month level until many months later. This child might show age-appropriate symbolic play, lack language, and display aberrant or absent vocal development. However, on theoretical grounds, there would be nothing to prevent development of strong language comprehension skills leading to a sudden productive spurt when the missing biological transition(s) occurred. We occasionally hear reports of children who remain nonverbal until 24 months or even later, then begin speaking in full sentences. A combination of earlier biological development allowing symbolization with delay in biological priming for articulation would lead to such a pattern.

Direct measurement of biological changes in the brain that affect development remain elusive. Therefore, the first strategies for evaluating the proposed model must be behavioral. My own efforts to date have involved small longitudinal and moderate-size cross-sectional samples, and are suggestive of how the model I have outlined might be employed rather than definitive in evaluating it. Results will soon be available from a larger longitudinal and cross-sectional study (McCune, in prep.).

Examples from Longitudinal and Cross-Sectional Studies

In our longitudinal study (McCune-Nicolich & Bruskin, 1981), five girls were studied from early in the single-word period until their language was predominately combinatorial (two- or three-word sentences). Two transitions in play and language development were evaluated. First, all five subjects exhibited combinations in play (Level 4) either at the same time as or prior to using language combinations. Second, following the children's development of Level 5 play, a number of related language developments occurred: Positional regularity in language combinations began; number of types of multiword utterances used increased sharply; and mean length of utterance also increased sharply.

In our cross-sectional study (Adler, 1982), subjects were 24 middle-class children, evenly divided by sex, who ranged in age from 19 to 24 months. Each child was observed in his or her own home during a half-hour play session with the mother, using a standard toy set. Measures of symbolic play and language were recorded and later analyzed.

The results confirmed that Play Levels 1 through 5 on Table 1 form an ordinal scale, though it was necessary to pool the two lowest levels because some advanced subjects failed to exhibit Level 1. The results also supported the hypothesis of correspondence. In play, one subject exhibited only single symbolic acts (Level 3); 18 exhibited combinations (Level 4); and five exhibited both combinations and the more advanced play (Level 5) characterized by planning. The subject who showed no combinations in play also failed to combine words. Two-thirds of the 18 children who exhibited combinations in play showed corresponding combinations in language; the other third exhibited a decalage between these symbolic domains.

Separate Fischer exact tests revealed that the decalage group included significantly more children exhibiting unintelligibility of speech than the correspondence group. In addition, the decalage group showed one or more extreme features of mother-child interaction which were not observed in the correspondence group. Maternal directiveness has often been reported to be associated with slow language development. This was not the case in the present study. The five most directive mothers' children were distributed such that two were in the highest play/language group, one in the correspondence group, and two in the decalage group.

One could reason in several directions from these findings. Beginning with the children's low intelligibility, one might consider biologically based poor articulatory control, hence low frequency of speaking. The more active mothers of children in this group may be facilitating their children's language development, in that without maternal leadership their speech would be even less frequent. Other interpretations are equally plausible. Only longitudinal study and more comprehensive measures applied to large numbers of cases will eventually allow prediction of language onset and transitions from other variables.

The model and results presented here suggest one approach to understanding language development that goes beyond the concept of "cognitive prerequisites." In attempting to consider cross-domain correspondences in behavior with underlying symbolic developments, as this model suggests, it is essential to consider additional threads of development which contribute to language development.

DISCUSSION

Allen Gottfried: How did you get into the study of play, Lorraine? Wasn't language your original interest?

Lorraine McCune: When I was doing graduate work I took a year's course work with Lois Bloom. At that time, we were still at the height of the Chomsky conflict. We were being led to believe on the one hand that language came full-blown from nowhere, that it was not related to any other aspect of the child's development. On the other hand, we were being told by some developmental psychologists that language really depended on object permanence. There had been no empirical work done at that time. As a new graduate student, it seemed to me that this was something that could be empirically resolved. All you needed to do in order to show that Chomsky was wrong is show that the child does something equally complex in a domain other than language. So I did a little pilot work with object permanence and found that all children who were speaking had nearly completed object permanence development. That's how I came to play. It interested me so much that it has been hard for me to get back to language at all.

Judy Dunn: What do you think is going on when you don't get 100 percent correlation between levels of language and play? I've been puzzled by both ends of the lack of correlation. In one of our studies, we had a couple of children who were extremely sophisticated in terms of social cognition but behind on language. That's not what I was expecting. In several other studies, I've noticed very bright children, very ahead on language, who weren't much interested in fantasy playing. I don't see how to explain the lack of correlation.

Lorraine McCune: First of all, I don't really believe correlation is the right model for finding out about this. For example, a child who doesn't do very much pretend play and is speaking in syntactic language probably has the capacity for pretense and would show you one or two exemplars under the appropriate conditions. In fact, what may happen is that children who are really good at language may get themselves away from some of the action-oriented aspects of play. Maybe their play is going to be more socially and linguistically oriented because they're so good at that. When you talk about lack of correspondence, I'm more concerned when we don't see any exemplars of, say, language combinations in a child who's showing us very clear play combinations.

The way I talk about it in my paper is that what we're really trying to do is account for decalage. What that says to me is that we need to look at external variables that might possibly operate. Particularly with respect to children who are more advanced in play than in language, the relevant variable could be biological maturation. Another thing you'd wonder about would be the motivation to interact. It's possible that some children might have been in situations where they were deprived of interaction opportunities, and for them there could be a motivational problem.

Judy Dunn: The two children I mentioned who were so good at social cognitive things were intensely interactive. What they played with were very often social rules and social roles. But they weren't very head-on with language.

Jay Belsky: I'd like to express a point of view that hasn't been represented in our comments. In *The Second Year of Life,* Jerry Kagan wants to make the argument that basically these things are not connected. He says that we can have parallel developmental tracks that emerge around the same point in time, and therefore we can spin yarns to suggest that they are intertwined causally or functionally, but actually they may have independent origins. I'm talking basically about the language and play connection. I'm curious about how a theorist like you, Lorraine, responds to a critic who says, sure they might be temporally associated, but they're not quantitatively or functionally associated.

Lorraine McCune: That question gets down to the notion of coherence in science. If we have things that can be described as highly similar and they occur close in time, then what's the point of positing two different sources for them? You could say that. On the other hand, I think some of what motivates Kagan's view is really an entirely different theoretical goal from mine, and this is the goal of long-term prediction. He's interested in things early relating to things later. In the past he's sometimes been very disappointed, but in his recent work he's gotten some really strong results about certain temperamental indices.

Jay Belsky: I read the book as a real challenge to the whole language-play connection.

Lorraine McCune: Well, the connection is very weak. Very little has really been documented. My first study on it is only being written now. I've been saying a lot about these ideas for a long time without producing very much to support them.

Jay Belsky: I don't feel that Jerry's theories are compelling on this point. What impresses me is his saying, wait a minute, we're assuming association, we're assuming relationship, why don't we just question that. Jerry's good at turning things on in their head like that and giving us more to think about.

Allen Gottfried: Lorraine, how much error in measurement do you have in research on play? This may be a fundamental question. When 20 percent of a sample don't show this theoretical correspondence, how much of this is due to simple error in measuring play and measuring language?

Lorraine McCune: You really never know. It's a very serious problem. One of the ways I get around it is by requiring several exemplars, because what I'm interested in is whether the child has the underlying construct. In my latest work, I've developed two useful measures of play, an onset measure and a consolidation measure. For the consolidation measure, the child has to show two different exemplars at a certain level, neither of which imitates the mother or has been suggested by the mother (I have the mother right there all the time). You get really interesting differences between onset and consolidation level because many, many of the children's early play behaviors are imitations.

Language is even harder to measure than play. Let me play you tapes of three 18-month-olds, and let's see how many of us are going to agree on what words are on that tape. I'm working on that problem with a colleague at Stanford now, just trying to quantify the bases for how sure we are that the child has a word.

Jay Belsky: Another issue about onset and consolidation is that those indices might relate to different things themselves.

Lorraine McCune: Yes, they might. For instance, a single instance needed for onset might often be produced in imitation of the mother and might not reflect child competence at all.

INTRINSIC MOTIVATION FOR PLAY

Adele Eskeles Gottfried, Ph.D.

Activities performed for their own sake are said to be intrinsically motivated; that is, pleasure is inherent in the activity itself (Berlyne, 1965; Deci, 1975). Play has been considered an intrinsically motivated activity, and intrinsic motivation has often been viewed as a defining criterion of play (Neumann, 1971; Rubin, Fein, & Vandenberg, 1983). Yet advancements in understanding specific conditions that influence intrinsic motivation in children have important implications for children's experience of play as an intrinsically motivated activity. In this paper, three approaches to intrinsic motivation for play will be summarized: cognitive discrepancy theories, competence (mastery) theories, and attribution theories. Their implications for the development of intrinsically motivating play experiences and materials will be examined, and an interactive conceptualization of intrinsic motivation for play will be advanced.

Cognitive Discrepancy Theories

Cognitive discrepancy theories emphasize intrinsic motivation that results when a child encounters stimuli that are discrepant from, or do not match, his or her existing cognitive structures. Children are motivated to reduce such discrepancies through curiosity, exploration, or play.

Much research and theory about intrinsically motivated play has focused on cognitive discrepancy. According to Berlyne (1960; 1965), stimulus properties such as novelty, surprise, incongruity, and complexity (called *collative stimuli*) can produce cognitive conflict and thereby increase arousal above an optimal level. This motivates the individual to reduce the arousal level, as by engaging in exploratory behavior in order to learn more about the collative stimulus. Exploration also occurs in response to levels of arousal that are below the optimal.

There is ample evidence, from infancy through childhood, that children attend more to stimuli with collative properties than to familiar stimuli (e.g., Nunnally & Lemond, 1973). For example, it has been found that toys characterized by novelty (Mendel, 1965) and complexity (Ellis, 1984; McCall, 1974) are preferred, or played with more.

Considerable attention has been paid to distinguishing between exploration and play. While some researchers question the need for this distinction because some forms of play may involve fantasy exploration (Weisler & McCall, 1976), others assert that exploration and play are different categories of behavior (Hughes, 1978; Hutt, 1970; 1981; Nunnally & Lemond, 1973; Wohlwill, 1984). Exploration, in this view, is more focused and stereotyped, and less joyful, than play; it tends to be oriented toward the properties of unfamiliar stimuli. Play, which involves children's own transformations of stimuli, is more variable and more relaxed than exploration; it tends to occur more readily with familiar stimuli.

One aspect of this debate that has been overlooked is children's subjective experience of an activity as play or exploration, and their perception of each type of activity as intrinsically motivating. The distinction between the two may have little subjective value for the child. For example, seeking information and reduction of uncertainty (exploration) may be experienced as "fun" while some forms of play, such as social pretend play, may have affiliative rather than intrinsic motivation as a foundation and may involve negative affect.

The major significance of the cognitive discrepancy view of play is that it helps define the characteristics of play materials and play experiences that increase arousal and facilitate play. Novelty, incongruity, complexity, and surprise are prime candidates. However, what surprises one child may not surprise another, and as yet there are no parameters for matching a certain toy or stimulus property with specific cognitive abilities. In addition, curiosity and exploration are multidimensional, not unitary or global traits (Henderson & Moore, 1979; Kreitler, Zigler, & Kreitler, 1975; Vidler, 1977). Thus, children's curiosity and exploration show low interrelationships across a variety of tasks.

The multidimensional nature of intrinsic motivation and the difficulty of matching toy properties to individual children's development suggest that the best play environment for infants and young children may be one characterized by variety of stimulation. This environment would include toys and other objects, people, and opportunities for experiencing a variety of play modalities. Variety of stimulation in children's environment has been shown to be positively related to young children's cognitive development (Gottfried & Gottfried, 1984; Ulvund, 1980). Variety maximizes the opportunity for cognitive discrepancies and may facilitate transitions between exploration and play.

Competence Theories

Another orientation to the intrinsic motivational aspects of play is the competence or mastery perspective. According to this view, children play in order to experience effectance in their environment. White (1959) provided the foundation for competence theories by proposing that children seek to interact effectively with their environment and that such interactions yield feelings of mastery. This is an intrinsic motive, since there is no external reward. White specified play as a mastery-oriented activity. Bruner (1972; 1973) proposed that play provides an arena in which new combinations of actions can be tried without concern for consequences. Implicit in his conception is a motive to achieve mastery.

Central to the mastery view of intrinsic motivation is the concept that the child experiences him- or herself as a causal agent of outcomes in the environment (Hunt, 1981; Piaget, 1962; White, 1959). Another theme is that the environment should be responsive to the child's activity in order for the child to experience mastery. It has also been suggested that mastery is facilitated by optimally challenging experiences (Harter, 1978).

In the mastery view, motivation derives from the child's activity, which strives toward effectance and mastery in the environment, rather than from a motive based on arousal reduction. Central nervous system arousal reduction is not a component of competence theories.

Research investigating competence motivation has supported the view that infants and children are motivated to master their environment. From infancy on, children experience pleasure in learning to control toys (Watson, 1971; Nuttin, 1973). Responsivity of play materials is a consistent finding related to mastery motivation in play in infancy (e.g., Yarrow et al., 1982; Jennings et al., 1979). Environmental stimulation from caretakers also appears to relate to mastery motivation, but it is unclear whether this stimulation needs to be responsive to the young child's actions. Research indicates that both contingent and noncontingent caretaker stimulation enhances or relates to mastery motivation. Challenge is a dimension that enhances mastery motivation of play during childhood (Csikszentmihalyi, 1975; Eiferman, 1972), and this dimension needs to be investigated for young children as well. Overall, play experiences that provide the child with a sense of control and feedback contingent upon the child's own activities are likely to enhance mastery motivation. Social, object, and symbolic play would all be included.

Attribution Theories

A third perspective on intrinsic motivation emphasizes children's attributions: their ideas about the causes of their behavior. Research on attributions has focused on the distinction between intrinsic and extrinsic motivation. An intrinsically motivated activity is inherently pleasurable. An extrinsically motivated activity is performed for an instrumental reason, such as to receive a reward or achieve some other desirable outcome not inherent in the activity itself. Whether play is perceived as intrinsically motivating by a child depends in part on the attributions the child makes as to why he or she is playing. Play could be engaged in for instrumental reasons (e.g., peer approval, affiliation, competition) whereas nonplay activities may take on play-like qualities when they are experienced as "fun" or "interesting."

The attribution perspective on intrinsic motivation has received relatively little attention from play researchers as yet, though it has significant implications for play. Attributional research to date has focused mainly upon the effects of rewards on intrinsic motivation. In general, the findings indicate that when children attribute their behavior to their own efforts, competence, or self-selection of goals, intrinsic motivation is likely to be enhanced. On the other hand, when children attribute their behavior to external influences such as rewards, or parental or teacher demands, intrinsic motivation is likely to be diminished.

Early research indicated that rewards had an undermining effect on intrinsic motivation. Lepper, Greene, and Nisbett (1973) found that nursery school children who expected and received a Good Player Award for drawing with felt pens (an intrinsically interesting activity) subsequently used the pens less during free play than children who received no award or who unexpectedly received an award. When children are offered an external reward for performing an intrinsically interesting activity, their intrinsic motivation declines. Because they attribute their interest to the reward rather than to the task itself, the researchers concluded, they will engage in the task less on subsequent occasions, when the reward is no longer available.

Since this study was published, there has been a great deal of research showing that rewards do not always decrease intrinsic motivation. The effects of rewards depend on such factors as the type and purpose of the reward and the child's initial interest in the activity. In some instances, rewards may increase intrinsic motivation.

In other words, rewards have complex effects on intrinsic motivation, and whether a given reward increases or decreases intrinsic motivation depends on the meaning it has for the child. The crucial factor seems to be the influence of the reward on children's perceptions of their own competence and of their self-determination in choosing the activity (Deci & Ryan, 1980; Lepper, 1983; Pittman, Boggiano, & Ruble, 1983). Rewards that enhance these perceptions tend to facilitate intrinsic motivation.

An Interactive Approach

Three different theoretical orientations to intrinsic motivation have been outlined. The cognitive discrepancy perspective emphasized novel stimuli and the motivation to reduce arousal; the competence perspective emphasized effective interaction with the environment; the attribution perspective emphasized the child's perceptions of the reasons for his or her behavior. It is my view that intrinsic motivation for play is an outcome of complex interactions and interrelationships between features of all three perspectives. For example, encountering a collative stimulus may produce cognitive discrepancy resulting in exploratory play. Resolution of the cognitive discrepancy may result in the child's experience of mastery. The consequences of the behavior, such as praise or disapproval from parents, will influence the child's perception of play as relatively intrinsically or extrinsically motivated.

Any play activity may emphasize one or more aspects of intrinsic motivation, and the three aspects of intrinsic motivation may or may not operate at the same time. For example, in infancy it is likely that cognitive discrepancy and mastery aspects of intrinsic motivation are most relevant to play. As social and cognitive skills develop during the preschool years and later, attributional aspects of intrinsic motivation would become more salient. Further, initiation of a play activity could be due to any of the three aspects of intrinsic motivation and the basis for intrinsic motivation may change within a sequence. For example, a child may start to play with a toy because of its novelty and continue to play with it because it provides responsive feedback and a sense of mastery.

This interactive conception of intrinsic motivation differs in certain respects from prior views of intrinsically motivated play. First, intrinsic motivation in play is viewed as a result of multivariate factors, whereas in prior conceptions a single orientation has been espoused. Second, intrinsic motivation is viewed not as a criterion of play but as a result of the stimuli, mastery, and consequence conditions of play. Finally, the child's experience of intrinsic motivation in play is an important dimension that needs to be accounted for.

DISCUSSION

Phyllis Levenstein: I have a comment and a question. The comment is that I'm fascinated by the way you have gone into the details of something that J. McVicker Hunt wrote about some 18 years ago, the problem of the match. He was talking principally about matching materials and work to the developmental stage of the child and didn't hint at any of these other very important complexities that you've ferreted out. So I congratulate you.

The question is, isn't there a point where extrinsic motivation can become intrinsic motivation, as through the praise of a beloved figure like the mother?

Adele Gottfried: That kind of a contingency itself would not be part of intrinsic motivation but would enhance the child's perception of intrinsic motivation in the activity. On second thought, from the mastery perspective, a child might be intrinsically motivated to interact with the person who's providing positive outcomes and become more effective in play interactions with that person. So, from that perspective, one could shift and say that significant others might become part of an intrinsic motivational component of social play.

Phyllis Levenstein: There's a fine line, perhaps even an osmosis.

Helen Schwartzman: Have you some ideas about how children change from playfulness to workfulness and back while performing the same activity? That might be one of the most interesting aspects of an investigation along the lines that I think you're suggesting.

Adele Gottfried: Your question makes me think of my own son's preschool education and of the whole question of academics in the preschool. As a believer in cognitive stimulation, which is a component of intrinsic motivation, I think we should be stimulating children to learn the alphabet, or numbers, and so on. But I see that stimulation as very different from the sort of stimulation many preschools are providing. Many preschools are implementing "stimulation" in a way that has created a pressure to achieve. This is an external sort of requirement that takes the intrinsic motivational quality out of learning. At one point a certain activity might be stimulating and fun because it challenges the cognitive level of the child, and the child experiences control over his own activities. But when the peer group, teachers, or parents start forcing the child to achieve a criterion of excellence, whatever it may be, then the motivation shifts into work rather than into play and interest.

Theodore Wachs: I have a comment on variety and the whole notion of optimal discrepancy, which I think cuts across two of the three motivational areas that you delineated. Concerning variety, it's very important to make the distinction that I and other people have made between long-term and short-term variety. Most people who talk about variety essentially mean short-term variety, that is, the number of different objects available to the child at a given time. Not nearly enough attention is paid to the change in objects over time.

This is important, because it relates to the whole notion of match or optimal discrepancy. I agree with Phyllis that it's a marvelously intriguing concept. It has persisted despite virtually no empirical evidence to support the existence of the phenomenon. I think what variety does, both short-term and long-term, is maximize the probability that the child will be able to select objects that are optimally discrepant for this child. Obviously, as the child gets older, if there is no change in objects, this probability is reduced.

Jay Belsky: One of the most impressive things about a really first-class toy is that it develops with the child. The Fisher Price toy telephone is a perfect example. Initially, it's a toy you play with functionally. You can move it back and forth. Then all of a sudden you can put the receiver down, and there's a functional relationship. Then you can go into self-pretend and talk into it, and later, when you're three or four, it makes a nice sociodramatic play prop. It's an object with great inherent versatility, so that the child can create variety over time.

Allen Gottfried: When a child comes back to a toy a year later, that toy has a new meaning for the child. The child will relate to it in a different way. Blocks, at first, are action things; later, you create things with them.

Adele Gottfried: One reason children come back to certain toys after a long period of time is that their cognitive or social development has changed to the point that they are able to relate to the materials in a different way.

Lorraine McCune: We can provide variety, but the child is the only person who can solve the problem of the match.

Greta Fein: Part of the idea of kids organizing their play worlds from the odd things they find around them, as Helen Schwartzman described in her paper, is that child-structured play requires children to impose their own organization on the materials. This kind of play is creative and fun; the main problem with it is that the settings and play materials children have available to choose from may confront them with some realistic dangers.

Brian Vandenberg: Another problem, related to variety, is that overstimulation in terms of providing a large number of toys sometimes produces chaos in the environment, and group play deteriorates instead of developing constructively. I don't know how much research has been done on this, but my own observations suggest that there's a point at which too many toys, too much concern with cognitive stimulation, seem to produce very fragmented, disjointed kinds of play episodes.

Theodore Wachs: Susan Gray made a similar point about 15 years ago. She said the worst thing you can do with children from very disorganized home environments is put them in a room with lots of toys. You're recreating the home situation. It's far better to put the child in a room with an adult and one toy.

COMPUTER PLAY

Daniel W. Kee, Ph.D.

Surprisingly little formal interest has been show by educators and psychologists in children's play with the personal computers and other microprocessor-based devices that now pervade our environment. In this paper, the new phenomenon of children's computer play is examined, beginning with a brief characterization of computer toys and computer-related activities. The second section of the paper identifies some emerging research themes in new studies of children's computer play. Finally, early results from our own research on parent-child computer activities are presented.

Computer Playthings

A visit to a local toy store will reveal how popular computer devices for children have become. One major chain of toy stores has separate display aisles for computer toys, microelectronic learning aids, video games, home/personal computers, and computer software. Early computer toys such as "Merlin" and "Speak & Spell" have been joined by larger toys such as "Big Tracks," a tank that can be programmed to traverse a room and fire its cannon in a prearranged sequence. Desk-top computer devices include the ubiquitous video game machines and an assortment of desk-top microcomputers for the home.

A significant number of children have video game machines in their homes (Greenfield, 1984; Loftus & Loftus, 1983; Mitchell, 1984) and personal computers are also becoming popular. Sales of over 4.4 million personal/home computers were anticipated in 1984, an increase of 22 percent over 1983 (Richter, 1984). Surveys indicate that the public believes home computers will be as commonplace as televisions in the near future (Friedrich, 1983).

Research Themes

Review of the extant research concerning children and the new microcomputer devices shows an emphasis on learning, education, and schooling issues. "Computer play" per se has received little attention, although the impact of video game playing on human development was the topic of a recent Harvard symposium (Baughman & Clagett, 1983). Also, both the psychology of video game playing (e.g., Loftus & Loftus, 1983) and the potential impact of computers on social and psychological development (see Turkle, 1984) have been recently treated. In this section some emerging themes in early research on children's computer play are identified.

1. *The computer as free-play "toy."* How will children's play be affected when personal computers become a part of their home environments? Levin and Kareev (1980) provide a useful illustration of computer play in the home. The following incident shows how two boys, aged seven-and-one-half and six, assimilated the computer into their more general play activities.

> They had been using a sketching program to create drawings on the computer screen, which they then saved for later viewing and modification. One day, they had a drawing displayed on the screen, an assortment of dots scattered about. They huddled in front of the computer and carefully moved the cursor (a dot that can be moved to indicate the current position for drawing) from one dot to another. The boys then ran from the living room into their playroom, where they played for a while. Then they ran back to the computer, carefully moving the cursor over next to yet another dot, and again ran to their playroom. This sequence was repeated several times. Finally, when asked what in the world they were doing, they patiently explained that they were playing "Star Trek." With the computer as "control room panel," they were "warping" from one star to another, then "beaming down" to the planet to explore (in their playroom). (p. 17)

In the home, a computer can be a "free" rather than a "scarce" resource. Whether similar play behaviors will emerge in classroom environments will depend on such factors as the duration of computer use, ratio of computers to children, nature of the resource (free vs. scarce), and kinds of software activities supported.

An important problem for future research will be to evaluate how play in classroom environments changes with long-term computer use and with different kinds of software activities (see Campbell & Schwartz, 1984). Furthermore, the effectiveness of software designed to foster group play in classroom should be evaluated (see Goodman, 1984).

2. *Media influence on play.* Initial research by Silvern, Williamson, and Countermine (1983; in press) shows no significant differences in level of aggression, fantasy play, or prosocial behavior in children after playing video games. However, these findings should be viewed cautiously, as the children were exposed only briefly to a limited range of video game activities.

3. *Turning play into work.* As indicated by Adele Gottfried (this volume), intrinsic motivation can be undermined by external constraints such as rewards, directions and surveillance of the activity (Lepper & Greene, 1979). However, two recently completed studies (Kee, Beauvais, & Whittaker, 1983; Wood & Kee, in press) using "Speak & Spell," the highly engaging hand-held device that supports different spelling and word games, failed to demonstrate reward effects on children's interest in spelling activities or spelling performance. These findings, which are consistent with Arnold's (1976) results concerning adults' computer game play, suggest that computer activities which are extremely high in intrinsic motivation may not be subject to negative reward effects.

4. *Gender differences in fantasy play.* A recent report by Revelle and colleagues (1984) indicates gender differences in the frequency of fantasy involvement in computer games. In-depth interviews with 24 children (10 females and 14 males) at a computer camp showed that "boys almost always reported engaging in vivid fantasies while playing computer or video games, and that girls almost never did." Experimental research (Malone, 1980; Malone & Lepper, in press) concerning what makes computer games fun also indicates gender differences in the kinds of fantasy children find appealing.

Gender differences have been reported for other aspects of children's computer activity as well. Boys show a greater interest in computer use than girls (Silvern, Countermine, & Williamson, 1982); boys hold more favorable perceptions of computers than girls (Williams, Coulombe, & Lievrouw, 1983); girls are less confident in their computer game playing skills than boys (Mitchell, 1984); and for some kinds of computer activities such as strategy games, girls prefer to know the rules prior to participation while boys enjoy the process of learning the rules by playing (Revelle et al., 1984). Additional analysis of gender differences in children's computer play should have high priority in future research.

5. *Play and computer microworlds.* According to Lawler (1982), "Microworlds are in essence 'task domains' or 'problem spaces' designed for virtual, streamlined experience. These worlds encompass objects and processes that we can get to know and understand."

Rich and exciting graphic and text-based microworlds can be established for children on personal computers. These microworlds can provide the basis for adventure games (Greenfield, 1984); simulations of dangerous activities such as nuclear reactor control (e.g., "Scram," marketed by Atari); and play within different worlds such as music, art, and logic (Levin & Kareev, 1980; Watt, 1983; 1984; Bateman, 1984).

Computer languages like LOGO can be used by children to create graphic microworlds for play (Papert, 1980), or such worlds can be created for them. For example, Lawler described a beach microworld based on LOGO that he created for his three-year-old daughter to facilitate language acquisition skills. In addition to fostering spelling skills, this beach microworld offers an exciting electronic environment for fantasy play.

In studying children's computer microworld play, verbal protocol techniques may be useful in unlocking some of the spontaneous covert fantasies engaged in by children. In addition, computers can be programmed to record the child's interactions within the microworld. Relating these data could provide some exciting insights. Indeed, the computer provides a unique laboratory in which play variable can be manipulated and their effect on the nature of play and related behaviors recorded.

Parent-Child Computer Activity

In this last section I describe some current work on parent-child computer activities conducted with Pat Worden (Kee & Worden, in press; Worden & Kee, 1984). We believe that many young children, ages two and three, will be exposed to computers in the context of a joint parent-child play or learning event. We wondered how this parent-child computer activity might compare with a traditional parent-child activity such as alphabet book reading.

We videotaped 20 parents (10 mothers and 10 fathers) and their three-year-old sons and daughters, using a software program called "My First Alphabet," marketed for Atari computers. All the subjects were computer-naive. In "My First Alphabet," a keyboard entry directs the computer to draw a colorful picture of an appropriate object or animal, draw the letter selected, and present words that begin with the letter, while playing a brief musical tune. For the book activity, three alphabet books appropriate for three-year-olds were provided and parents were instructed to read to the children as they would at home. The computer and book sessions were 12 minutes each.

At this time, only data from ten mother-child pairs have been thoroughly analyzed. Although linguistic complexity did not differ for children in the computer and book conditions, major differences were found in volume of interaction. For example, more letters were reviewed in the book condition (mean = 40) than in the computer condition (mean = 18), and the number of verbal exchanges between parent and child was also greater in the book condition. These differences are probably due to subjects' reading the alphabet books at a faster pace than was possible in the computer activity. After a key-press on the computer, about 20 seconds was required for the screen to complete its presentation of the display. During this period, most parents and children simply waited for the screen display to finish. We were surprised that parents did not make better use of this time, as by prompting their children to guess the identity of the object the computer was drawing. This kind of parental strategy might develop with more familiarity with the activity.

Analysis of verbal activity revealed that mothers gave a greater proportion of identifications and requests for identifications in the book condition; in the computer task they made more comments and more directive and negative remarks. The high rate of controlling and directive statements was probably due to the need to talk about how to operate the computer keyboard and to "wait for it to finish" before entering new letters.

Our study did not focus on play, and no evidence of play behaviors was observed in analyses of verbal or behavioral indices. However, I would anticipate that as parents and children become more familiar with the program, play behavior would begin to appear. My three-year-old son Matthew, who has played with "My First Alphabet" for a year and a half, enjoys "calling up" pictures in both storytelling and pretend activities. For example, when the letter *U* is pressed the computer produces a picture of raindrops falling on an umbrella. Matthew might tell me it's going to rain, then push the *U* key and say, "We need a 'brella.'"

My own observations also suggest that as young children become more familiar with computer activities, they will often ignore the objective of software programs. For example, Matthew enjoys deliberately mismatching the colors—different-colored dinosaurs with corresponding color rectangles in a "jungle" scene—in a new learning game called "Colorasaurus," developed by The Learning Company. Each mismatch causes a dinosaur to fall to the bottom of the screen. Asked what he was doing, Matthew explained he was making the dragons fly through the jungle.

In summary, our study provides a preliminary sketch of parent-child interaction with computers and how it differs from a more traditional parent-child activity. The results have implications for the design of software and for effective parental involvement in young children's computer activities.

DISCUSSION

Allen Gottfried: In our longitudinal study, we found that 25 percent of all five-year-olds now have a personal computer available to them at home —a wide range of middle-class families. My question is, is the computer a new toy, a futuristic toy, or is computer play really a new vehicle or tool for giving us greater insight into the construct called play?

Daniel Kee: It can be both.

Allen Gottfried: It tells us about representation, but children's drawings can tell us about representation. In what way do you think computer play suggests a new methodology?

Daniel Kee: I don't know that it's going to revolutionize the field, but it certainly offers a way to conceptualize play and to uncover new facets of play behavior. For example, variables such as complexity or familiarity can be easily manipulated within a computer microworld and we can look at how this affects children's exploration or play patterns. Furthermore, the personal computer is ideally suited for collecting a detailed account of certain kinds of play activities.

Brian Sutton-Smith: An array of responses to an array of programs might lead to a model of mind that is quite different from the ones we've already got. They might actually give us a new kind of theory of play.

Brian Vandenberg: It puzzles me that we so often seem to assume that new tools and technologies enter our lives without changing them. I see computer play as a continuation of a general increase in an asocial-cognitive-sedentary lifestyle. It's like some sort of historical culmination: a final point where people are all sitting in front of flickering terminals talking to each other through a billboard located somewhere else. What that does to our social life and so on, I think, has potential significance for us as human beings, as it also does for the study of play.

Jay Belsky: I advance that sort of hypothesis myself sometimes, Brian, and I've found that when you test it you may get just the opposite. That is, what about the children who might apparently have an asocial inclination because they're very analytical, very solitary. All of a sudden they have a big shared world, something shared that they're experts in, and they become the computer hackers who develop their own social group.

Before we buy into a new myth that we're going to isolate ourselves, let's recognize some of these other possibilities as well.

Daniel Kee: As Jay suggests, children may not be isolated. For example, new kinds of social interactions, electronic social interactions, may be created. That's a very exciting possibility. Imagine a classroom in which children are seated behind terminals or their own personal computers. What kinds of social activities will emerge in such a situation, and will they be different from the social patterns found in more traditional classrooms? There's some evidence on this in a paper called "Playworlds and Microworlds," by June Wright (in press). She had children working on two separate computers, using a drawing program, and one child is trying to get his picture to look just like the other child's picture. This is very different from a view that suggests that children will be isolated in a solitary environment.

Greta Fein: As educators, we have choices. We can set up computers so that the terminals are separated, or we can encourage cooperation. We can select programs that are stultifying, or we can select programs that are energizing and exciting. I think the distinction between drill-and-practice programs and the more imaginative, creative LOGO programs is one we can talk about and promote.

Some follow-up work that we've done relates to the question of what computers can help us learn about children's play. We used an open-ended graphics program with a cursor that would draw colored lines and make splotches of color appear and go away. The children converted those capabilities into animation and created animated stories, like animated cartoons. They made things happen on the screens. Wolves were going down into dark caves. Two people were sewing. I would not have realized, without seeing that, the degree to which these children could create dynamic forms. When they crayon or paint, you don't see the dynamic qualities. That's why I like to study pretend play. But you can see the same kind of dynamic, integrative, constructive things happening on the computer. Of course, it's also easier to code, and so forth.

Robert Bradley: Precisely the same thing can be seen with good programs for creating music. I've seen children having more fun than almost anything that I've watched them do, spending hours side by side together, creating musical forms one after another and having a wonderful social encounter. So I think computer play is a medium that has the potential both for what Brian is suggesting as almost antisocial and for creating some brilliant new kinds of social interchanges. I think it will be wonderful for some children.

Jay Belsky: It's a new domain to be an expert in, besides sports and how well you dress. It creates a new currency, a new economy, and some children who wouldn't have made it socially in my elementary school now have high value because they're in touch with this medium. Children who used to be social isolates may end up mainstream children. There are new social structural possibilities.

Dan, when you described your child's play and some other children's play, it suggested that the computer was really being used as a prop in a larger scenario. I hadn't thought of that; I'd thought of computer play as sitting at the console and interacting with it. Are there data on how often the computer is used in these two different ways?

Daniel Kee: Not that I'm aware of. That would be interesting to sort out. I suspect that children will find many uses for computers as "partial props" in their play. With older children, the phenomenon that intrigues me is that, after they've learned to program, they begin to adapt video games and tailor them to their own activities. They really personalize them and take off on their own. Rather than using the computer as a prop per se, they exploit it as a medium for play.

Kenneth Rubin: Should we be worried about sex differences in computer use and attitudes toward computers? Statistics show fewer girls than boys registered in computer camps, and I know at Waterloo, which has a very extensive computer program department, the faculty is something like 80 percent male and 20 percent female.

Daniel Kee: One issue is differential access and another is potential performance differences, given equal exposure. I think that differential access is a problem right now because boys are more attracted to the technology and appear more comfortable with its use.

Kenneth Rubin: You suggested that home computer use often starts with games, and many of them are action-oriented games that boys are attracted to but girls might shy away from. Boys therefore get to explore the unit and become familiar with it. Perhaps we need to develop software that will attract females.

Robert Bradley: I think more males are writing software. It's hard to know where to break into the circle.

Brian Sutton-Smith: I would hate to see computer play become a masculine realm. Women have been deprived of the games world for hundreds of years.

ORIGINS AND DEVELOPMENTAL PROCESSES OF PLAY

Brian Sutton-Smith, Ph.D.
Discussant

This conference is about play materials, parental involvement, and play interactions. The first of these has attracted less attention from psychologists than the other two, although the reverse is probably true for the public at large. The public takes its play materials very seriously, whether as toys or as playgrounds.

Even famous intellectuals often have strong feelings about play materials. Here is Roland Barthes (1972), the noted French structuralist and semiotician, talking about the modern manufacture of toys:

> The bourgeois status of toys can be recognized not only in their forms . . . but also in their substances. Current toys are made of graceless material, the product of chemistry, not of nature . . . A sign which fills one with consternation is the gradual disappearance of wood, in spite of its being an ideal material because of its firmness and its softness, and the natural warmth of its touch . . . Wood does not wound or break down; it does not shatter, it wears out, it can last a long time, live with the child, alter little by little the relations between the object and the hand. If it dies, it is in dwindling, not in swelling out like those mechanical toys which disappear behind the hernia of a broken spring. Wood makes essential objects, objects for all time. (pp. 54-55)

This speaker has not remembered his childhood splinters! Much the same rhapsodic viewpoint is found in a 1980 UNESCO French publication on children's play:

> More serious still is the fact that an industrially made toy, stereotyped and technically perfect, forfeits much of its value

as a plaything. It is a closed object, setting up a barrier against creativity and imagination. In almost all instances an elementary plaything is preferable, be it stick or pebble, which the small player can turn into a musical instrument, a tool, a weapon, a car or a boat, a doll or an animal, as his mood dictates. (p. 11)

I found nothing in the present papers to support these prejudices, interesting and widespread as they are. There is no evidence that modern children are either more or less creative with their current "plastic" playthings than were their predecessors with bits of wood or stones. We do know that today's child is somewhat more domesticated than were those of the last century, somewhat less cruel and savage than they were with toys and in play activities.

The writers of these two quotations seem to assume that one can simply look at toys and make predictions as to how they will be used and what their effects will be on human creativity. It is very doubtful if that is possible. One needs to know the context in which toys are used to know much at all about their effects.

I make these preliminary remarks in order to suggest that as psychologists we might ask ourselves whether our own work with play materials is in any way relevant to such issues of claimed public relevance. I believe the prototypical/nonprototypical distinctions made by some conferees probably are. Realism in play materials appears to facilitate pretense at an earlier developmental level, but not at a later one (Fenson, this volume; Fein, 1984).

It is my reading of the literature that we as psychologists take the issue of parental involvement more seriously than we do the issue of play materials. Here we are ahead of the public rather than behind in our practical concerns. I believe we could probably claim that either parental or peer involvement accounts for the greater part of the play variance in the first two years of life, and that there is not much solitary play at all unless it has been so shared or modeled. There may be a lot of solitary intelligent activity, exploration, and mastery, but there's not much play.

It is clear that some of us are using the word *play* globally for almost anything that children do. Others are separating play from mastery, imagination, and exploration. I favor these more specific differentiations. We implicitly deny infants their intelligence and realism by calling everything play.

With respect to play interaction, the third topic of this conference, it is my view that we more often deal with such things empirically than embed them theoretically into our conceptualizations of play as, say, we would if we looked for theory to Mead or Vygotsky rather than to Piaget. This lack of a social interactive epistemology is, I think, our most critical theoretical handicap, and I will speak of it again later.

The Origins of Play

I turn now to the way in which play is framed by the first three speakers, who dealt with the origins of play. Brian Vandenberg has passed beyond ethology to an insistence upon the importance of fantasy in human life. His assertions of the primacy of fantasy in human affairs is refreshingly different from the usual approach in our field—except that it may be, after all, just the old cultural-evolutionary argument about the primacy or primitivity of fantasy, its recapitulation in children (as savages), and its replacement by mature thought. The Freudian and Jungian passage from primary to secondary process had similar evolutionary overtones.

Still, the assertion of primacy doesn't need to carry those historical residues. Bruner (1984) has also been satisfied, in effect, to give fantasy equal time with logic as a mode of thought. Making narrative or fantasy a *mode* of thought has its limitations, of course. It suggests a psychologistic encapsulation for fantasy. It could be just another of those mentalistic mechanisms (traits, IQs, egos, and the like) with which our field is littered.

After 2,000 years of Platonic disenfranchisement, however, this new emphasis on fantasy as an epistemological form seems well taken. There are many play or fantasy metaphors available to us, and I agree with Vandenberg that we should not be too much impressed by those of problem solving alone (Sutton-Smith, 1979). The history of play provides a positive shower of potential metaphors, including irrationality, as in the early Greek notions of the gods playing randomly with our lives; uselessness, as in the Platonic epistemology just mentioned; dissimulation, as exemplified by Machiavelli on the one hand and Rabelais and Cervantes on the other. From Romanticism we get the metaphor of play (and art) as especially sublime and as well we get the key concepts of voluntarism and "fun." Our current notions of intrinsic motivation owe as much to Schiller and Wordsworth as they do to our own empiricism.

What intrigues me more than intrinsic motivation as a postulate, I should say in passing to Adele Gottfried, is our almost desperate concern to have it associated with children's play. Why must freedom be so important to our conception of childhood? In the nineteenth century, artists were sometimes viewed as the only truly free and therefore authentic beings (Trilling, 1971); now it is children. Why? I think this question is as important as our observation that they *are* free in some sense.

Part of the fascination of Bateson's (1972) view of play as metacommunication is that it applies to both animals and humans. Since one criterion for the evaluation of a metaphor is its fertility or comprehensiveness, metacommunication has, in my view, a mythic edge over Vandenberg's hope at this point.

Helen Schwartzman's paper has the healing power that anthropologists always exercise. One contrary example, and our universals collapse to the ground. Her assertions are:

1. *That child work doesn't preclude child play.* Although this is probably true, I doubt if anyone ever put the matter quite that dichotomously. Obviously, child work does affect the amount of time left over for play, and the energy one has for play. I have the unpublished tables from the Whitings' six-culture study showing a very clear negative relationship between number of chores and amount of observed play. I imagine TV affects the amount of street play in the same negative way, though solitary imaginative play (in front of the TV) may increase.

2. *That disadvantaged children do not play less complexly or less imaginatively.* Again, this question cannot be settled by a case here or there. Shirley Heath and I (1981) have taken the approach of seeking to differentiate between kinds of imaginative play, instead of defining it only in ethnocentric middle-class terms. There is a difference between the decontextualized literary fantasies we induce in our children and the more contextualized ones of nonliterate peoples. In the latter, narratives do not stand aside from speaker and hearer but include them in the content.

3. *That multi-age peer groups are more collaborative, and perhaps more beneficial, than single-age peer groups.* This point is well taken, except that my own historical examples are full of multi-age cruelties as well. So the real issue may be multi-age groups in a frame of constraint of some sort.

4. *That children do not need space and toys to be imaginative.* This is like the proposition about work and play earlier. Did anyone ever say it in quite this singular way? Isn't it rather that these variables account for a small, significant piece of the variance in some modern samples (e.g., Singer, 1973)?

We have in the past fifty years made sensory stimulation into a vogue term. For good or for bad, we have convinced many people that their children can be hastened forward with the right kinds of parental and object stimulation. We have a scattering of findings, like those of Caldwell,

Bradley, and Wachs presented at this conference, showing that the right kind of objects can be correlated with the right kind of growth. And yet if one looks at our textbooks in child psychology, or even at the writings of those who have attempted to consider toys systematically, as Dick Chase and Burton White (1975) have, it is amazing how limited the information actually is. There is next to no systematic work on the environment as specific objects. In short, although we are a technological society that pours objects on and around its infants en masse, we have no psychological technology of objects. There is some sense, apparently, in which we don't believe specific objects make much difference.

My own empirical reconciliation to date is that there is evidence both that some toys make little difference and that some make a lot of difference. In a recent study (1985), I found it useful to distinguish between three classes: toys of acquaintance, toys of stereotype, and toys of identity. The last group, at least as reminisced about by their owners, made an enormous difference and were a very heterogeneous group of objects: tennis racquets, music recorders, toy first-aid kits, bicycles, Barbie dolls, and many kinds of soft toys that were cuddled in bed literally for decades.

For years Greta Fein has been both keeping us up-to-date on pretense and keeping us on our toes. One strength of the present paper is that she looks in some depth at longitudinal rather than experimental data. Some of her formulations are most exciting. For example, I like her skepticism about scripts as play, because the notion itself is so tied to correspondence theories about truth.

My only quarrel is with such metaphors as "transformational mechanisms" and "affective templates." These impute an aggregate of internal psychologistic mechanisms, whereas the data she supplies us with are a dialogic series of happenings between two or three players, who use centripetal and centrifugal moves with great fluidity. Dr. Fein's is a study of interaction par excellence; its paradox is that its leading concepts are not interactive so much as monistic after Piaget. I believe Greta has now really left Piaget behind and needs Bakhtin (1981), whose dialogic theory of the imagination seems a more fitting paradigm.

In sum, the origins of play presented to us to this point stress:

1. The omnipotence of fantasy

2. The relativity of our concepts

3. The existence of a metacognitive sphere of play sui generis, quite unpredictable by our usual modes of thinking about the subject as cognitions or as literal scripts.

Developmental Processes

But I have also been given the task of discussing developmental processes. We do have a goodly representation of recent work on developmental processes in the papers by Fenson, Fein, McCune, and Bretherton. For economy, I will not retrace the steps by which the present systems of McCune, Fein, and Fenson have developed out of and owe lineage to Piaget's series of symbolic steps in his *Play, Dreams, and Imitation in Childhood* (1962). They have all contributed immensely to a more detailed picture of the development of play in the first two years of life than we had before.

My major criticism of this preliminary mapping is that, although it is beneficially influenced and instigated by Piaget, at the same time it is limited by his structuralist metaphors of human development. Whatever he may say about interaction, in my opinion Piaget's work is within the main structuralist tradition of this century as exemplified in linguistics by Jacobsen, in anthropology by Levi Strauss, and in narratology by Barthes and others. This work, despite its virtues, has often argued that underlying the description of sequential and universal systems of cognition, culture, and narrative, there are internal cognitive operations (schemas, templates, binary oppositions, functions, deep structures) which propel the whole thing forward. These mental homunculi always seem to end up becoming reified as relatively autotelic mentalisms. As has been illustrated here by our panel, this leads in practice to a belief in the virtue of tracing structural sequences, not just for a beginning of description but as an end point.

Recent criticism of Piaget, arguing that his descriptions of sequence have been artificially drawn from nonrepresentative situations (in the laboratory) or from solitary children, suggests that children function much more competently than he realized when seen in natural contexts. Further, when they are seen within an interaction, we get a view of mind as it usually works. The mind working in more abstract circumstances may be a more abstractive mind, but it is by no means a typical one, nor, therefore, the best source for understanding even cognition, let alone play. To put it another way, if we take Piaget's structural metaphor, we reify as operations apparently universal cognitions derived from an aggregate of subjects in a limited array of highly abstracted human situations. But if we study children continuously, as Greta did, in order to discover *processes* of individual *change* in the social or individual structurings that we temporarily describe, we are much more likely to discover the course of development, with all its individual variety, multilinearity, and mobility of operations.

PART III
THE SOCIAL SIGNIFICANCE OF PLAY

PRETENSE: PRACTICING AND PLAYING WITH SOCIAL UNDERSTANDING

Inge Bretherton, Ph.D.

Of all forms of early play, symbolic play or pretense has received most attention from investigators because Piaget (1962) regarded it — along with language and deferred imitation — as a hallmark of an emerging ability to engage in mental representation. By drawing on detailed observations of his own young children, Piaget was able to illustrate that the development of make-believe play is characterized by a growing distance between the persons and objects that are used as symbols and what the symbols are meant to represent. For example, a baby first reenacts everyday activities such as sleeping or eating, later feeds a doll or puts it to bed, and later still uses blocks as cars and sticks as spoons. In the course of development, the child's symbols become more and more dissimilar and distinct from those which they are meant to represent. Thus, pretense can serve as a gauge of a young child's developing representational ability.

However, Piaget did not recognize pretense as an actual *contributor* to cognitive development. In Piaget's view, the primary role of pretense in development is affective. As young children make dolls relive their own unpleasant past experiences, or transform reality in line with their desires, they can get a sense of mastery over a world they cannot yet control in reality. In this interpretation, Piaget is very close to psychoanalytic writers such as Erikson (1963) and Peller (1954).

My view of pretend play is not incompatible with Piaget's description of sensorimotor development during the first two years or with his views about the affective significance of pretense. It is incompatible with his belief that pretend play reflects cognitive development rather than producing it and with his views about the preschool child's egocentric and incoherent thought processes. In what follows, I will argue that early pretense can be regarded and studied as a form of event representation, that event representation in pretense becomes increasingly coherent over the course of infancy and toddlerhood, and that even very young children practice and play with pretend representations of the social world in ways that further cognitive development.

Event Representation: Roles, Actions, and Objects

In pretending, children simulate and transform routine events of family life. Later, they draw on other sources as well. I will discuss the development of early pretense in terms of roles, actions, and props (objects), even though these three dimensions are not completely independent.

Piaget (1962) outlines a systematic developmental progression of pretend roles, from self-representation to the representation of multirole structures. As previously noted, Piaget saw in these findings evidence for an increasing ability to distance or sever the symbol from what it symbolized. Viewed from the perspective of event representation, the same data illustrate toddlers' developing ability to play roles other than their own and to collaborate in role-play with playmates. Although Piaget made his initial observations on just three children, his findings have since been corroborated by others (e.g., Fenson & Ramsay, 1980; Kagan, 1981; Nicolich, 1977; Wolf, 1982; Watson & Fischer, 1977; 1980). There are a few disagreements about the finer distinctions that we ought to make in describing pretense, but the level of agreement among investigators is impressive. Table 2 outlines the development of roles as it pertains to replica play and to sociodramatic play.

Table 2. The Development of Pretend Roles in Replica and Sociodramatic Play

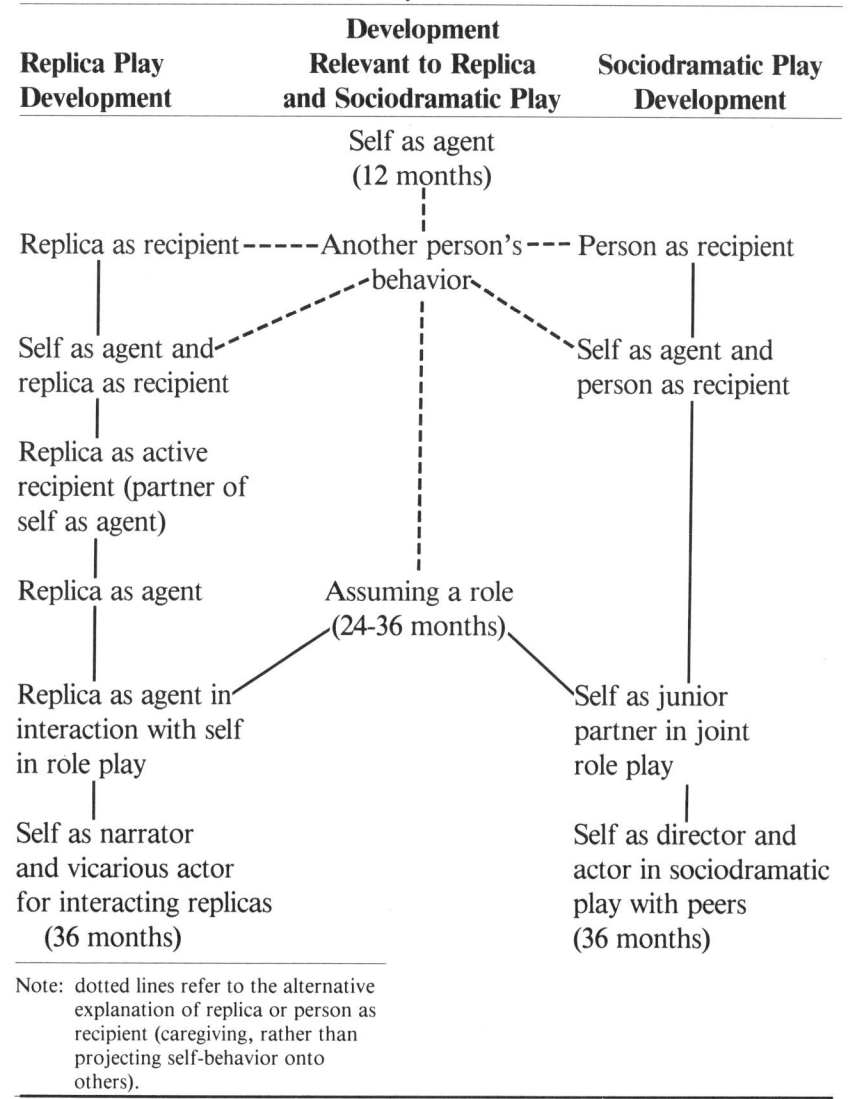

Replica Play Development	Development Relevant to Replica and Sociodramatic Play	Sociodramatic Play Development
	Self as agent (12 months)	
Replica as recipient -----	Another person's behavior	--- Person as recipient
Self as agent and replica as recipient		Self as agent and person as recipient
Replica as active recipient (partner of self as agent)		
Replica as agent	Assuming a role (24-36 months)	
Replica as agent in interaction with self in role play		Self as junior partner in joint role play
Self as narrator and vicarious actor for interacting replicas (36 months)		Self as director and actor in sociodramatic play with peers (36 months)

Note: dotted lines refer to the alternative explanation of replica or person as recipient (caregiving, rather than projecting self-behavior onto others).

It is evident from the table that some forms of role-taking and playing are present as soon as the infant goes beyond self-representation. These activities include, in the second half of the second year, use of replicas as experiencers as well as agents (Wolf, 1982). At the end of the third year children are capable of much more. In performing a drama including several interacting dolls, the child has to play several roles. In joint make-believe the situation is comparable. The child has to coordinate her or his viewpoint of the make-believe event with that of other children.

As in the description of role-play, there is a large measure of agreement among investigators on the development of pretend actions. A baby's initial pretend actions consist of single behaviors. Later in the second year, toddler's action sequences are based primarily on everyday experiences (Wolf, 1982). Although a group of three- to five-year-olds studied by Garvey (1977) had a considerably larger repertoire, much of their sociodramatic play continued to revolve around family life. The older children also incorporate more out-of-home and fictional material into their joint pretense. A few general themes accounted for the greater proportion of make-believe events: treating-healing, averting threat, packing, taking a trip, going to the store, cooking, having a meal, and repairing were especially popular. A *theme,* it should be noted, is a more abstract framework than a basic-level event schema. For example, a number of very different event schemas or *scripts* may be used to enact the theme "averting threat" (the threat can be a monster, fire, or getting lost).

Infants' first efforts at pretending appear to require prototypical objects such as realistic spoons, telephones, or baby dolls (Piaget, 1962; Vygotsky, 1966; Nicolich, 1977). Later such realism is less and less necessary to sustain the make-believe reality, although many children seem to need tangible placeholders to stand for imagined objects. Empty-handed miming tends to be infrequent in spontaneous play until at least the middle of the third year.

The findings of Nicolich's (1977) longitudinal study of 14- to 19-month-olds suggest that progress in role representation (making others the recipients of one's action, enacting others' behavior) generally occurs before children begin to enact action sequences, and that object substitution is acquired last. It seems sensible to hypothesize, however, that there may be a trade-off between the three dimensions (roles, actions, and objects). For example, a toddler might be able to represent two interacting roles without sequenced actions, or to act out a sequence with realistic but not with substitute objects.

Metacommunication: "This Is Play"

In sociodramatic play, children not only enact make-believe sequences but plan, negotiate, and coordinate their joint enactment. The term *metacommunication* was coined by Bateson (1955; 1956) to refer to messages that inform coplayers that "this is play" as opposed to not-play. Bateson pointed out that such messages are logically paradoxical, saying in effect, "These actions in which we now engage do not denote what the actions for which they stand would denote" or, to put it more concretely, "This nip is not a bite."

Because acts of pretense can look and sound quite "real," it is necessary to mark the make-believe reality as simulation or fiction to avoid misunderstandings. Metacommunication in pretense becomes very prominent during the fourth and fifth years, but precursors of this ability can be traced to infancy, although systematic studies of metacommunicative signals during the second and third years are still lacking. The management of play at two conceptual levels (communicating outside the play frame about actions to be performed within the play frame) has been examined in several studies.

Garvey and Berndt (1977) go beyond Bateson in their definition of metacommunication. They emphasize that the joint creation of a make-believe reality requires more than the message "This is play." In order to pretend with companions, children need techniques for negotiating about content: what theme or script is to be played, and where as well as how the theme is to be realized. Garvey and Berndt studied 48 pairs of children ranging in age from 34 to 67 months and developed a system for categorizing metacommunicative behaviors (mostly verbal statements) by which children coordinate sociodramatic play:

1. Mention role	Other's	"Are you going to be a bride?"
	Own	"I'm a lady at work."
	Joint	"We can both be wives."
2. Mention plan	Other's	"Pretend you hate baby fish."
	Own	"I gotta drive to the shopping center."
	Joint	"We have to eat. Our dinner's ready."
3. Mention object	Transform	"This is the train," putting suitcase on sofa.
	Invent	"Now this is cheese," pointing to empty plate.
4. Mention setting	Transform	"This is a cave," pointing to wooden structure.
	Invent	"We're there," about imaginary picnic site.

Garvey and Berndt also observed that exits from the pretend world are explicitly negotiated by negating make-believe roles ("I'm not the Dad"), actions ("I'm not dead"), props ("That's not a car"), and settings ("We're not at the beach"). Especially interesting are back-transformations ("It's not a cake anymore"; "Please don't push me 'cause I'm not the dragon anymore").

What is so fascinating about sociodramatic and replica play is that the logically clear distinction between the acts of planning (or describing) and acting is deliberately blurred once it has been mastered. Statements that look like acting are really or simultaneously metacommunication about play. Likewise, real-world action and pretend action are logically distinct. As Bateson aptly stated, "The map is not the territory," but map and territory (pretense and reality) have a strange way of becoming tangled in play. Frightening make-believe themes may become so "real" that a player feels compelled to step outside the play frame or refuses to enter it.

Not only does pretense sometimes become "too real," real-world concerns intrude into the make-believe world in a number of ways. For example, Schwartzman's (1978) study of collaborative play in a daycare center showed that the children's relationships outside the play context (friendships, dominance) affected the content and process of sociodramatic play. High status children could join ongoing play by imperiously adopting a role or defining an activity. Low status children had to ask for permission to join the group or play particular roles ("Can I be the witch?"). The roles children played tended to reflect the actual authority structure of the group, with the most popular children frequently playing mothers and fathers and less popular children often assuming the role of pet (kitty or doggy).

The Representation of Subjunctive Events

A separate aspect of pretense is the transformation rather than recreation of reality through simulation. The roles children play are often not their own; the objects serving as props are frequently not what they purport to be; and the scripts may represent physically impossible worlds. Event schemas and specific memories provide the raw material for make-believe scenes, but most play is not an attempt at faithful reproduction. Rather, make-believe consists of making new maps by transforming old ones.

The term *make-believe* has two meanings: "as if" behavior, which simulates everyday reality, and "what if" behavior, which creates new worlds where a spoon can be a telephone, toddlers can be mommy and daddy, and people can fly or become invisible.

Hofstadter (1979) has pointed out that human beings constantly manufacture mental variants on the situations they encounter. These unconsciously manufactured "subjunctives" represent some of the richest potential sources of insights into how human beings organize and categorize their perceptions of reality. Hofstadter proposes a hierarchy of conditions for transforming aspects of reality, ranging from simple pretend actions through elaborate play worlds in which gravity is denied, time contracted or expanded, and causality and values turned upside-down. Toddlers do not deliberately toy with the laws of time, space, and causality, but high-level "what ifs" become increasingly common during the preschool years (Scarlett & Wolf, 1979). As these researchers put it, fantasy (not only real-world understanding) undergoes cognitive development.

The Development of Social Understanding

In considering pretense in terms of tangled levels of reality and subjunctive thought we have moved a long way from the discussion of make-believe in terms of "as if" or mere simulation. In what way are these phenomena related to the development of social understanding?

I would like to suggest that the ability to engage in "serious" mental trial and error—"What if I did it this way, rather than that way?"—and the ability to engage in make-believe are but two different facets of the same representational function. Organisms that can create mental alternatives prior to action are ipso facto able to play with this ability, just as organisms with great control over motor actions can and do play with their motor skills (Fagen, 1981). Piaget (1962) makes much the same claim. I differ from him only in believing that subjunctive skills are of cognitive, not purely affective, significance.

Not all children seem willing to play with their representational ability to the same degree (Wolf & Grollman, 1982). Beyond infancy the imaginative disposition appears to be more a matter of cognitive style than of cognitive level. Some individuals refuse to contemplate fanciful ideas or repress them before they become conscious, while others enjoy toying with subjunctive thoughts, however outlandish these might be. Nevertheless, the quality of fantasy that an individual can produce ought to be related to the coherence and sophistication of his or her real-world social understanding of people, their intentions, motives, feelings, and actions. The ability to create imaginary worlds (even of the low-level "what if" variety) should not, I believe, simply be taken for granted.

A second major component of make-believe is the ability to engage in subjunctive event representation for and with others. This creates both the potential for sharing one's inner world with companions and the potential for deceit or pretense. Make-believe is linked to the capacity to lie, to "put on a show," to deceive, and, at the other end of the value scale, to engage in sacred ritual. In the case of lying, the communicator hopes that the addressee will not perceive the deception. In the case of make-believe and ritual, the participants jointly agree to create an alternative reality.

It is presumably because of its close association with deceit that children's make-believe play creates unease as well as enchantment in adult onlookers. A further reason for unease is the incompleteness of the map-territory distinction. By claiming that "it is only pretend," children can surreptitiously act out real-world antagonisms. The real can sometimes parade as make-believe. This process can also work in the reverse direction. What started as deliciously thrilling make-believe can become frighteningly or distressingly real, even for adults. The tendency for map and territory to blend and tangle may be an inevitable part of the capacity to simulate reality in order to entertain alternative courses of action.

I want to conclude by proposing that the ability to create symbolic alternatives to reality and to play with that ability is as deeply part of human experience as the ability to construct an adapted model of everyday reality. I suggest that we ponder why the ability to think of the other-than-the-case emerges so early in life, what it means for human development that even a two-year-old is able and eager to proclaim "I a daddy."

DISCUSSION

Brian Sutton-Smith: Your central metaphor for play is event representation, but when you speak of "putting on a show" or engaging in ritual or what you call subjunctive play generally, you also suggest a theatric metaphor. You haven't elaborated it, but I think it's exciting. The data you've reviewed seem to show that children get less literal with age. I wonder if they really do, or whether that's merely our perception of what they do. It seems to me there must be some other basis for early roles than the literal. Children adopt them too early. How could an 18-month-old base the role of mommy and daddy on the literal?

But parents are already acting in play with their babies at two months. They make a funny face and the baby responds. If you're a stimulating kind of parent, you do a lot of acting with a baby, and in return the baby adopts a role too, at least for a second. The theatric situation of parent and child could well be the model from which the whole set of changing roles you've described is derived. Event literality is another stream of phenomena, and only one of them. We haven't done enough yet with the theatric metaphor.

Inge Bretherton: You may be right. Certainly it's true that the theatrical is there very early, and it requires metacommunication. The infant has to distinguish between somebody frightening and Daddy doing something that seems to be frightening but isn't really.

Brian Sutton-Smith: Funny faces games are only fun with a face you know you can trust, as it were. You can't trust strangers who make funny faces.

Lorraine McCune: I'd like to offer another way of looking at Piaget's interpretation of the play stages that we've been discussing. As I see it, his major interest was in the development of operative intelligence, and so he conceptualized the operative aspects of the sensorimotor period in terms of the logic of action. In order to go from the logic of action to a logic of propositions, actions must be internalized, and you have to develop a representational system that will allow you to proceed to this next operative level. Consequently, there is a long period of figurative development, which was not of compelling interest for Piaget as it is for us. I don't think he discussed how play acts would move one forward, but he did say that play allows the child to assimilate reality to the structures that he or she already has available, and we know that assimilation is one of Piaget's requirements for progress.

Inge Bretherton: Piaget calls pretend play "assimilation of reality to the ego," and he says that before about age four play includes a lot of distortions and so on. At that time, it becomes more realistic and has to be accommodated to reality, which makes it useful in terms of cognitive development. I think it makes a major contribution to cognitive development before then. Furthermore, "assimilation of reality to the ego" doesn't explain some things I think must be explained, such as wishful thinking. Wishful thinking is one of our most amazing capacities, and I don't think you can just say it's assimilation to the ego. How is the ego able to conceive of such things?

Lorraine McCune: Piaget didn't address play much before the age of four. To me it's similar to the case of language. Piaget has not really addressed language extensively either, but some people wish to impute a particular linguistic theory to him. Although he says very little about how the capacity for play develops and how it related to logic, that doesn't mean he didn't believe it was important.

Inge Bretherton: He did think it was important. It was important because it gives you power over the world when you don't have any. In other words, you can make reality conform to your wishes, which as Brian Vandenberg pointed out is not something that stops with infancy. We continue to make reality conform to our wishes when we take placebos and get well, for example. What I'm saying is that I think it's far more likely that some of these logical operations actually develop out of earlier event representations, so that there is a continual reconstruction throughout this period, than that you're starting with a confused figurative network of representations on which you then impose some order because at a certain age you're suddenly able to perform logical operations.

Greta Fein: I have two serious concerns about event representation as an approach to play. First, the Schank and Abelson model, which was a deliberate attempt to design a computer program that met the Turing test, doesn't meet the Turing test. This test says that the computer program has to respond in such a way that if you didn't know it was a computer program, you'd think it was a human being. Schank and Abelson developed the restaurant scenario, and the artificial intelligence people have torn it apart. It doesn't meet the criteria of good psychological modeling. It isn't able to account for what I consider the most primary, the most fundamental, capacities to experience life—from birth on—in an affectively profound, moving, emotionally salient way. If it can't do that, on its own grounds, why are we bringing it in as an explanation for even more primitive processes?

Inge Bretherton: I think that event representations *are* affective; that we have left affect out of representation, unfortunately; that every time you enact, for example, a script of abandonment, you actually feel sad. You feel sad when you talk about it and when you think about it, which is why we don't like to think about unpleasant things sometimes. It's true that Schank and Abelson did not build that in, but it would be very easy to build in. Furthermore, other models of representation are in no better state. The event representation model does have one advantage. It's the only model that preserves enough relationships for it to be used to explain planning, acting, understanding, and so on. The logical categories do not help you do that.

Greta Fein: Let me speak to that issue. As I see it, event representation is essentially a linguistic model. When you discuss actions and objects, for instance, you're presupposing something like parts of speech, something like verb categories and noun categories. Now, if that isn't classification, I don't know what is. I don't think you can finesse the problem by saying that we're going to take it as a given, and then move to something called events. Buried in the events are taxonomic assumptions, and the problem isn't solved by embedding the assumptions in the model. That's my other concern about event representation.

I also have reservations about imposing a semantic-linguistic model on preverbal children. I am not sure that what we know about language is adequate or appropriate for use in accounting for nonlinguistic phenomena. Piaget is wonderful for this, because of his very well-formed notion that language cannot be used as a model of thinking. It certainly can't be used as a substitute for a model of thinking, and I believe that's what event representation is trying to do.

Inge Bretherton: You could say it the other way around, and some people do. Maybe the structure of language is as it is because event representation is a very basic necessity. It's more important than logic, although I agree with you that we categorize. We categorize events, so you have taxonomies of events, but they hang together in ways that you can operate on.

Greta Fein: I think you're departing from Brian Vandenberg's rule. You're implying that a myth, a theoretical proposition called event representation, is not a myth but is what is.

Inge Bretherton: No, I'm not that naive. I realize it's just one myth, but I happen to think it's a useful one. The only way you can use your myths is to believe for a moment that they're true.

PRETEND PLAY IN THE FAMILY

Judy Dunn, Ph.D.

There are striking differences between mothers in the interest and enthusiasm that they show toward young children's pretend play. Some join in with alacrity; others simply are not interested. Still others actively discourage pretend play:

> He'd make up stories . . . It got so bad that I tried to stop it, because I didn't want him to go from an imaginary story to a

downright lie—because there's not much difference between the two.

He's got a . . . I'll tell you what it is—it worries me sometimes—he's got a vivid imagination; and it goes on and on and on until he *lives* it; and sometimes, these imaginary people, you have to *feed* them with him, do you see what I mean? It worries me. (Newson & Newson, 1970)

How important and how widespread are such differences in maternal interest in children's early symbolic play? What are the developmental consequences for a child who grows up in a family in which the parents are uninterested in or actively discourage make-believe?

To begin to answer such questions, we have to study children playing at home in their usual way rather than during structured laboratory "play" sessions with standardized toys. The home studies reviewed below have yielded data of central importance to those interested in children's play from either a developmental or a clinical perspective. For developmental psychologists the findings suggest, first, that we greatly underestimate children's abilities if we study play solely in more public contexts such as the school, playground, or laboratory. Second, they demonstrate that the importance of *social* pretend in the development of symbolic activities has been misunderstood, and that the developmental sequence of solitary to social pretend outlined by Piaget may well be misleading.

For clinicians, studies of children playing at home in the family can help correct an overemphasis in the research literature on pretend play and *cognitive* development. Pretend play has a role in children's emotional and social development as well, and it is obviously important that we understand this role more clearly. Manuals for parents do encourage parents to become involved in children's pretend play (White, 1980). But do we in fact know enough to justify this recommendation?

Findings from four studies of very young children playing at home with their mothers and siblings bear on these issues. The studies all employed unstructured observations. Study I (Dunn & Wooding, 1977) focused upon firstborn children aged 18 to 24 months; Study II (Dunn & Kendrick, 1982) upon firstborn children followed longitudinally through the infancy of their siblings; Study III (Dale, 1983) upon second-born children aged 24 months; and Study IV (Dunn & Dale, 1984) on second-born children aged 18 and 24 months.

Mothers and Symbolic Play

What part do mothers play in the development of children's abilities to pretend? From experimental work such as the elegant study of O'Connell and Bretherton (1984), we know something about the teaching role that mothers commonly adopt during laboratory play sessions. What happens at home, when mothers are busy with household tasks but are also free to join their children's play when they wish?

First, we will consider the question of how frequently mothers participate in their children's pretend play. Our studies show that, on average, mothers are involved in many of the very young child's early assays into symbolic play. In Dale's study (Study III), for example, 59 percent of pretend play episodes included some participation by mother or sibling. In all four studies, however, there were very wide individual differences in the participation of mothers — a topic to which we will return.

A second issue concerns the character and significance of interaction with the mother during pretend play. According to our data, mothers' contributions were frequently didactic in nature. The mothers used joint pretend play to explore concepts of size and shape, to encourage classification skills, and especially to discuss the functions and appropriate uses of objects. Their questions and comments frequently focused on bringing fantasy play into line with reality. Mothers would draw the child's attention to the question, Is that how it *is* at the shops, or at bedtime, or when Daddy goes to work? Here is an example (Dunn, 1980):

Mother:	Are you going to the shops for me?
Frances (age 3):	No. I'm going to the shops for Judy first. I got some. They're fish. Now I'm getting some for Mummy. My scooter fall down...
Mother:	See if you can find a space to park the scooter, then you can go and find me some fish in the market.
Frances:	I *got* some fish. It's in the cupboard.
Mother:	Oh. I don't think that's a very good place for it. Can you put it in the fridge for me?

Inge Bretherton has drawn attention to the interesting distinction between "as if" fantasies and the more exploratory "what if" fantasies (Bretherton, this volume). Mothers' suggestions are most commonly of the "as if" kind.

Another characteristic feature of early social pretend games between mothers and children is the tutoring mothers provide for role play. Miller and Garvey (1984) have traced the importance of mothers in a particular role game, that of nurturing a baby, or "playing mother." Dale's study confirms that maternal involvement in nurturing games is common with 24-month-olds.

In our ongoing Study IV, we find mothers becoming involved not only in nurturing play but in a range of role games. In these exchanges mothers usually act as spectators, offering guiding comments from the perspective of a detached observer rather than joining in play as equal partners. This is, as we'll see, in marked contrast to the behavior of siblings during role play.

A final interesting feature of the collaboration of mother and child in joint pretend play is the frequent explicit discussion of the inner state and feelings of other people. Pain, sadness, cold, warmth, hunger, tiredness, or sleepiness — not only mothers but children as young as 24 months discussed such feeling states during fantasy play. This finding suggests that discussion with the mother in the context of joint pretend provides a forum in which children explore the causes and consequences of such states.

Individual Differences Among Mothers

In the United Kingdom, at least, differences between mothers in their involvement in pretend play with young children are marked and widespread. To illustrate, when the children in our current longitudinal study were 24 months old, the differences ranged from mothers being involved in joint pretend play in no observation intervals to involvement in 35 percent of them. These differences were *not* closely related to differences in forms of joint play other than pretend play. However, they did correlate with differences in the ways the mothers conversed with their children. In Study II, for instance, mothers who made frequent pretend suggestions were likely also to use language in more elaborate ways with their children, and their children were more likely themselves to use language in a relatively mature fashion.

Interview studies show that some individual differences in mothers' interest and involvement in pretend are linked to social class and educational differences. In the Newsons' (1970) interview studies of 700 Nottingham families, a significant minority of working-class mothers disliked, disapproved of, and tried to discourage their four-year-olds' fantasy play, usually because they associated it with lying. A follow-up of these 700 families when the children were seven years old showed even more marked concern and anxieties about children's fantasies (Newson & Newson, 1978).

Siblings and Symbolic Play

Our two most recent observation studies, which included siblings, highlight an important and hitherto neglected point. It is not only mothers—or even primarily mothers—who are involved in very young children's pretend play. For some children, siblings are extremely important partners.

In some families there is frequent pretend play with both mother and sibling; in others it is only with the mother; in others it is only with the sibling. Although sibling-child pretend play was common in only a third of the samples in Studies III and IV, it had features that give it special developmental interest. First, the nature of the collaboration between siblings in joint pretend differs markedly from that between mother and child. Mothers, as noted, usually act as spectators and rarely enter the game as full partners. In play between child and sibling, in contrast, siblings take complementary roles. Their play involves a close meshing of actions and themes by two equal partners.

Second, children as young as 24 months take part in joint role enactment in play with a sibling. They can make explicit a transformation of their own identity and can share a framework of pretend play with the other child. This is remarkably mature behavior for such young children, and it has not been observed with mothers or fathers. The arguments about play roles that two-year-olds have with their siblings, and the pronouncements they make, show how seriously we may underestimate children's abilities by failing to study them in their family world.

Third, there are important differences in the themes of pretend play shared with mother and with sibling. With siblings, pretend games often concern much less mundane experiences than shopping, cooking, eating, and the bedtime routines commonly played out with mothers. With a sibling, fantasy play takes the child into space, into lands of monsters and killing, to the bottom of the sea, to desert islands, to the moon.

Children with highly participant mothers and those with highly participant siblings have quite different experiences, it seems. Further, our data suggest that growing up in a family with a mother who is uninterested in and unsupportive of pretend play will not necessarily be a disadvantage, if the family includes a friendly and affectionate sibling. Indeed, siblings may have more influence on developing children's interest in pretend than mothers.

Developmental Implications

Four implications of these observational studies stand out.

1. In assessing the relative significance of solitary and social pretend play in development, we must study social play, not simply solitary play. The widely accepted view that "solitary leads to social" must at least be reconsidered. Valentine (1937) pointed out nearly fifty years ago that children play make-believe "at a much earlier age in the intimate life of the family than has been reported in the observations made of children in groups."

2. To suggest that children under three cannot negotiate or communicate about rules and roles in a shared pretend game is to underestimate their capabilities, as shown in home play with siblings.

3. Individual differences in mothers' interest in pretend are extremely marked. They are linked to differences in conversational style and social class that are likely to be associated with differences in children's verbal and representational skills. However, a warm and affectionate older sibling will often introduce a child to a rich and exciting world of pretend very early, with all the possibilities for exploring social roles and rules that this implies.

4. The significance for emotional development of parental involvement in children's early pretend play urgently needs our attention. Until we know more, we are hardly in a position to pronounce on the importance of encouraging parents to become involved in children's early pretend play.

DISCUSSION

Allen Gottfried: I'm surprised that mothers were involved in such a small percentage of pretend play episodes. What individual differences or characteristics have you found in the mothers that might account for the differences in involvement?

Judy Dunn: First, there are language differences. Mothers who do and don't engage in a lot of pretend play with their children talk to the children differently in other contexts, too. The second point, which Vonnie McLoyd will be talking about, is the thorny area of social class. As I said in my paper, the Newsons' study of 700 families in Nottingham found that a large minority of working-class parents—and I think class was defined on the basis of mother's education rather than father's occupation—actively discourage fantasy play. Although only one of my own studies included families from the lowest social strata, we found the same negative attitudes that the Newsons did in some of these lower-class mothers. The small size of our sample makes me cautious, but I do think parent involvement in pretend play is linked, at least in England, to social class. I wouldn't want to generalize to America or anywhere else.

One surprise to me was that an interest in pretend cut across the child-rearing variables we had thought were important, such as interest in playing with the child and permissiveness. It seems to tap a different dimension.

Allen Gottfried: I'd like to push you a little on the issue of intervention. Almost everything that's been said at this Round Table so far seems to suggest that play is a good thing, a positive thing, and that it tells us a lot. It's an index of social-emotional maturity, an index of cognitive functioning. The higher you are on the play ladder, the more socially, emotionally, and cognitively advanced you are.

Suppose that instead of doing observational studies we ran some experimental intervention programs oriented toward pretend play. How do you think they could be conducted?

Judy Dunn: Interventions focusing on role play have been done with older children, but nothing has been done with children as young as those in my studies. I think it's terribly important to bear in mind how young these children are—under two, a lot of them. Once they are three, they seem to be on a trajectory. If they've had early experience with a supportive mother or sibling at getting into the world of pretend, they can do it on their own. Intervention might be helpful, but I have a lot of caution about it.

Lorraine McCune: I don't think intervention has to necessarily wait for firm demonstrations of positive outcomes, though. Even without firm evidence on causal links, you can suggest what I like to call a gentle intervention—one you know isn't going to do any harm and probably will help the mother-child dyad learn more about each other. Mothers could be encouraged to see pretend play as a way of enriching their lives and those of their children, though they should not be given the impression that pretend play is an essential daily activity. People do differ in the extent they want to do that sort of thing.

Judy Dunn: My main concern about intervention, and maybe Vonnie will talk more about this, is that how a mother feels about joining in a child's fantasy life is something so deep, so much part of her whole way of relating to the child and her culture, that I hesitate to just wade in there and tell her what to do. Perhaps, if we offer "gentle intervention," the emphasis should be on gentleness.

Theodore Wachs: We usually look on intervention with a main effects model, but I strongly suspect based on your data and those of others that we should use a covariance model instead. For certain kinds of mothers, you can recommend certain kinds of interventions, but for other kinds of mothers, those same interventions aren't going to work.

Jay Belsky: Have you examined individual differences in the extent to which mothers play with the child on the child's own terms, accepting the child's theme and so on, as opposed to maintaining an "adultocentric" perspective that might be intrusive and interfere with play?

Judy Dunn: No, but that would be interesting to look at. I do know of a study that compared a five-year-old boy's pretend play when he was alone, with his mother, and with his best friend, and he behaved very differently in the three situations. When his mother got involved, she was tremendously didactic and turned the play into a teaching situation. The little boy complied. He made all the right moves and fit in, because this was how they did it together. But in other situations he could play in other ways.

It may be difficult for mothers to fit in with some of the fantasies young children like to act out. If a two-year-old is pretending that Teddy is peeing here and there around the house, would you really expect a mother to join in and keep the game going without being didactic?

Kenneth Rubin: Maybe fathers would find that game more acceptable.

Judy Dunn: Ah. We tried to observe fathers. It may be something about English men, though it's probably more general than that, but the fathers were much more self-conscious when we were around than the mothers. They tended to be either very inhibited or very active in their participation, in which case the mother might say, "Oh, you should come every day — this doesn't usually happen."

From what we did observe, the fathers seemed to be less good than the mothers at getting into the children's pretend because they were less familiar with the child's current interests. Some of the mothers were brilliant about that. They know how compelling these themes are.

I had one child who was a railway engine for two weeks, and so the mother knew all about this engine. She could make just the right kinds of comments. The father couldn't, because he was out of the house all day.

Kenneth Rubin: Fathers may play with their babies in a different way, too: more rough-and-tumble play, more ghosts and monsters, more shooting and killing people.

Jay Belsky: I suspect you're right, Judy, that fathers are less tuned in to what's going on. They are going to be more concerned with the formal script: you're shot, you fall down, and you wait five seconds before you get up. A script that said you're shot, you say you're dead, and the next thing you know you're flying through the air might not appeal to them as much.

Daniel Kee: Did the mothers in your study correct the dads when they saw them "dropping the ball" during pretend episodes?

Judy Dunn: We didn't study that systematically, and the individual differences were huge, as you can imagine. Some mothers were very cynical about their husbands' uselessness; others were more supportive; some even said, "Well, he's better at it," but then they'd add, slightly resentfully, "Of course, she's daddy's girl."

Daniel Kee: Did you ask the moms what they would tell the dads to do in a hypothetical situation?

Judy Dunn: Well, no. Most English mothers don't tell their husbands how to play with their kids.

Brian Vandenberg: Your comment bears on a point that I think is very important, Judy, and that is power. If you look at much of your data in terms of power, didactic interventions on the part of the parents can be seen as reinforcing the social order. The reason parents don't join in pretend play about peeing Teddy bears and so on is that the parent's role is that of a powerful figure, a social agent who enforces the status quo and communicates the accepted social order. I think dads don't get into fantasy play with their children because of the role-status-power implications of it. To break the role of being father by playing with the child as a mother does would be a serious power-status violation. As I interpret it, these issues also relate to the ways in which siblings differ.

Judy Dunn: I think power relations is a particularly good way to think about individual differences in siblings. An older sibling who gets into pretend has to be prepared to relinquish some power and let the younger child do some of the contributing and negotiating. Usually, the older ones are very managerial and bossy about play. But the little ones, even though in power terms they're at the bottom, are very good at one thing: terminating pretend play. If something gets out of hand or they don't want to do it, they just walk off. They do have quite a lot of power in that sense.

Theodore Wachs: Have you looked at frequency differences in siblings' play as well as in mother-child play?

Judy Dunn: Not yet, but I think that's important. One of the puzzles for me, and I hope we'll hear more about it here, is why some children are so riveted by pretend and others are much less interested. It's not that they can't do it. Maybe they're more interested in objects than in persons; I don't know.

With some siblings, what determines participation in pretend with a younger one is the quality of the relationship. Others just are not that interested in fantasy. Those who are, though, are real sophisticates. When a three-and-one-half to five-year-old gets into pretend, it's like a magnet for a two-year-old. It's much more exciting than anything the mother could do, and I think that's why it works so well.

PLAY, PEER INTERACTION, AND SOCIAL DEVELOPMENT

Kenneth H. Rubin, Ph.D.

Children's play is now serious business for academicians. A quick count shows some 450 citations in the new Carmichael *Handbook of Child Psychology* chapter on play (Rubin, Fein, & Vandenberg, 1983), over half of them with post-1975 publication dates. Despite this intense recent interest in studying play, the idea of using play to identify children who may deviate from normality in some way has received little attention. Not all forms of children's play are adaptive; indeed, the very frequent display of certain forms of play at certain ages may be an early warning signal that a child is at risk for socioemotional problems.

Play Observation Scale

The first Waterloo observational studies of preschoolers' free play were conducted about ten years ago (Rubin & Maioni, 1975; Rubin, Maioni, & Horning, 1976). In planning the research, we had been aided immensely by Smilansky's (1968) volume on the sociodramatic play of Israeli children. Smilansky, borrowing from Piaget (1962), defined the following four categories of play:

1. *Functional play.* A child simply repeats the same movements, with or without objects, as when manipulating and exploring toys during infancy.

2. *Constructive play.* The preschool child moves from handling and exploring materials to using them to construct or create something that remains after the child has finished playing, such as a road of blocks.

3. *Dramatic play.* This type of play, which also develops during the preschool years, has received a great deal of attention at this Round Table and from researchers. Pretend play is nonliteral. It involves symbolic transformations and the production of decontextualized behaviors.

4. *Games with rules.* To play games, children must accept a division of labor and a set of prearranged rules. Rarely evident during the preschool and kindergarten years, this type of play generally develops at about six or seven and continues into adulthood.

Although these four types of play were thought to develop in the order listed, it's important to note that constructive play and dramatic or pretend play actually emerge at about the same time.

To develop the Play Observation Scale, my colleagues and I combined the cognitive play forms just described with Parten's (1932) familiar social-participation categories of solitary, parallel, and group activities. The play coding frame is illustrated on page 90.

The Play Observation Scale has been used to gather large amounts of developmental data (Rubin, Fein, & Vandenberg, 1983). Our findings on the developmental progression of play from age three to age five can be summarized as follows:

1. The frequency of parallel play decreases; group play increases. Conversations with peers increase, and children spend less time watching others or doing nothing.

2. The frequency of functional play decreases, while dramatic play and games-with-rules increase.

Major Categories in the Play Observation Scale	

SOLITARY PLAY
  Functional
  Constructive
  Dramatic
  Games
	GROUP PLAY
	  Functional
	  Constructive
	  Dramatic
	  Games

PARALLEL PLAY
  Functional
  Constructive
  Dramatic
  Games
	OTHER BEHAVIOR
	  Unoccupied
	  Onlooker
	  Reading
	  Conversation
	  Transitional activity
	  Rough-and-tumble
	  Exploration

3. The frequencies of solitary-functional, solitary-dramatic, parallel-functional, and parallel-dramatic play decrease. Group-constructive play, dramatic play, and games increase.

Developmental Correlates of Children's Play

Can observations of children's free play provide us with telltale information concerning their social, emotional, and cognitive development? We have obtained some interesting correlations between particular play forms and various developmental measures. For example, we found that children in preschool, kindergarten, and grade one who produce a high frequency of solitary-functional play (the least mature form of play) perform more poorly than others on social and impersonal problem-solving tasks and on measures of verbal IQ. Furthermore, their teachers rate them as socially incompetent and their peers dislike them. (Peer rejection was assessed by observation and by administering a sociometric battery to the children.) Second, children who engage frequently in solitary-dramatic, parallel-functional, and parallel-dramatic play fare similarly to the solitary-functional players. That is, they are rejected by peers, rated by teachers as socially maladroit, and perform poorly on measures of perspective-taking and social problem solving (e.g., Rubin, 1982; Rubin & Clark, 1983).

Why is it that these relations occur? In the case of functional play, the answer is simply that this is a rather immature form of behavior for four-, five-, and six-year-olds. The dramatic play data may surprise psychologists and educators who believe that *all* forms of pretense are "good for" young children: Clearly this is not the case. In early childhood, dramatic play occurs most often in group settings. Thus, nonsocial pretend play produced frequently in group (classroom) settings is a nonnormative form of behavior. In numerous other reports, nonnormative (e.g., immature, aggressive) behaviors have been associated with peer rejection and social-cognitive deficits (Coie & Kupersmidt, 1983; Dodge, 1983).

Which forms of play are associated with developmental maturity and adaptation? Parallel-constructive play (such as seatwork, art, and puzzle-type activities) is related positively to peer popularity, teacher ratings of social competence, and both impersonal and social problem solving in preschool and kindergarten. High frequencies of sociodramatic play in preschool and kindergarten are associated positively with popularity, social competence, perspective-taking, and social problem-solving skills. The category of play in kindergarten and grade one that correlates most strongly with measures of peer popularity, social competence, and social-cognitive development is group-games-with-rules. This category is, of course, theoretically, the most mature form of social and cognitive play in the Play Observation Scale hierarchy.

Targeting At-Risk Children

My own interest in children's play centers on how and whether peers can play an active role as socialization agents. I am less concerned with the connection between play and the development of symbolic representation than with the *social* benefits of play. I decided to use the Play Observation Scale to try to target small numbers of children who deviate from the normal play patterns of their peers. The children who attracted my attention in the Waterloo Longitudinal Project were those who interacted very infrequently with their peers during free play periods.

Peer interaction has long been thought to have special importance for cognitive and social development (e.g., Piaget, 1932; Schwarz, 1972). In addition, children who have been identified as isolated from or rejected by their peer group appear to be at risk for school dropout, antisocial behavior, and psychopathology in adolescence and early adulthood (Cowen et al., 1973; John, Mednick, & Schulsinger, 1982; Roff, Sells, & Golden, 1972). Four years into the Waterloo Longitudinal Project, we have data suggesting that severely withdrawn young children may be at risk for particular psychosocial problems.

Initial Findings: Preschool and Kindergarten

Basically, I am interested in children who deviate in some extreme fashion from their age-group and classroom social-play norms. My first research efforts included children attending a large number of preschools and kindergartens in Southwest Ontario. Through the use of the Play Observation Scale, I devised a targeting scheme that identified three sociability groups: isolate, average, and sociable children. The first and last groups each represented approximately 15 percent of the population.

The concomitants of extreme "isolate" status can be summarized as follows:

1. Isolate children produce more transitional, "off-task" activity than their more sociable age-mates. They are also less boisterous in their play.

2. The quality of solitary play by isolates and nonisolates differs. Withdrawn preschoolers engage in more solitary-functional and solitary-dramatic play than others but in an equal amount of solitary-constructive play. These data have special interest because of our earlier findings that solitary-functional and solitary-dramatic play are associated with peer rejection and social maladjustment.

3. The quality of group play by isolates and nonisolates also differs. During group play, the sociable children are more likely than isolates to participate in dramatic play and games. Given the significance that many developmental psychologists attach to sociodramatic play and social games, we might expect infrequent participation in such play to predict lags in social-cognitive development.

4. Extremely withdrawn children do not receive significantly more negative sociometric ratings than children in other groups, though teachers rate preschool isolates as more fearful and anxious than others.

5. On a social problem-solving measure (see Rubin & Krasnor, in press), isolate children produce fewer alternative solutions and are more likely to suggest "adult intervention" strategies than their more sociable age-mates.

6. Isolate children are more likely than average or sociable children to talk to themselves or to an imaginary playmate during free play with another child.

7. When isolate children direct requests to another child, they tend to be "low-cost" (e.g., "Look at this"). Sociable children make more "high-cost" requests (e.g., "Give me that"). Even so, isolates experience less compliance to their directives than do other children. Furthermore,

when their requests fail, isolate children are less likely than sociable ones to modify their original strategies.

In short, our data portray young isolates as somewhat anxious, deferent to their peers, less mature and boisterous in their play, and perhaps more dependent on adults to solve social problems than their more sociable age-mates. Because young isolates are not disliked by their peers, some psychologists have suggested that they are not at risk for later problems and that we focus our attention instead on rejected children, who are known to have more psychological and academic problems in adolescence and young adulthood.

It is true that our initial data do not allow us to conclude that severely withdrawn young children are at risk. In part, we cannot draw this conclusion because it will take time to assess the stability and the long-term correlates of early isolate (nonsocial) behaviors.

Early Follow-up Findings: First and Second Grades

Many of the kindergartners who participated in the first year of the Project were followed into grades one and two, where they were again rated as isolate, average, or sociable. Initial analyses reveal that over 60 percent of the isolate kindergarten children who remained in the study were similarly classified in grade two. (Interestingly, even more of the sociable kindergarten children — over 80 percent — maintained stable status.)

Stable isolates are as popular among their peers sociometrically as their more sociable age-mates. They can also think as well about solutions to social dilemmas involving object acquisition and friendship initiation. However, isolate children do not believe themselves to be socially competent. They also perceive themselves as less competent in academic and physical-motor-performance than do their peers. Despite objective indicators of social competence, then, there appears to be a breakdown in the self-system.

What could be happening to produce significant negative self-perceptions in this group? Recent data concerning children's role relationships during play provide us with some possible direction. Isolate children, when they engage in dyadic free play with a nonisolate partner, are more likely to take on deferent, submissive roles. Furthermore, when they attempt to play dominant roles (e.g., manager or teacher), they are more likely to be rebuffed than their more sociable counterparts. Finally, they are "easy marks"; their more sociable play partners are extremely successful in gaining compliance from them. This combination of social deference and social failure may help explain why isolate children have poor perceptions of their own competencies.

It is my belief that consistently withdrawn children do represent an at-risk population. However, they are probably not at risk for the same problems as rejected children. The latter group is characterized generally by aggressive acts and poor social-cognitive problem-solving skills: They appear to be at risk for externalizing problems. Our group of stable isolates seems quite different from rejected-aggressive children. The data suggest that they are at risk for internalizing problems such as depression or anxiety disorders.

To sum up, early longitudinal work with the Play Observation Scale has allowed the identification of a small group of children who may be at risk for later socioemotional problems. Future research efforts will center on (1) why some three- and four-year-olds come to be identified as severely withdrawn relative to their age-group norms, and (2) what psychologists and educators can do to prevent or ameliorate the problems associated with social isolation in childhood. Our work is obviously cut out for us.

DISCUSSION

Greta Fein: Ken, could you describe what a solitary-dramatic player who was classified as an isolate would be doing?

Kenneth Rubin: Perhaps a whole lot of fantasy, using little figures, within a group context.

Greta Fein: So these are children who are in a group but are not interacting?

Kenneth Rubin: Yes. Let me give you an example from one of our dyadic situations. We had a Sesame Street Clubhouse that we put in the middle of a very attractive playroom in the lab. The average child, in the room with another child, says "Hey, come play with me. Look, here's Bert and Ernie!" The isolate child takes a look at the objects, says "Yeah, these are neat," then takes Grover over into the corner alone and talks to him. In that situation, the materials themselves are supposed to be pulling for interaction, but it isn't happening.

Inge Bretherton: So it's not so much that the play itself is maladaptive as that it's maladaptive in the social setting.

Kenneth Rubin: That's right. Another way of looking at it is that these extremely withdrawn children are displaying behaviors that are typical of younger children.

Allen Gottfried: Ken, do you have any speculation as to directionality? Does play develop slowly in children who are isolates, or is it that children whose play is developing slowly become isolates?

Kenneth Rubin: Both, I suppose. If you engage in nonnormative behaviors, which solitary-functional and solitary-dramatic play are in a group context beyond a certain age, I think that leads other children to look at you and say, Hey, there's something a little wrong. Your peers don't reject you for solitary play in early childhood, but as you get older the solitary nature of your play, if it continues, becomes increasingly salient to the peer group. It will be observed to be increasingly nonnormative. In school-age children, certain forms of solitary play are associated with peer rejection.

Jay Belsky: Does the peer group really notice the solitary nature of the activity at younger ages? I can envision an isolate as perhaps lacking social skills and feeling anxious about relating to others, so anxious that the child can't really gather together her cognitive resources very well. She's her own worst enemy because she's so insecure, and it shows in her self-system. But all the time her peers don't regard her as unpopular, because ultimately they don't see her. As you suggested, it's an internalizing problem: It's not that they are doing it to me, it's that I'm doing it to myself.

Helen Schwartzman: Going back to Inge's point about the importance of setting, it seems to me that you're really focusing on maladaptive play styles as something that exist within children and paying less attention than you should to how you can assess and understand maladaptive play *situations*. What maladaptive play contexts might be interacting with qualities of the child? You seem to locate the problem in the individual as opposed to the context or situation.

Kenneth Rubin: That's true, I do.

Lorraine McCune: A student of mine has just obtained some findings that are similar to yours, but from the other direction. She compared language-delayed kindergartners with nonlanguage-delayed kindergartners on sociodramatic play, looking at roles, themes, length of episode, object information, and other variables. She got very clear differences between the language groups in all the sociodramatic play indices except those that were purely action-based. The language-delayed children also tended to play alone more often than others.

Jay Belsky: That raises the question, might some of the deficits in isolates' social skills be attachment-based?

Kenneth Rubin: I think so.

Robert Bradley: Did you notice anything different about the children who were classified as isolates in the early age period but not later on?

Kenneth Rubin: The most interesting thing about that group—children who were withdrawn in kindergarten or grade one but not in grade two—is that as second graders they showed no deficit in any realm, including the self-system. It's the children who are continuously withdrawn, who are consistently very insecure in their peer relationships, that I think are the problem.

Jay Belsky: Do you have any idea what distinguishes withdrawn children who later become more sociable from those who remain isolates?

Kenneth Rubin: Not yet. One thing we're trying to look at right now is whether the children who changed acquired a friend somewhere along the line. Finding someone else who is like you can be critical. Wyndol Furman at Denver has demonstrated, for example, that you can change the behavior of severely withdrawn children quite readily by pairing them with similar children. You force a dyadic situation on them.

To conclude things, let me tell you a bit about some of the rejected children we've been following over the years. In second grade, after being identified as highly aggressive and rejected by their peers for several years, these children don't have any problem in the self-system at all. In fact, their egos are inflated. That's a major social-cognitive problem for those children.

I should also mention that the group of children I'm targeting as extremely withdrawn over the years is very small, only 10 of the 150 children we started with. This is not a large number of children at all, but it's a group that has not been properly identified in the past and a group we ought to be concerned about.

SOCIAL CLASS AND PRETEND PLAY

Vonnie C. McLoyd, Ph.D.

In *The Effects of Sociodramatic Play on Disadvantaged Children* (1968), Smilansky compellingly set forth an issue with which scores of researchers have since wrestled, namely, the ways in which position in the class structure of society affects the imaginative play of children. Smilansky's work led her to three major conclusions: (1) that lower-class children engage in less and poorer quality sociodramatic play than their middle-class counterparts; (2) that these deficits develop because of parental attitudes and practices and are related to verbal, cognitive, and social abilities; and (3) that training by adults in the techniques of sociodramatic play can ameliorate these deficits and positively affect verbal, cognitive, and social skills.

What do almost twenty years of research since the publication of Smilansky's book tell us about the pretend and sociodramatic play of children from different socioeconomic backgrounds? The first section of this paper reviews the findings to date. It is followed by a discussion of factors that militate against drawing firm conclusions from this body of research and ways future research might proceed. Finally, in keeping with the theme of this Round Table, research on social class differences in maternal attitudes and practices regarding pretend play, sparse though it is, is briefly summarized.

Amount and Quality of Play

Most, but not all, studies of sociodramatic play report that middle-class preschoolers engage in sociodramatic play more frequently than do lower-class preschoolers (Fein & Stork, 1981; Griffing, 1980; Rosen, 1974; Udwin & Shmukler, 1981; White, 1978). A minority of studies report no differences (Golomb, 1979; Stern, Bragdon, & Gordon, 1976) or a more complex pattern of findings (Rubin, Maioni, & Hornung, 1976). One study of the amount of time children spend in sociodramatic play actually reported differences in favor of lower-class children (Eiferman, 1971).

Some researchers have found that middle-class children enact longer episodes of sociodramatic play than lower-class children (Griffing, 1980; Smilansky, 1968, Study 1). Others have found neither length of sociodramatic episode (Fein & Stork, 1981; Smilansky, 1968, Study 2), length of pretend play episode, nor complexity of pretend play (Golomb, 1979) to be related to social class. Fein and Stork (1981) found the overall quality of sociodramatic play among middle-class children to be higher than that among lower-class children.

The findings regarding social class differences in the use of objects during pretend play are also mixed. Some studies report that economically advantaged children show greater imaginary and elaborated use of objects, an increased tendency to invent imaginary objects, and less use of objects in ways dictated by their form (Griffing, 1980; Smilansky, 1968, Study l; Smith & Dodsworth, 1978). Other studies report no relationship between social class and the frequency with which preschoolers use objects as though they possess imaginary properties, use representative and nonrepresentative objects as referents, or invent imaginary objects for which concrete referents are absent (Fein & Stork, 1981; Smilansky, 1968, Study 2; Stern et al., 1976).

Taken as a whole, studies of social class differences in pretend and sociodramatic play are inconclusive. There is far less evidence of lower quality than of depressed frequency of sociodramatic play among economically disadvantaged children, though findings with respect to the latter have not been univocal or particularly robust.

Methodological Problems

Irrespective of the findings themselves, this body of research is inconclusive because of problematic data gathering and processing procedures, confounding classroom and school variables, and insufficient consideration of how the primary medium of sociodramatic play, namely verbal behavior, may be affected by ecological variables. Even studies that report no significant social class effects are characterized by a number of problems that undermine their validity and generalizability.

Future research should make vigorous attempts to eliminate potentially confounding variables and methodological biases so that systematic variation between children from different social classes, if found, can be confidently attributed to social class rather than a host of contaminating factors. When social class differences are found, researchers need to press even harder to understand their source. As Smith (1983) has reminded us, social class is an umbrella variable which should serve only as a conceptual way-station on the road to identifying more proximate variables that cause or underlie the observed differences.

Mueller and Parcel (1981) recently criticized the imprecise, often impressionistic, criteria psychologists use to identify social class levels, and the use of outdated measures (e.g., Hollingshead). Their suggestions regarding specific alternative measures of social class merit careful attention. Future research should also make greater differentiation among social class groups, especially within lower-income strata. The life circumstances and conditions of the underclass are different from those of the more stable upper-lower and working-class segments of society (Billingsley, 1968; Higgins, 1976), and these factors may well affect children's pretend play.

Previous studies are plagued by a number of other methodological flaws and ambiguities. One of the most troublesome aspects of the majority of studies is the confounding of social class and classroom factors such as curriculum, materials, space, and affective environment.

With one exception (White, 1978), children in all the reviewed studies were observed in school or daycare settings, usually during free play. Recent research indicating systematic variation in children's pretend play as a function of school and situational factors makes reevaluation of these studies obligatory.

A few researchers have eliminated the confounding of social class and classroom factors by observing lower- and middle-class children within social heterogeneous classrooms (Fein & Stork, 1981; Rubin et al., 1976). Their findings indicate higher frequencies of sociodramatic play among middle income children. Observation of lower and middle-class children in socially heterogeneous classrooms does not necessarily ensure elimination of possible confounding factors such as unfamiliarity with play materials and feelings of apprehension, both of which are known inhibitors of pretend play (Fein, 1981; Hutt, 1970). Perhaps social class differences in pretend play should be assessed only after systematic attempts have been made by the researcher to familiarize lower-class children with play materials, their teachers, and the school environment in general (Fein & Stork, 1981). Ideally, the success of these attempts should be empirically verified.

Another possibility is to assess social class differences in pretend play and symbolic competence at home instead of at school. The casual observations of scholars not necessarily interested in children's pretend play suggest that we may gain much insight into the imaginative lives of poor children when we study them in home settings. For example, in the course of his field work with poor families and children in eastern Kentucky, Looff (1971), a clinical child psychiatrist, encountered a 13-member family living in a three-room shanty. Despite an existence so bleak that the crew of a Walter Cronkite television program chose them in the winter of 1963-64 to portray Appalachian life to the nation, the children in this family appeared to have a rich fantasy life.

One other strategy merits serious consideration. Rather than attempting to control motivational and affective differences within one setting, a different setting might be chosen for each group precisely because of its facilitory effect on pretend play (Fein & Stork, 1981). For one, the highest level of symbolic competence may be expressed in a home or neighborhood setting and, for the other, in a school setting. Alternatively, both groups of children might be observed in the same two settings, one chosen to be optimal for each group. Implementation of this research strategy, of course, requires more knowledge than is currently available about the ecological determinants of pretend play for lower-and middle-class children. As a beginning, observations of lower- and middle-class children should be conducted in an array of settings. The information gained would not only inform researchers about where pretense is most likely to occur for each group and thereby allow designation of optimal settings but permit distinctions between "typical" and "best" displays of pretense (Fein & Stork, 1981).

Lower-class children's verbal behavior varies substantially as a function of the situation (Cazden, 1970) and may be mediated by, for example, suspicion that their behavior will have adverse consequences (Labov, 1972). Such variability may pose validity problems in the study of children's pretend play, since verbalizations, and to a lesser extent vocalizations, elucidate the symbolic content of play. Huttenlocher and Higgins (1978) have argued quite strongly that without verbal evidence that play behavior is meant to designate an absent model or object (e.g., "Pretend I am the mother"), symbolic processes need not be involved. The child's behavior may reflect nothing more than exemplification or practice of social skills, a toy's limited potential or functional substitutability, or what the child has learned about the appropriate use of toys. The importance of their argument is their call for a more rigorous and unifying definition of symbolic behavior.

Though Huttenlocher and Higgins were concerned with overestimation of symbolic competence as a result of inadequate operational definitions, there is also reason to be concerned about underestimation. Because lower-class children are more likely to speak nonstandard English, they are more likely to be admonished about their speech patterns in the classroom. The potential inhibition of spontaneous verbal behavior, then, constitutes another reason that the classroom may be a less than optimal setting for studying pretense in lower-class and working-class children. In addition, some of the communication patterns of lower-class children have been ignored in previous research. Among Afro-Americans, especially lower-class groups, verbal communication is laced with distinctive nonverbal expressions and frequent displays of affect (Hannerz, 1969; Kochman, 1972; Akbar, 1974).

Maternal Practices and Attitudes

Because it is both scanty and conflicting, existing research does not provide a firm basis to judge whether the attitudes and practices of lower- and working-class parents regarding pretend play differ reliably from those of middle-class parents. Smilansky (1968) reported that lower-class parents were less likely than middle-class parents to join in the games of their children, teach them how to play, provide toys suited to dramatic play, encourage them to abandon the "real" world when playing, or praise them when they succeeded in sustaining a game. Some studies of working-class and middle-class families in England tend to support Smilansky's conclusions; other findings appear contrary to this pattern. Interestingly, home observations by Dunn and Wooding (1977) showed that working-class mothers were less likely than middle-class mothers to play with objects with their 18- to 24-month-olds but equally likely to become involved in the child's pretend play.

Clearly, more effort should be devoted to understanding the role of parents in the onset and development of pretense in children. Future research also should give attention to the contribution of siblings and other members of the household. If a mother spends only a modest amount of time in playful exchanges with her child, this does not necessarily indicate that the child has a dearth of playful interaction with adults or older children, especially in lower-class families where households tend to be larger.

DISCUSSION

Allen Gottfried: I've just written a paper for the *Merrill-Palmer Quarterly* dealing specifically with socioeconomic status indices in child development research, and what you say, Vonnie, is definitely true: Current SES indices, including some that we've used in our own research, are notoriously bad. They are not flexible enough to deal with such issues as SES differences in different racial or ethnic groups, differences in family structure, changes in the women's work market. I find it incredible that people keep using the Hollingshead two-factor index when in 1975, Hollingshead wrote papers saying that it should no longer be used.

The second point I want to make is that some researchers have, in fact, gone beyond SES and focused on proximal variables. It's amazing that so few play researchers are using these tools that have been proven to be reliable and valid.

Theodore Wachs: Based on the variability in social class results summarized in your paper, Vonnie, how comfortable would you be with the idea of abandoning SES as an explanatory construct? Is it time to get rid of the umbrella, to use your phrase — to drop this whole nonsense of social class—and start looking for more relevant explanatory constructs?

Vonnie McLoyd: That's what I'm inclined to do in my own work. I don't think I am interested in using SES as a major independent variable in any of my work.

Dante Cicchetti: I've seen so many papers in *Child Development* that describe a sample as "predominantly middle class." You might think that meant the researchers had conducted demographic interviews, but it doesn't; it usually means that they sent out a card and it came back from a "middle-class neighborhood." Those of us who study psychopathology or deviant samples need to know what's going on with class precisely and in as much detail as possible, because we want to separate factors associated with membership in a particular class from factors associated with the problem we're studying.

Implicit in what's been said about studying different cultures and ethnic groups, I think, is that we need more people from these groups doing the research. We have an obligation to try to recruit as many black and other minority students as we can to go on and get doctorates in child development. There are so few, and I think that's one reason good, sensitive research with these different ethnic groups and minority populations is not that common.

Brian Vandenberg: I'm struck by how closely related people think speed and competence are in our culture. Not long ago, I heard a child at the zoo say to his mother, "Oh, look at that turtle! It's moving so slow, it must be really dumb."

When we talk about fantasy and developmental lags, there is an implicit evaluative quality in there. There's an assumption that we're watching some kind of competence unfolding, rather than emerging at different times, and then we place evaluative labels on "stages of competence" even when there's no empirical reason to do that. One of the things Ken Rubin has done, I think, is find some instances in which delays are, in fact, related to competence problems. Another part of what he did was show that there are delays that are not related to competence problems. We need to be careful about calling a difference a "lag," and therefore implying incompetence.

Vonnie McLoyd: We also assume that lower- and working-class children are less intellectually competent, and that this ought to show up in their pretend play.

Brian Vandenberg: In other words, turtles are not only dumb because they're slow but slow because they're dumb.

Dante Cicchetti: Because of clinical experiences I've had, I strongly agree with the suggestion that we must study children in multiple contexts. Varying the contexts and the measures helps you learn more not only about lower-class children or black children or (in my case) maltreated children but about all children.

Greta Fein: It's hard to give up the hope that there is some one best setting for the study of children and all we need to do is identify it. I'm intrigued by home studies, but I'm not sure that the home is the ultimate place where children experience life. There are backyards and neighborhoods, as Helen Schwartzman has emphasized; there are beaches and playgrounds. Methodologically, it is easiest to study children in a lab or at least in a stable setting such as a schoolroom or home. It's very hard to track children through the backyards or the streets, coding reliably as we go, no less. Our methodological requirements sometimes force us into radical departures from real life. When we try to explain sibling effects like those Judy Dunn reported, for example, don't we need to know what happens outdoors? What are the children getting from other children in the neighborhood? Observations in one setting open up questions about others rather than giving us neat answers.

Judy Dunn: The main reason for looking at very young siblings—toddlers and preschoolers—at home is that that's where they spend most of their time together. This point about context, which has come up again and again, is a very important one. In a beautiful study of four-year-old working-class and middle-class children at home and at school, the researcher has shown, among a host of other interesting findings, that the working-class children spoke brilliantly at home but were virtually silent at school. All the familiar class differences were evident in the school situation, but they were not evident at home. At home, these children would have the same elaborate conversations that the middle-class children were having, and so on. So I agree that school is a peculiarly limiting situation.

I also agree, Greta, that gang life or street life is important. It isn't impossible to study it, either. We have a graduate student who became part of a group of lower-working-class children. These children spent most of their time on the streets from the age of three, and she really became part of their gang. They would tell her where they were going and she'd go through hedges with them, with her tape recorder on. She has amazing stuff.

Vonnie McLoyd: It's a problem that there's so much cost associated with doing that kind of work, not only in terms of money but in terms of whether you can get it published, quite frankly. If you spend a large amount of time studying a small number of children, you're more likely to have difficulty getting your work published, particularly in the journals that would give it most visibility.

Helen Schwartzman: Those are the real issues: What kind of research is regarded as convincing or unconvincing? What kind gets published and heard, and what kind doesn't get listened to? I don't think the problem with research in natural contexts is really a shortage of methods or tools for collecting and analyzing data. Anthropologists have those.

Jay Belsky: The politics in science are as real as they are any place else, but I'm sure there's some different work out there—work that none of us can replicate but all of us will cite, just because it's compelling. We have to hope that eventually, as happened with Piaget, the good work — the cream — will rise to the top.

PART IV
PARENT-CHILD INTERACTION IN DIFFERENT POPULATIONS

CAREGIVER-INFANT INTERACTION: THE STUDY OF MALTREATED INFANTS

by Dante Cicchetti, Ph.D.

Research directed toward maltreated children and their families has a particular urgency given the number of individuals who are affected. Over one million children are maltreated each year, according to recent estimates (National Center on Child Abuse and Neglect, 1981). Although child maltreatment research has focused almost exclusively on physical abuse, Giovannoni and Becerra (1979) have documented through case review that most children experience more than one type of maltreatment. Attention to the diversity of types of abuse and neglect, and to their interacting effects, is crucial to an accurate understanding of the causes and consequences of child maltreatment.

The etiology of child maltreatment has been investigated in several recent studies. Research on etiology is important in order to develop parent treatment programs and major preventive techniques, but it is equally important to document the ways in which maltreated children may be impaired by their experiences.

Maltreatment per se does not constitute an emotional disorder; however, the experience of being maltreated places the infant at high risk for both current and future developmental dysfunction (Aber & Cicchetti, 1984). Maltreatment involves multiple factors, including parental psychopathology, environmental stress, child characteristics, and social isolation (Belsky, 1980; Cicchetti, Taraldson, & Egeland, 1978). It is *not* a "within the child" disorder and must be studied by employing a transactional model of development that emphasizes the mutual, ongoing, dynamic nature of the transaction among infant, caregivers, and environment (Cicchetti & Rizley, 1981). The chaotic home setting and stressful circumstances in which many maltreated infants are reared, and the inconsistent or abusive patterns of care they experience, place them at an extreme on the continuum of caretaking environments. Maltreated infants are at high risk for the negative consequences of "caretaking casualty" (Sameroff & Chandler, 1975), and their study can illuminate the role or influence of environmental factors on the organization of emotional development.

Socioemotional Competence in Maltreated Infants

According to the organizational perspective of development, as proposed by Werner and Kaplan (1963) and elaborated by Sroufe (1979), the early years of life can be segmented into developmental periods, each characterized by a pivotal task that must be resolved by the child before progression to the next period. While each task remains important over the life span, it is most salient during one developmental period (see Cicchetti & Schneider-Rosen, in press). Each task includes related elements from the social, emotional, and cognitive domains. Among the most salient developmental issues of the infancy period are differentiation of affect and the formation of a secure attachment relationship, discussed below.

An organizational framework emphasizing pivotal tasks is particularly useful when considering the construct of competence. According to Waters and Sroufe (1983), the competent child is one who is able to utilize internal and external resources in order to achieve a favorable developmental outcome. External resources are positive environmental influences such as stimulating play objects and social relations. Internal resources are specific skills and individual characteristics that enable the child to capitalize on environmental resources.

Differentiation of Affect

Among the very few investigators to focus on abnormalities in the development of affective communication between maltreated infants and caretakers are Gaensbauer and his colleagues (1980). They have identified four relatively consistent negative affective patterns: (1) developmentally and affectively retarded (showing lack of social responsiveness, emotional blunting, and inattentiveness to the environment); (2) depressed (showing inhibition, withdrawal, aimless quality of play, and sad and depressed facial expressions); (3) ambivalent/affectively labile (showing sudden shifts from engagement and pleasure to withdrawal and anger), and (4) angry (showing active, disorganized play and low frustration tolerance, with frequent angry outbursts).

The work of Frodi and Lamb (1980) indicates that maltreating parents may have different psychophysiological responses to the cries of infants, thereby suggesting that these parents are less effective than nonmaltreating parents in responding to the affective expression of their infants. Inadequacies in the infant's communicative system may also contribute to deviant patterns of interaction and atypical developmental outcomes. In future research, it is essential that the contribution of both caregiver and infant to early developmental deviations be considered, with the aim of illuminating the transactional nature of maltreatment.

The Development of Attachment

Since Bowlby's (1969) seminal exposition on attachment theory, there has been general assent among developmental psychologists that the establishment of a secure attachment relationship between infant and caregiver is one of the primary tasks of the first year of life. According to Bowlby's formulation, the attachment relationship has both a physical and a psychological function. It has evolutionary survival value in that the caregiver protects the infant from potential physical harm. Diverse infant behaviors, such as smiling, vocalizing, and clinging, promote physical proximity to the contact with the attachment figure. In addition, the relationship has the psychological set-goal of "felt security" that will enable the infant to explore both the social and inanimate worlds (Sroufe & Waters, 1977).

Contemporary elaborations of attachment theory have emphasized the latter function of the relationship, stressing the enduring affective tie between infant and caregiver. Rather than focusing on individual behaviors emitted by the infant, researchers have examined the organization of attachment behaviors; the quality of the relationship is seen to depend upon the quality of interaction between the dyad during the first year of life.

Based upon their behavior during the "Strange Situation," a procedure developed by Ainsworth and Wittig (1969) to assess the quality of the attachment relationship, infants can be classified into one of three categories. Infants in Groups A and C are considered insecurely attached to the caregiver. During reunion episodes, they either avoid her (Group A) or manifest angry, resistant behavior alternating with proximity-seeking or passive behavior (Group C). In contrast, securely attached infants (Group B) greet the caregiver positively during reunions and use her as a secure base from which to explore the environment. In nonclinical samples, approximately 70 percent of infants are classified as securely attached to the primary caregiver, while 30 percent (20 percent A and 10 percent C) are classified as insecurely attached (Ainsworth et al., 1978).

Five recent empirical studies have examined the relationship between maltreatment and quality of attachment, two cross-sectional in design (Crittenden, in press; Schneider-Rosen & Cicchetti, 1984) and three longitudinal (Egeland & Sroufe, 1981a; 1981b; Schneider-Rosen et al., in press). All five studies used the same theoretical approach, and all five employed the Strange Situation procedure as a means of assessing attachment. These uniformities permit increased confidence in the consistent finding that maltreated infants are significantly more likely to be insecurely attached to their caregivers than comparison infants.

When Ainsworth's three-category system was used to classify infants' behavior in the Strange Situation, however, it appeared that a number of maltreated infants were securely attached to their caregivers. Crittenden's investigation addresses this somewhat surprising finding. Crittenden derived a fourth category, characterized by anxious behavior combined with moderate to high proximity-seeking, avoidance, and resistance. When this additional category was used, *none* of the neglected or abused infants was classified as secure, while 88 percent of comparison infants were so classified.

Insecure attachment was associated with distinct patterns of behavior on the part of both members of the dyad. The maltreating mothers were less sensitive and responsive, more hostile, and more inconsistent with their infants, while the maltreated infants were more difficult or passive than the comparison infants. This study vividly illustrates the mutual nature of the attachment relationship and highlights the contributions made by each member of the dyad.

The three longitudinal studies have demonstrated the instability of the attachment classifications of maltreated infants, particularly those who were classified as secure upon the initial assessment. Their results suggest that early secure relationships, where they exist, tend to be transient. Changes in quality of attachment may occur when the ongoing transaction between the infant and the caregiver is disrupted in any way. The durability of the relationship may not be sufficient to withstand the stress of factors external to the dyad, such as poverty or family illness, or within it, such as the experience of maltreatment.

Schneider-Rosen and her colleagues have developed a model that highlights the ongoing transaction between a variety of factors that may support or inhibit competent behavior at any point in time. The model distinguishes between two broad influences on competence: potentiating factors, which increase the probability of manifesting incompetent behavior, and compensatory factors, which increase the likelihood of manifesting competent behavior. Potentiating factors may be enduring or transient; similarly, compensatory factors may be long-term or temporary.

This model provides a way of conceptualizing stability or change in attachment not only in a population of infants at risk (such as maltreated infants) but in all infant-caregiver dyads. It also helps explain the finding that some maltreated infants achieve secure attachment relationships. Rather than assuming that this is impossible, as Crittenden does, this transactional model illustrates the multiplicity of influences that support or inhibit attachment at any one time.

The Role of Infant Competence in Later Adaptation

The organizational approach to development conceptualizes competence as the child's successful resolution of stage-salient developmental tasks. Accordingly, we must ascertain the relationship between competence/incompetence on these stage-salient developmental tasks and current and future adaptation or maladaptation.

While there has been no research on the relationship between incompetence on stage-salient developmental issues and the later development of psychopathology in maltreated infants, several recent prospective studies with nonclinical populations of infants suggest that emotional incompetence in infancy may be predictive of later maladaptation (Sroufe, Fox, & Pancake, 1983; Sroufe, 1983; Lewis et al., 1984). These studies also show that not all insecurely attached children inevitably develop later problems. Thus, a linear, main-effects model of psychopathology is inaccurate; what is needed is a dynamic, transactional one.

Early maltreatment may lead to later competence or incompetence. Many factors may mediate between early and later adaptation or maladaptation and allow alternative outcomes to occur. For example, early successful resolution of developmental tasks may be interfered with by environmental factors, inhibiting competence at a later stage. Conversely, early problems or deviations in the successful resolution of a developmental task may be countered by major changes in the child's experience, resulting in the successful negotiation of subsequent developmental tasks.

Our broader conceptualization of infant emotional disorders places dysfunction in the context of an insecure attachment relationship between infant and caregiver. Thus, emotional dysfunction is not a static syndrome that is present or absent within the infant but rather a transactional process that is influenced and modified by environmental factors.

DISCUSSION

Bettye Caldwell: In the work using the Strange Situation that you summarized, did you use the same criteria in assigning the attachment ratings A, B, and C to the children at 12, 18, and 24 months?

Dante Cicchetti: No, we did not.

Bettye Caldwell: I think that's critical. During the Strange Situation, the separation experience means something quite different to a 24-month-old child and a 12-month-old.

Dante Cicchetti: One of my ex-students, Karen Schneider-Rosen, and I have developed new criteria to classify quality of attachment at both 18 and 24 months, and I'm currently working on criteria for 30 through 40 months. I think that this is absolutely essential, because so little work has been done on the development of attachment beyond infancy.

Bettye Caldwell: My second question is, have you looked at your secure and insecurely attached dyads in relation to broader ecological variables? Let's take, for example, the children who have been abused. What is the rest of the caretaking like in those families?

Dante Cicchetti: We are just beginning to analyze the vast amount of data we have collected on the ecology of maltreatment, so I can't give you a definitive answer. However, in a preliminary analysis Vicki Carlson and I have found that single risk factors do not necessarily discriminate maltreating from demographically matched nonmaltreating families. We believe that it is the cumulative and especially the interactive stresses, without buffers, that do differentiate maltreating from nonmaltreating families and securely from insecurely attached mother-infant pairs.

Ken Rubin: What's the relation between the security or insecurity of children's attachment and the later development of competence? Is there a connection between feeling secure and developing more adaptively?

Dante Cicchetti: As you know, Ken, this is an important issue. While much work remains to be done, there is growing evidence that, given a stable caretaking environment, securely attached youngsters have a higher probability of functioning more competently on a variety of stage-salient developmental issues. These include the development of symbolic play, self-development, problem solving, syntactic and pragmatic development, and early peer relationships, to name a few. However, throughout development there will also be those children who, despite an early secure attachment, develop poorly, as well as those who rise above an early insecure relationship to develop well. Much more must be done before we can answer your question fully.

PLAY IN THE HOSPITAL

Jerriann M. Wilson, M.Ed.

Hospitalization can be traumatizing for a child, leading to problems even after the hospital stay. Increasingly, health-care workers in pediatric settings are concentrating on children's secondary or psychosocial needs as well as their primary physical needs. Because a child who is hospitalized is still a child, it is particularly important to include familiar activities like play in the strange and frightening world of the hospital. Play has a vital place in the life of the pediatric patient.

Children's Reactions to Hospitalization

Distress signs noted in the hospital include crying, fear, withdrawal, destructiveness, regressive behaviors, and sleeping poorly. There are several causes of this pyschological upset: (1) separation from parents, (2) age of child at admission, and (3) unfamiliarity of hospital setting (Vernon et al., 1965). Hospitals can ameliorate the impact of all these with some special planning.

The separation of parents and children is easily corrected. In many hospitals, parents are accorded 24-hour visiting privileges as well as live-in accommodations, and they participate in some care of their children. It is difficult to control the second determinant, the age at which a child is hospitalized, although Mason (1965) suggests postponing elective procedures until after the critical preschool years. Evidence indicates that children from six months of age to four or five years generally deal least well with the hospital experience. The presence of parents makes a significant difference for these younger children.

The third major cause of psychological upset is the unfamiliarity of the hospital setting. The people, equipment, and routines that pediatric patients typically experience in the hospital are foreign to them. A child can encounter over 50 staff members in the first 24 hours; that number should be reduced. Unfamiliar equipment should be kept in storage areas. Most routines of the hospital are not like those at home but can be made more familiar through orientation. The truly familiar routines, such as play, school, and group meal times, must be planned for in a pediatric setting. Having a routine helps children adjust to their day.

It is interesting to note that not every child has a negative hospital experience (Azarnoff & Flegal, 1975). For some children, hospitalization is a period of positive growth as they learn to cope *successfully* with a new environment, separation from family members, and other stresses.

Play Setting and Activities

Certain conditions must be satisfied in order to create a setting in which good play can occur (Chance, 1979). First, the playroom and decor of the pediatric unit should create a child-welcoming climate. The playroom should have space for wheelchairs and intravenous poles to move; this encourages play (Piserchia, Bragg, & Alvarez, 1982). Second, play materials and creative media that are familiar but varied should be present. Medical play equipment, though not necessarily familiar, is essential.

Third, a supportive, consistent adult must be present. This individual, who should be responsive and interactive, can enhance play by participating in it (Pearson et al., 1980). Researchers have discussed who this person should be. Ideally it would be a parent, particularly the mother. As this is often not possible, a mother substitute can be considered, such as a nurse, a volunteer, or a child life specialist (Bolig, 1984). A child life specialist is a member of the health-care team who focuses on the emotional and developmental needs of hospitalized children, using play and other forms of communication to reduce stress for children and their families.

Play can happen anywhere—on a treatment table during a dressing change, in the elevator on the way to x-ray, or as a child creates "caves" with the bed sheets — but the playroom offers a special setting. The playroom is a "safe place" where play, visiting with families, group meal times, and other familiar activities can occur. No painful treatments are given in the playroom, which serves as a link between home and hospital.

The playroom is open to patients and their parents and usually offers a variety of options in addition to free play. Play sessions can be one-on-one, group, or a combination. Toys and games appropriate to the children's developmental levels and physical conditions are available and special activities are programmed during the day, much as in any good preschool or school setting. The hospital play program should be well balanced and include:

- *messy activities* that children find so comforting like finger painting, pudding painting, clay, sand or water play, and bubble blowing
- *creative art*
- *crafts and games*
- *construction opportunities* with building and block sets as well as woodworking and building with junk for older teens
- *books and story records*
- *field trips* within the hospital to further the understanding of the institution, from the kitchen to the telephone paging room
- *music,* which is particularly relaxing for infants (Lindsay, 1981)
- *films* for entertainment as well as therapeutic/educational value dealing with hospitalization (Melamed & Siegel, 1975)
- *dramatic play* with home and hospital garb
- *tape recorder* for parent-recorded stories and conversations to be played in absence of families (McCain, 1982)
- *closed circuit television* offers entertainment, a chance to be on television, and an interactive opportunity between playroom and isolation room playing call-in BINGO (Guttentag & Kettner, 1983)

— *video games* offer interactive opportunities and distraction from treatment, decreasing anxiety and unpleasant physical symptoms (Kee, 1981; *Pediatric News,* 1982)

— *animals* for the comfort a child can receive from taking care of a pet in the playroom (Wilson, 1979a)

— *outdoor play* whether a child is ambulatory enough to swing and slide or tend a raised garden from a stretcher (Wilson, 1979a)

— *education* as part of play helps children build a sense of mastery and to increase their knowledge while in the hospital (Wilson, 1979b; Rae, 1981)

The presence of a child life specialist as a facilitator tends to make the play more constructive and positive (Williams & Powell, 1980) and assures that adult help is available if questions or concerns arise. Adult supervision guarantees a sense of order and a routine in the daily play events. Children who come from chaotic home settings with limited opportunities for enrichment can thrive and grow in the richness of a well-developed play program (Rae, 1981).

Medical Play

In a hospital setting, medical play is especially important. It can heighten a child's awareness of hospital experiences, offer new information, help with the expression of feelings, reveal the child's misunderstandings so that they can be corrected, and bring child, parents, and staff closer together. A medical play corner should be supplied with many of the tools of medical care, including plastic syringes (without needles), anesthesia masks, x-ray viewing boxes, stethoscopes, and IV arm boards and tubing. Hard and soft dolls, family and medical puppets, and doll hospitals should also be available. Fein (1979) suggests having play equipment that offers varying degrees of definition and realism — both real medical equipment and replicas, for instance — to give children a choice.

Medical play usually concentrates on sensory and concrete experiences. A child may use a syringe to simulate an injection, look at x-rays to discover that the machines only take photographs and do not read minds, or apply a cast to a doll to duplicate one the patient will receive the next day.

The degree of structure for the medical play setting will vary with the anxiety level of the child. A less anxious child will more easily go to the play materials than a child experiencing conflict, who may need adult guidance and direction. Children need to be reminded that there is a reason for each procedure, and for the hospital stay, too. If misconceptions arise, the child life specialist can explore the areas of confusion and correct the information (Chan, 1980). For example, holding an anesthesia mask to a doll's face may help draw out a child's fears of being put to sleep permanently.

Medical play differs for the various age groups. Toddlers and older infants seem to understand the placement of a stethoscope or anesthesia mask on a doll. Preschoolers benefit from handling safe medical equipment. Early school-age children often become involved in detailed medical dramatic play, with gowns, masks, and lots of paraphernalia. Older school-age patients are comfortable creating a drama with a "visible man" and a miniature operating room table, while teenagers have made video or audio tapes to "help other kids" get ready for surgery. Adaptations of medical play make it meaningful to a wide age range of pediatric patients.

Particularly for preschoolers, fear is reduced when parents join in play. Parents may also acquire new information that allows them to become allies in the child's treatment. Research shows that as parents feel more comfortable in the hospital setting, they experience a greater sense of well-being and seem to pass it on to their children (Skipper & Leonard, 1968). These children appear to recover faster, as demonstrated by their physiological signs (temperature, blood pressure, and pulse rate) returning to normal sooner after surgery.

Restrictions on Play

Restrictions on play in pediatric settings include (1) immobility because of physical restraints, (2) dull environment (e.g., isolation), (3) overstimulating environment (high technology units), and (4) fear because of separation and unfamiliarity (Crocker, 1981). The fear element must be dealt with constantly in all facets of hospitalization; the other three occur in special circumstances.

Bed rest is a confining circumstance that is dictated by a need for traction or for very limited movement to facilitate healing. Children who must stay in bed can be cut off physically from participation in group activities, although some orthopedic surgeons allow and encourage their traction patients to be moved to a playroom. Two children who cannot be moved can be placed together in one patient room so that they can play side-by-side, or occasional playroom activities can be held in the patient's room with the mobile children joining in.

Intravenous apparatus (IVs), catheters, drainage tubes, casts and bandaging are encumbrances that inhibit hospital play. Restrictions must be anticipated and activities planned with special creativity. For example, one child who was badly burned and had heavily bandaged hands chose to "fingerpaint" the only way she could — with her feet.

Isolation restrictions severely limit play because the group experience is impossible, the environment is dull, and routines are repetitive. Sensory deprivation can be extreme in this setting. O'Connell (1984) discusses the environment of the Laminar Air Flow Room and the role of play. Because the routine in these special isolation rooms varies so little from day to day, children enjoy the choice of activities offered by a play program. Parents also benefit from the play programming. A child life specialist can help both patients and parents discover new activities that alleviate the tedium of long periods in the isolation room.

Intensive care typifies the other extreme — an overstimulating setting with a myriad of medical activities occurring simultaneously to several patients in the same room. A lack of curtains or the urgency of medical interventions may expose a patient to a terrifying array of events. The typical patient may withdraw and is not easily involved in play. Toys are not enough to encourage play here (Pearson et al., 1980). Children seem to attend more to play and toys when a child life specialist or other facilitator is present.

Infant Units and Outpatient Areas

Two prospective play areas deserve special mention: infant units and outpatient areas. The infant's experience can be particularly passive, especially if a child life program has limited resources and does not include infants. "Stranger anxiety" makes unfamiliar environments, unknown caregivers, and uncomfortable procedures an overwhelming emotional challenge. Furthermore, the child's need for exploration and stimulation is a powerful motivating force in healthy development. Infants need familiar, experienced caregivers and play materials appropriate to their level of development. Plastic mirrors at eye level, activity boards attached to crib rails, and mobiles containing interesting items that can be touched and manipulated are some of the possibilities.

For preterm infants, "infant stimulation" is a controversial topic as researchers and developmental pediatricians try to determine how much extra stimulation should be presented to prematures, who are in the process of adapting to an already overstimulating life. A concerted effort with very young, very ill prematures may indeed be to *reduce* handling and to keep stimulation to a minimum. Although some stimulation programs seem to have benefits, placing stuffed animals and other toys in isolettes may be more a response to adult needs than in the infant's best interest.

Outpatient services take place in several different settings, which all can benefit from play programs. The outpatient and emergency areas often give children and their families their first view of the hospital. These areas should make a positive impression. Play activities can be the same as those offered in inpatient areas. The benefits to children are obvious and have been documented (Williams & Powell, 1980; Zilliacus & Enberg, 1980).

As Golden (1983) summed up, "Play intervention for children in hospital settings is an unqualified necessity . . . in helping a child leave the hospital healthier than when he or she arrived."

DISCUSSION

Brian Vandenberg: Hospitals could use some sort of play program for adults, too, I think. When I was in the hospital, I used to sit and watch TV while I envied the children down the hall, playing with toys.

Allen Gottfried: The hospital environment is hard on adults. Peter Suedfeld's book *Restricted Environmental Stimulation* discusses this, and a recent article in *Science* described a study showing that just having a room with a window made recovery from surgery faster.

Jerriann Wilson: We need research of all kinds that will help us justify child life programs in hospitals. We're having real difficulties with funding in these times of cost containment, as you can imagine. Some child life programs in this country are being dissolved as we speak.

Robert Bradley: The question of cost does come to mind, since a play program requires an investment in terms of persons, equipment, and so on. Have there been any studies of costs showing whether you get outcomes that justify the additional expenditure?

Jerriann Wilson: The Association for the Care of Children's Health is conducting research now to show that a child life program reduces the length of stay. That's the magic formula now, to reduce the LOS.

Brian Vandenberg: I've seen research showing that preparing children for hospitalization through medical play and so on before they enter the hospital reduces length of stay, but I think only for first-timers. For children who've been in the hospital before, "preparation" just invokes a lot of memories and makes things more difficult. Did you find much difference between first-timers and those who'd been there before in terms of their responses and use of the play program?

Jerriann Wilson: What we see from children who are hospitalized more than once is sort of a love-hate reaction. They just love seeing their same nurse and child life specialist on the unit, but they know what it's going to feel like to have a bone marrow or an IVP, and that's not easy. It doesn't hurt any less the second time around.

Douglas in England has done some research on the long-term effects of repeated hospitalizations during early childhood. He found that children who were hospitalized repeatedly or for more than one week between the ages of four and seven often had serious problems as teenagers—reading problems, school difficulties, some delinquency.

Brian Vandenberg: Norman Cousins' experience with laughter, and some empirical work as well, suggests that joy may promote health. Unfortunately, hospitals tend to be joyless places. Historically, the rise of the hospital is meshed with the rise of the factory. Hospitals used to be way-stations, but in the late nineteenth century the factory became their institutional model. Patients are treated rather like parts on a production line.

Leila Beckwith: Norman Cousins literally laughed his way out of his illness, he says. He actually made himself laugh by watching slapstick movies and the like. Have you tried anything like that, Jerriann? The guidelines you're using seem to emphasize catharsis and mastery over trauma, and some distraction also. But perhaps the idea is just to reduce the anxiety. Trying to get the child to joy might be too much.

Jerriann Wilson: I think so. Often members of the staff don't feel they've succeeded unless they make a child laugh, but who wants to laugh in intensive care? We're not demanding that the children laugh. If we can get them involved and playing, we feel we've made a step. If they happen to laugh, that's nice, too—and sometimes they do. As they get involved in play they really do laugh and seem rather joyful.

Jay Belsky: You have to have them engaged to get the possibility of laughter.

Jerriann Wilson: Yes, but we don't want to keep them involved every minute. I think we do children a disservice if we try to distract them and take their minds off being in the hospital; it's better to help them deal with what's happening to them, to capitalize on and enhance the experiences. We do provide some diversion, but that's not our main goal.

Bettye Caldwell: Still, diversion might be something to look at. It's an important way of dealing with pain. I wouldn't concentrate on length of stay in an evaluative study, because it really cannot be shortened for certain illnesses. The rate of time it takes for the skin to grow back after a serious burn is difficult to change. But if you've got humble little measures like parental satisfaction and less anxiety in the children and even, perhaps, self-reports from the children of less severe pain, that will help. To have to prove the merits of what you're doing through length of stay seems rather like having to prove the merits of nutrition by doing outcome research on mental development. It isn't necessary, because by and large it's better not to be hungry than it is to be hungry, regardless of what it does to the brain.

Jerriann Wilson: I agree with you. It's just that the financial pressure is so great that I think we need to look at everything at once, including length of stay.

Greta Fein: What Bettye may be saying, Jerriann, is that because the diagnostic categories are very complicated it's not just a question of neutral findings. If you select the wrong measure, it's conceivable you could do your case a disservice.

Instead of length of stay, you might consider another hospital measurement possibility. For example, what happens at night when the lights are down and it's supposed to be quiet? I suspect this may be the time to find out how children are dealing with things. How many times is the nurse called? How much crying do you get, and what kind? Fairly uncomplicated measures like these could be persuasive, because they involve staffing issues. Upset children take up a lot of nursing time.

Jay Belsky: Can you monitor pain and demonstrate that with and without a play program you get more or less pain?

Jerriann Wilson: That would be wonderful.

Brian Vandenberg: Research on pain control with children on burn units shows that a hypnosis-like procedure similar to dramatic play helps make the children much more manageable. Painful procedures take less time and are much easier.

Jerriann Wilson: In that case, play would serve as a relaxation technique and also as a distraction, which I didn't mean to suggest was a bad thing. It's just not our main goal.

THE SOCIAL SIGNIFICANCE OF PLAY

Jay Belsky, Ph.D.
Discussant

My task this afternoon is to bring together all, or at least much, of what we have heard today. Thus, the challenge is mine to see how the coordinates go together and whether the whole is greater than the sum of the parts.

I think we are all in agreement that the investigation of play is a good idea and that it may serve as a "window" on a variety of aspects of the child's world, including cognitive and motivational abilities, social skills, and relations with others. For me, then, the best way of organizing what we have heard and learned about the social significance of play comes from thinking in terms of its characteristics, consequences, and determinants. I plan to be brief in my comments, merely painting the broad brush strokes of this organizing structure rather than delving in detail into any particular presentation. Let me start by considering the characteristics of play.

Characteristics

From Inge Bretherton's presentation it is clear that play actions reveal much about children's ability to represent events and thereby tell us a great deal about their cognitive functioning. Play, as she told us, can serve as a "window" on the child's notions of roles, actions, and objects. By analyzing play in this manner, Inge's work is nicely related to that of Lorraine McCune and Larry Fenson. All share a focus on cognitive functioning and things done by most children at different ages.

In the talks by Inge, Larry, and Lorraine we learned much about the characteristics or the nature of object play. Judy Dunn made us look at another characteristic of play—its social side. It was striking to discover, though in retrospect we should have known it all along, that siblings and mothers are quite different as playmates; the child obviously lives in at least two social worlds. The people in these different worlds know the child to differing degrees and, as a result of this knowledge and their own agenda for what they want to do, relate to him or her differently. We really have our work cut out for us in charting this terrain, especially when we realize that what transpires in one situation is not necessarily similar to what transpires in another situation — even if the playmate is the same person. I remain of the opinion, however, at least until convinced otherwise, that there is coherence in the different patterns of play observed with the same person in different situations. As we search for such coherence, the issue that repeatedly comes to mind has to do with the benefits that accrue from playing with one partner rather than another of different social status (sibling, mother) and of playing with certain mothers or siblings.

One of the most intriguing of Judy's findings involved the variability in pretend play across mother-child pairs. Is it possible that mother and child "negotiated" the play domains they engaged in — with some selecting pretense and others focusing more on spatial phenomenon, for example — or did one partner lead and the other follow? Whatever the answer is, it would be nice to believe that each relationship finds a kind of activity in which it can play — that is, in which the partners can enjoy each other and learn things about each other and the world.

Before moving past Judy's work, I must mention my admiration of her methodology and the patience and scientific integrity it reveals. Like all great scientists, Judy is first a watcher — and clearly an extraordinarily good one. The kind of work she does takes much time, is expensive, and requires an ability to delay gratification; by no means is it "quick and dirty." I think it's important to remember, however, that most methods are not inherently better or worse. It always depends upon the question. If one wants to know, as Judy does, what the child's everyday experiences are, then obviously the naturalistic context of the home environment is the place to be. But the lab can also be useful, as Inge and others have demonstrated, if one wants to control the scope of activities and see what the child may be capable of doing.

Consequences

Play, as Ken Rubin showed us, occurs not only in the lab and in the home but beyond the family as well — in peer groups. At the very least we have to conclude that play is ubiquitous. By modifying Parten's traditional peer play categories just a bit, Ken has asked a new question: Is play a window on the emergence of developmental psychopathology? In terms of my framework for discussion, this question concerns the consequences of play. I am persuaded by Ken's data that the answer to the question may well be yes. Some of his socially withdrawn children were avoiding social contact, not merely showing greater interest in the nonsocial world. Indeed, I wonder if the two groups of withdrawn children could be distinguished by "wiring them up" and obtaining psychophysiological measurements. I suspect that the internal feeling states and the concomitant physiological indicators of the truly withdrawn children would show them to be quite uncomfortable: anxious, and even possibly lonely. What we do not know, of course, are the mechanisms that lead to socially withdrawn behavior. Do these children lack skills to engage others, or do they make attributions about others and themselves that keep them away, like "I can't do that," "They don't like me," "They won't want me to join them."

Now, of course, it may be the case, if we think about Judy's work, that some children play well with mothers, others with siblings, and others with peers. But what happens when we find children whose play across all partners seems to lack the enthusiasm, ease of action, and fun that we associate with the term *play*? And is it possibly the case that play, or its absence, with one set of partners is more developmentally informative than play with another set?

Determinants

As we think about Ken's different types of players, we need to wonder about more than where they are going developmentally, that is, about more than consequences. We also need to wonder about determinants. Where does a socially withdrawn style come from?

One possibility, of course, is that these different social orientations are temperamental, inborn, even heritable. After all, there is evidence that sociability is inherited. Jerry Kagan, one proponent of the temperamental argument, has contended that extreme inhibition in the face of arousing stimuli, including unfamiliar age-mates, is biologically based and relatively stable over time.

While I am sure that there is some truth to this, particularly with the extreme groups Kagan studies, I am also persuaded by Dante Cicchetti's work and those of his Minnesota colleagues, and by Ken Rubin's theorizing and the theorizing of others, that the origins of the withdrawn social style may lie in the early mother-infant relationship. This is not to say that the attachment relationship dictates the child's eventual relations with peers, but only to contend that there is a linkage. It seems quite conceivable that the social skills and trust learned in a harmonious reciprocal parent-infant relationship — the "breeding ground" of a secure attachment — will carry over to some extent to relations with age-mates.

Still, development in plastic, and even well-established developmental trajectories are susceptible to deflection and redirection. A major question then, is whether the arena of peer play, or play with others, can be used not only to diagnose risk for later problems but also as a target for clinical intervention. Play therapists have long argued that this is possible. The fact that play can be used to support functioning even with short-term goals in mind was nicely demonstrated by Jerriann Wilson. As I listened to her I was not only impressed with the thoughtful program she implemented, but I also felt proud — proud that scientists studying play have contributed in such a practical way to fostering the well-being of children.

But I think, as Judy Dunn warned us, that we have to be careful not to intervene too quickly. Good intentions alone are not sufficient. But by the same token it is often more appropriate to act and try than to do nothing at all. Play is probably an arena in which to act.

In closing this discussion of the characteristics, consequences and determinants of play, I must underscore Vonnie McLoyd's critical evaluation of social class studies of play. I am in total agreement with Vonnie that social class offers us very little as an explanatory construct, whether we are trying to account for variation in play or for other behavioral phenomenon. While SES may enable us to predict — and Vonnie's review clearly suggests otherwise — it is a tremendously ambiguous construct when it comes to explaining. For the minute we attempt to explain social class "effects," we are forced to move to less macro constructs such as attitudes, housing, and socialization practices. Why not just work with these as determinants, then? We are all familiar with work showing that the variation within and across social classes is huge. When we look beyond this macrosociological construct we get not only more precise prediction but better explanation as well.

PART V
CONSEQUENCES OF PLAY MATERIALS AND PARENT-CHILD INTERACTION

PLAY MATERIALS AND INTELLECTUAL DEVELOPMENT

Robert H. Bradley, Ph.D.

The importance of the social environment for children's development is widely acknowledged. A rich literature exists describing the relation between cognitive, social, and emotional functioning and various aspects of the social environment. Much less is known about attributes of the physical environment and their relation to children's development.

The purpose of this review is to focus on one aspect of the relation between the physical environment and development in children: the relation between play materials and intellectual development. Piaget postulated that much of children's early learning occurs as a result of direct encounters with the physical environment. Because of Piaget's great impact on cognitive psychology, child development researchers became interested in the significance of toys, games, and materials as contexts for intellectual development during childhood.

In this paper, I will summarize findings from observational research done in the homes of young children that addresses the relationship between the availability of toys and other materials in the home and children's intellectual development. The review will be split: Part one will overview the findings of others; part two will focus on our own research.

A Review of Empirical Findings

Perhaps the most intensive home observational studies of the relation between the presence of toys and materials during the first two years of life and children's intellectual development have been those done by our next presenter, Ted Wachs (e.g., Wachs, Uzgiris, & Hunt, 1971; Wachs, 1976). The first study done by Wachs and his colleagues involved 102 predominantly lower-class children. Observations in the homes of these children revealed that the availability of books and toys during the second year of life was significantly correlated with several scales from the Infant Psychological Development Scale at 22 months, but not at 15 or 18 months. Research done on a second sample of 39 children showed a substantial relationship between the number of audiovisually responsive toys and children's performance on object permanence and the development of schemas throughout the second year of life. In a follow-up study, Wachs reported that the presence of audiovisually responsive toys in the second year of life was correlated .6 with IQ at age 30 months.

Clarke-Stewart (1973) found evidence that the availability of toys, even during the first year of life, was related to subsequent intellectual development. Her study involved repeated observations of 36 predominantly low-SES children and their mothers in home and laboratory settings. Infant competence was assessed throughout the period of 9 to 18 months. The observations revealed that children's dependency on the mother diminished over that period while their interest in aspects of the physical environment increased. By age 17 months, children spent an average of 34 percent of their time interacting with their mothers and about 50 percent of their time playing with, looking at, and investigating objects (about 20 percent toys and 30 percent other household objects). Clarke-Stewart observed a correlation of .39 between the number of toys available to the child in the home and a conglomerate measure of competence derived through factor analysis. Variety of toys was correlated .34 with the competence measure, while the child's actual use of toys and objects was correlated .46. The variety of toys was correlated .47 with Bayley MDI at 17 months; and the use of toys and objects was correlated .36.

Among the most comprehensive studies of the relation between the availability of play materials early in life and later intellectual development is that reported by Barnard, Bee, and Hammond (1984). The study involved 163 working-class and middle-class families from the Seattle area. The Play Materials subscale of the Home Observation for Measurement of the Environment (HOME) Inventory was administered when children were 4, 8, 12 and 24 months old. Bayley Scales were administered to the children at ages one and two years and the Stanford-Binet at age four.

Correlations between the Play Materials scores and measures of intellectual competence were low but significant. Correlations for a subgroup of well-educated mothers were low; those for mothers with less than a high school education were a little higher. Correlations were clearly higher for boys (.3 to .5) than for girls (.2 to .3). When maternal education and SES were partialled out of the correlation between Play Materials and intellectual competence, some attenuation was noted but the partial correlations remained significant (.2 to .3).

Another study of interest is Siegel's (1984) longitudinal study of preterm and full-term infants from working-class backgrounds in Hamilton, Ontario. Negligible correlations were observed between 12-month scores on Play Materials and concurrent scores on the Bayley and the Uzgiris-Hunt Scales. However, three-year scores on Play Materials showed low to moderate correlations (.3 to .5) with three-year Stanford-Binet and Reynell Language scores for both preterm and full-term samples. Similarly, five-year scores on Play Materials were correlated .5 with concurrent scores on the McCarthy General Cognitive Index. Twelve-month Play Materials scores were also correlated with three-year IQ scores but only for preterm children.

While most studies of normal children have reported significant correlations between the availability of toys and objects during the first three years of life and children's cognitive development, there have been exceptions. A good example of such an exception is the research of Gottfried and Gottfried (1984). Their study of predominantly middle-class white families in California showed few instances of significant correlations between Play Materials and children's intellectual development.

An especially revealing longitudinal study of older (ages 8 to 14) handicapped children was conducted by Nihira, Meyers, and Mink (1980; 1983). It involved 114 seriously retarded children from southern California who were living at home. The home environments of the children were assessed with a variety of measures including the HOME Inventory, the Family Environment Scale, the Home Quality Rating Scale, various indices of family adjustment, and various demographic and structural descriptions of the home. The child was assessed using the Adaptive Behavior Scale and parental ratings of social and psychological adjustment.

Three canonical analyses were performed on the data: (1) home environment vs. child characteristics; (2) home environment vs. family adjustment; (3) family adjustment vs. child characteristics. In analysis I, the first canonical variate was between the overall "harmony and quality of parenting" and the "social adjustment of the child." Highly loaded on this factor was stimulation through toys and equipment. In analysis II, the first canonical variate was between overall "harmony and quality of parenting" and "observed coping level." Again, stimulation through toys and equipment was highly loaded (.60) on the first factor.

In a follow-up three years later, Nihira, Meyers, and Mink (1983) attempted to further delineate the relation between home environment, family adjustment, and child competence by looking for direction of effects among the environmental and developmental variables. Improvements in Personal Maladaptation over the three-year period were significantly related to the subscale, Stimulation through Toys, Games and Reading Materials, with the effects of initial maladaptation and all other environmental variables partialled out (-.35). Relatedly, children whose initial cognitive status was highest had parents who provided more stimulation through toys, games, and materials three years later.

In essence, there appears to be a kind of reverberating circuit, with the provision of cognitively stimulating experiences through toys, equipment, and materials leading to higher levels of social and personal adjustment. Simultaneously, children with better cognitive and social skills appear to elicit from their parents greater cognitive stimulation (including the provision of more advanced toys and materials) — in sum, the maintenance of a more nearly optimal environment. The degree of optimality appears positively related to maternal education and negatively related to the number of children present in the home.

Little Rock Longitudinal Studies

During the past two decades we have been involved in two research studies that have particular relevance for the topic of this report: (1) the Longitudinal Observation and Intervention Study (Caldwell, Elardo, & Elardo, 1972); and (2) the consortium study on home environments and child development.

The Longitudinal Observation and Intervention Study, hereinafter referred to as LOIS, was designed to explore the question of exactly when the decline in development so often observed in economically disadvantaged circumstances begins. Recruitment of subjects for this study commenced in 1970. Some 130 children were involved in the observational (nonintervention) groups for the project. Approximately 60 percent of the participants were black, the remainder white. Both racial groups were heterogeneous with respect to SES. However, the black sample was from mostly lower-class and working-class backgrounds, whereas the white sample was from mostly working-class and middle-class backgrounds.

Participants entered the study at about age six months. They were periodically assessed with developmental measures through age 54 months, then with achievement tests after school entry. Their home environments were also periodically assessed using the HOME Inventory. The Infant version of HOME, used up to age three, is a 45-item combination observation/interview procedure done at home with both the infant and primary caregiver present. The items are clustered into six subscales: (1) Maternal Responsivity, (2) Avoidance of Restriction (Acceptance of Child), (3) Organization of the Environment, (4) Play Materials, (5) Maternal Involvement, and (6) Variety in Daily Stimulation. Among the six subscales, Play Materials has shown one of the most consistent relationships with intellectual development as shown in Table 3.

Table 3. Correlations between 6-, 12-, and 24-month HOME Scores and Mental Test Scores Gathered at 1, 3, and 4½ Years

HOME Subscales	\multicolumn{3}{c}{Time of HOME Assessment}					
	\multicolumn{3}{c}{6 Months}	\multicolumn{3}{c}{12 Months}	\multicolumn{2}{c}{24 Months}
	1-yr. MDI[b]	3-yr. IQ	4½-yr. IQ	1-yr. MDI	3-yr. IQ	4½-yr. IQ	3-yr. IQ	4½-yr. IQ
1. Responsivity	.09	.25*	.27	.15	.39*	.34*	.49*	.50*
2. Restriction	.13	.24*	.10	.01	.24*	.21*	.41*	.28*
3. Organization	.20	.40*	.31*	.20	.39*	.34*	.41*	.33*
4. Play Materials	.05	.41*	.44*	.28*	.56*	.52*	.64*	.56*
5. Involvement	.08	.33*	.28*	.28*	.47*	.36*	.55*	.55*
6. Variety	.27*	.31*	.30*	.05	.28*	.32*	.50*	.39*
Total Score	.16	.50*	.44*	.30*	.58*	.53*	.71*	.57*
Multiple Correlation[a]	.30	.54*	.50*	.40	.59*	.57*	.72*	.63*

* $p < .05$
[a] This represents the multiple correlation of all six HOME subscales.
[b] MDI - Mental Development Index from Bayley Scales

Beginning at age three, the 55-item Preschool version of HOME was administered. The items are clustered into eight subscales: (1) Toys and Materials, (2) Language Stimulation, (3) Physical Environment, (4) Pride and Affection, (5) Stimulation of Academic Behavior, (6) Modeling of Social Maturity, (7) Variety of Stimulation, and (8) Physical Punishment. Scores on the Toys and Materials subscale at 36 months correlated .47 with three-year IQ and .48 with 54-month IQ. Scores on the Toys and Materials subscale at age 54 months were correlated .55 with concurrent IQ scores. Correlations with first grade achievement test scores were between .4 and .5.

After reviewing sets of simple correlations between HOME subscales and subsequent mental test performance in our sample, we became interested in trying to further delineate the nature of the relationship. Our first effort was to examine gender and race differences in the relationship. Separating the sample into male and female groups provided some interesting results. To begin with, correlations for the two samples were higher than when the combined sample was used. Secondly, correlations between Play Materials and IQ for males were consistently high (.62 at 6 months, .74 at 12 months, .72 at 24 months). For females, the correlations started lower but attained the same level at 24 months (.49 at 6 months, .74 at 24 months).

Similarly interesting results emerged when the sample was separated according to race. For whites, the correlations between Play Materials and three-year IQ were essentially constant from six months (.46 at 6 months, .45 at 12 months, .47 at 24 months). For blacks, the pattern was slightly different (.28 at six months, .45 at 12 months, .51 at 24 months). In essence, there was some evidence for specificity of effect along gender and race lines; but there was also evidence that the association between Play Materials and intelligence was significant for all subgroups in our sample.

A second concern of ours was whether the observed relation between the availability of play materials early in life and later intelligence occurs because of the correlation between early environmental opportunities and later environmental opportunities or because of the particular salience of toys during the first year of life. To examine this issue, we performed a series of partial correlational analyses using Play Materials scores and three-year IQ. Separate analyses were done for males and females and for blacks and whites. For females, the evidence suggests that the observed correlation between Play Materials and IQ results because of a stable pattern of environmental opportunities. For males, the story reads somewhat differently. There is evidence that Play Materials available during the first year or so of life may have some unique value. For whites, the set of partial correlations indicated that scores on Play Materials at all three time points contribute about the same to three-year IQ (.2 to .3). For blacks, on the other hand, later scores on Play Materials were more predictive than earlier scores.

A related study concerned an attempt to find a set of predictors among environmental processes and cognitive processes measured during the first year of life that would provide the most efficient prediction of later IQ. To examine this issue, stepwise multiple regression analyses were done using six-month HOME subscale scores, 12-month HOME subscale scores, and 12-month cluster scores from the Bayley to predict three-year IQ. Separate analyses were done for females and males. For boys, the most efficient set of predictors included 12-month Play Materials scores, six-month Play Materials scores, and 12-month language use scores. For girls, the most efficient predictors were 12-month Play Materials and Maternal Responsivity scores.

Despite the fact that the stepwise regression analyses showed that Play Materials in the case of boys and Play Materials plus Maternal Responsivity in the case of girls provided for efficient prediction of three-year IQ, other findings within the data suggested that the mere availability of toys may not be sufficient for facilitating intellectual development. Specifically, Play Materials was significantly correlated with Maternal Involvement (.61 to .75). Thus, it may be the availability of appropriate play materials, in conjunction with consistent encouragement, that is useful for development.

Another focus for our studies of the relation of environmental processes to intellectual development was bidirectionality of effect. Cross-lagged panel analyses were done using Bayley Mental Development Index (MDI) scores at 6, 12, and 24 months as measures of intellectual development and HOME subscale scores at the same times as measures of the environment. Separate analyses were done for three HOME subscales: Play Materials, Maternal Responsivity, and Maternal Involvement.

The results in the case of Play Materials indicated that the primary direction of effect in the period from 6 to 12 months may be from child to environment (that is, more capable children elicit more appropriate play materials from their parents). However, in the period from 12 to 24 months, the effects seem about equal in both directions. The pattern of coefficients for Maternal Involvement seemed similar to that for Play Materials in the 6- to 12-month period, but seemed to reverse itself in the 12- to 24-month period (that is, the more encouragement from mother at age 12 months, the higher the MDI score at two years). No discernible pattern for direction of effect emerged for Maternal Responsivity. Despite skepticism expressed about doing panel analyses on developmental data, these findings offer some tentative clarification about the nature of the relationships among environmental processes and intellectual development during infancy.

A final study utilizing the Little Rock longitudinal sample that has implications for the relation between play materials and intellectual development in children has been reported (Bradley & Caldwell, 1984). In essence, it examined the relation between HOME subscale scores and family demographics when infants were one and two years old. This study was done to determine the extent to which the environmental processes tapped by the HOME might be attributable to common socioeconomic, family structure, and racial characteristics. More specifically, the study examined the relation between HOME scores and the following demographic variables: race, sex, SES, degree of crowding in the home, and birth order.

Multivariate analyses of covariance were done with demographic variables entered in the following order: degree of crowding, birth order, social status, sex, race, sex X social status, race X social status, and sex X race. Criterion variables were the six HOME subscales. Separate analyses were done for 12-month HOME scores and 24-month HOME scores. With respect to 12-month HOME scores, overall multivariate effects were noted for birth order and crowding. Significant univariate effects for Play Materials were obtained for crowding and birth order. With respect to 24-month scores, significant multivariate effects were noted for birth order, race X social status, and sex X race. Significant univariate effects for Play Materials were noted for crowding, birth order, social status, and race. For both time points, scores on Play Materials were strongest for family structure as compared to social status characteristics.

In sum, while part of the relation between Play Materials and intellectual development may be attributable to the relation between HOME scores and social status, most of the relationship does not seem attributable to such associations. The significant relationship between family structure characteristics and scores on Play Materials is of particular interest.

Consortium Study

In addition to the longitudinal study done on children from Little Rock, we have recently become involved in a research consortium study that is examining the relation between early environmental processes and children's development over the first five years of life. This consortium study involves pooling data from six sites in North America. Site I is Little Rock (lower- to lower-middle-class blacks, plus lower-middle to upper-middle-class whites). Site II is Houston (lower-class to working-class Mexican-Americans). Site III is Chapel Hill, North Carolina (middle-class whites, lower-class blacks). Site IV is Fullerton, California (middle-class whites). Site V is Seattle (working-class and middle-class whites). Site VI is Hamilton, Ontario (working-class whites). The data from these six sites were combined so that they could be jointly analyzed. The data sets were first brought together because of a large amount of overlap in both measures used in the individual studies and the ages at which major measures were administered. The total sample included over 1,500 children and their families — albeit full data sets were available for only a few hundred cases.

Among the more interesting analyses done on the consortium data set were path analyses involving environmental and developmental data at 12, 24, and 36 months, Stanford-Binet IQs being the outcome measure of focus. Variables included in these analyses were SES, Bayley MDI scores at 12 and 24 months, Maternal Responsivity and Play Materials scores at 12 and 24 months, Toys and Materials and Pride, Affection, and Warmth scores at 36 months, and IQ scores at 36 months. Since full data sets were not available on all participants, a total of three path analyses were done.

For the first analysis, Maternal Responsivity and Play Materials scores at 24 months were not available. We found significant paths running from 12-month scores on the Play Materials subscale to Bayley scores at both 12 and 24 months, a strong path from Play Materials scores at 12 months to Toys and Materials scores at 36 months, a significant path from Bayley MDI scores at 24 months to Toys and Materials at 36 months and to three-year IQ scores, and a significant path from 36-month Toys and Materials scores to 3-year IQ. In the second path analysis, 36-month scores on HOME subscales were not available. Path coefficients were similar to those in the first analysis, except that the path from 24-month Play Materials to three-year IQ was weaker than that from 36-month Toys and Materials to 36-month IQ; and the path from 24-month MDI to three-year IQ was stronger. Figure 1 displays the most complete path model. It generally shows a continuing influence of SES on the provision of toys and play materials (in the .2 to .3 range). It shows significant paths from Play Materials to mental test scores at all three time points (.20 to .36) and diminishing paths from the quality of the socioemotional environment to mental test scores (.23 to .06). There was a generally stable path between Play Materials scores across the three time points (around .4); and increasing paths among mental test scores (.29 to .47).

Overall, the path analyses seem to indicate that socioeconomic status influences the kinds of experiences (socioemotional support and objects) that a child has. The impact of SES on mental test scores appears to flow mainly through the kind of socioemotional support and cognitive stimulation provided in the home. The effect of these particular environmental processes shows up as early as the first year of life and seems to increase thereafter. In other words, the "reverberating circuit" between intelligence and the provision of play materials is begun as early as the second year of life. Having more appropriate toys and materials leads to more advanced cognitive functioning and more advanced cognitive func-

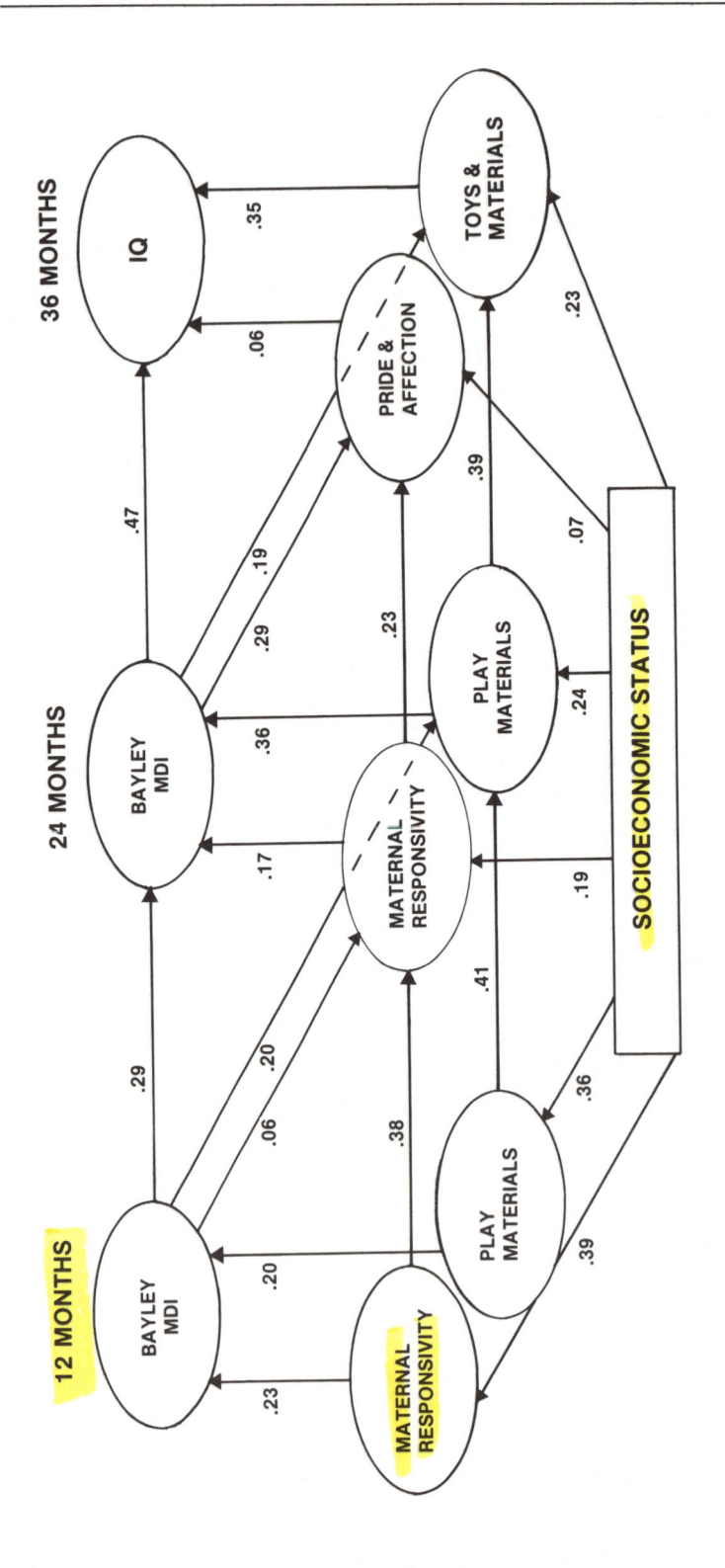

Figure 1. Path Model for Home Environment and Intellectual Development at 12, 24, and 36 months

tioning leads to the provision of more appropriate toys and materials. Throughout this period, the stronger path of influence appears to be from play materials to mental development.

An interesting finding from these analyses is that being brighter may lead to obtaining more socioemotional support. Indeed, the impact of "brightness" seems to be as great on the socioemotional environment as it is on the provision of appropriate toys and materials after the first year of life. The gap between the highs and lows gets wider, both in terms of measured intellectual performance and in terms of the quality of cognitive and socioemotional support available to the child. However, after age three, most of the increase in mental test scores appears to come from the provision of greater cognitive stimulation (in this instance measured by the provision of toys and materials but probably also in terms of direct encouragement of achievement and the provision of other educationally enriching experiences).

Conclusions

I have treated in rather synoptic fashion research on the issue of how play materials are related to mental development. Several tentative conclusions are offered regarding the relationship.

1. Young children tend to spend a considerable amount of time viewing and interacting with toys and other objects.

2. There is a moderate correlation between the availability and use of toys and children's mental test scores beginning as early as the second year of life.

3. The relation between play materials and intelligence appears to be reciprocal, with brighter children eliciting more appropriate play materials to interact with.

4. Part of the observed correlation between toys and intellectual development may reflect their joint relation to family social status and parental encouragement of development, but the total relationship does not seem attributable to these factors.

5. Toys and other objects frequently serve as the focus of social encounters — more fully social as the child matures. Such encounters afford numerous opportunities for direct and incidental learning.

6. Toys and other physical objects appear to have an inherent attractiveness for young children. They draw children into action and serve as a source of skill development and tool mastery.

7. Toys can serve as a catalyst for imaginative play and can serve to carry the meaning of the play situation to full realization. They may also help to provide a link between learnings derived from the imaginative world of play and the more concrete settings of the real world.

Much about the relation between play materials and intellectual development remains speculative. Much of the apparent strength of that relationship may derive from the fact that play materials frequently enlist three major intrinsic motives: curiosity, mastery, and affiliation (Yarrow, Rubenstein, & Pederson, 1975. As the child matures, he is likely to enlist a number of secondary motives as well. The heightened attention and persistence that flow from these motives increase substantially the likelihood of all types of learning, and in turn help drive development. As Caldwell cogently argued nearly two decades ago, the optimal environment for young children should include a wide variety of responsive objects and play materials.

DISCUSSION

Jay Belsky: What is the relationship between Maternal Responsivity and Play Materials? Is there a pathway, conceivably, from Responsivity to Play Materials and back? For the parent who is responsive, who is tuned in, who's sensitive, toy materials are one way of expressing it.

Robert Bradley: We find about a .5 correlation generally between Play Materials and Maternal Responsivity. We find a slightly higher one between Play Materials and Maternal Involvement, the direct encouragement, roughly .6 or .7. I think what you're suggesting is what we do see. It's not just the availability of the materials that matters, but how they're used. Parents who are sensitive to changes in their own children are responsive to those changes in providing materials.

Vonnie McLoyd: How do you define play materials in the HOME Inventory? Is the definition functional, so that anything the child uses in a playful way is classified as a toy?

Robert Bradley: Yes, the definitions are functional; play materials like pots and pans for stacking or a stool to push around would count, as long as they are available and accessible to the child.

Bettye Caldwell: The Play Materials scale covers several functions: materials for large muscle activities, small muscle activities, rhythm and music, cuddling and comfort, and so on.

Vonnie McLoyd: Does that mean that if the child uses a toy in a way that isn't included as a function in your measure, then the toy is not accounted as a play material?

Bettye Caldwell: Right, but I honestly do not think there are any major functions left out.

Vonnie McLoyd: You're not missing a number of toys because the child doesn't use them for the functions that you have delineated?

Bettye Caldwell: We could be missing some, Vonnie. Two points to remember are, first, that the HOME Inventory subscales were developed through successive factor analyses. There were originally some 20 items related to toys and over 300 items in the Inventory as a whole; now, the total number of items is 45. The ones that remain are those that correlate highly with the total score—the same kind of procedure you go through with any measure. Now, for some crazy reason, some of the toy items, including books, do not group with the toy subscale. But you have to do it the way the factor analysis gives it. I really think we have most of the functions covered.

Second, the Inventory measures the home environment. It's easy to fall into the trap of thinking it measures something in the children. It measures the quality of what is available and accessible to the child, and the instructions to the people who've used it are, "When in doubt, put yourself in the child's position." This means, for instance, that if the family bought a toy for an earlier child but it's still available, it counts.

Jay Belsky: It's the lag relationships that are intriguing to me, Bob.

Robert Bradley: I think they are, too.

Allen Gottfried: There are problems with lag analyses, though.

Robert Bradley: And with path models. We know that.

Greta Fein: You can use hierarchical regression.

Robert Bradley: Yes. We're trying to use all the techniques we can.

Jay Belsky: You're trying to address a modeling question with a variety of modeling tactics. As Bob McCall likes to say, a different analytic framework won't necessarily give you the same results but, if there are consistencies across approaches, it suggests you're onto something.

Robert Bradley: It's very interesting. For example, pairing Play Materials and Maternal Involvement gave us a very high multiple R. When we factored out all the rest, just those two were left. They're also correlated with Maternal Responsivity but, even when you move that out, we find very strong continuing multiple correlations.

To follow up on what's been said about siblings, I want to mention that how toys and play materials become accessible to children and how they're used varies tremendously. We've seen situations in which the parents aren't making a lot of things available but the siblings are great. They drag things out and involve the younger ones in all kinds of play. That's what has the power: The child is pulled into a social structure, not just an object environment.

Greta Fein: What I've seen in homes with several children is that you have sibling toys and baby toys. Several generations of toys are part of the setting and used by the different children in the family.

Judy Dunn: It's a repeated finding among studies of siblings that what the other child has acts like a magnet. They both want to play with the same thing. Often, they want to play together.

Robert Bradley: That's what we've seen, absolutely.

HOME STIMULATION AND COGNITIVE DEVELOPMENT

Theodore D. Wachs, Ph.D.

Recent theoretical reviews clearly indicate that the environment is not unitary but highly differentiated, containing a variety of specific subunits or levels (Bronfenbrenner, 1977; Wohlwill, 1983). My focus today will be on the molecular level, corresponding to what Bronfenbrenner has called the microsystem. Within this level, until very recently, most developmental research and theory has focused on the social environment rather than the physical environment. This one-sided emphasis is justified, it has been claimed, because the physical environment can have little impact upon development unless it is mediated by social variables (Provence & Lipton, 1962; Clarke-Stewart, 1973; Parke, 1978). This claim has gained wider acceptance than supporting data warrant (MacPhee, Ramey, & Yates, 1984).

After a brief review of known relationships between physical environment parameters and cognitive development, I will present four competing models that define relationships between the social and physical microenvironments and summarize data from two studies that help evaluate the models. Next, I will show why my study of the physical environment has led me to prefer specific models of environmental action to global, main-effects models.

Models of Physical-Social Relationships

Data from a variety of studies demonstrate the relevance of the physical environment to cognitive performance (Wachs & Gruen, 1982; Wachs, in press; Gottfried, 1984b). The seven dimensions of the physical environment most consistently found to be related to cognitive development during the first five years of life are shown in Table 4.

Table 4. Physical Environmental Factors Showing Consistent Relationships to Cognitive Development over the First Five Years of Life

Dimension	Direction of Relationship to Cognitive Performance	Comments
Availability of stimulus material	Positive	Primarily relevant in first nine months of life
Variety of stimulus material	Positive	As child gets older changes in available objects may be more critical than number of different objects available
Responsivity of the physical environment	Positive	
Ambient background noise	Negative	Particularly salient for males and at-risk infants
Overcrowding	Negative	
Regularity of scheduling	Positive	May be mediated by age and by ability under study
Physical restraints on exploration	Negative	

The *nature* of the relationship between the physical environment and development, however, has not been defined. Of particular interest is the question of whether the findings in the studies referred to above were due to an independent impact of the physical environment or due primarily to adults' mediating the physical environment for the child.

Figure 2 shows a series of simplified path models, indicating four possible patterns of interrelationships between the physical and social environments as these impact upon development. The physical and social environments could have independent effects (Model A); they could covary (Model B); the social environment could mediate the physical environment (Model C); or the physical environment could mediate the social environment (Model D).

Model A. Independent Effects

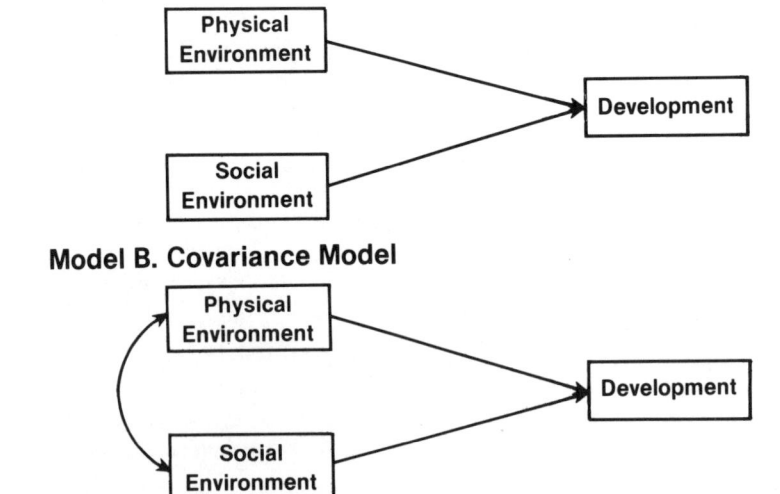

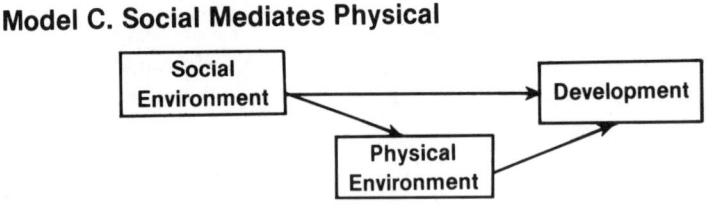

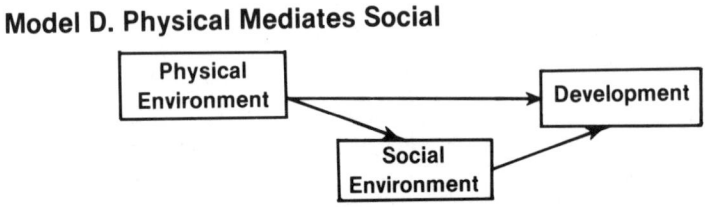

Model B. Covariance Model

Model C. Social Mediates Physical

Model D. Physical Mediates Social

Figure 2. Models of the Relationship Between the Physical and Social Environments

Two recent studies offer data that can be used for a preliminary evaluation of these competing models. In the first study (Wachs & Gandour, 1983), our subjects were 100 six-month-old infants. We used the Purdue Home Stimulation Inventory to measure the physical environment and the Yarrow Scale to measure the social environment. In our analysis, we emphasized five physical environment factors that are known to be consistently related to cognitive performance.

We classified these five factors into two categories: those that provide high affordances for the child and those that provide only limited affordances, as shown below. Gibson (1979) defines affordances in terms of the degree of fit between stimulus properties and behaviors which are naturally associated with these stimulus properties. For example, blocks may be said to be objects that afford a child the opportunity to place two physical surfaces together, as in stacking the blocks or hitting them together. Looking at the physical environment in terms of affordances allows us to make a distinction between aspects of the physical environment that provide multiple affordances to the child and those whose physical properties offer few affordances.

High- and Low-Affordance Factors of the Physical Environment

High-Affordance Factors

1. Availability of stimulus materials (e.g., number of small objects, papers, toys)
2. Variety of stimulus materials (e.g., new toys)
3. Responsivity of stimulus materials (e.g., number of audiovisually responsive toys)

Low-Affordance Factors

1. Noise rating
2. Crowding (number of siblings; rooms-to-people ratio)

To test the available models, we correlated eleven summary scores from the Yarrow Scale with the codes defining our two categories of physical environment factors. We found no relationship between adult interactions and high-affordance factors in the physical environment for our six-month-old subjects. These results seem to support Model A; that is, they suggest that high-affordance aspects of the physical environment operate independently of social mediation, at least at six months of age. Low-affordance stimuli, on the other hand, were negatively correlated with many social variables; interestingly, the relation of these low-affordance factors to development is also primarily negative, as noted earlier. At first glance, this latter pattern seemed to support Model B or C. When we looked closely at the items involved, however, a somewhat different picture emerged.

What the results show is that higher levels of ambient background noise are significantly and negatively related to amount of auditory stimulation, contingent parental vocalization, and reinforcement of the child's play activities. Similar findings are also seen for the number of siblings (a measure of crowding). Logically, I find it difficult to understand how low levels of contingency or auditory stimulation by adults can produce higher levels of background noise or crowding in the home. In contrast, I find it quite logical to view these findings as suggesting that the presence of noise or crowding *interferes* with parental reinforcement or auditory stimulation of the infant. Looked at in this way, these data offer little support for Model C (social mediates physical) but can be used to support either Model B (covariance) or Model D (physical mediates social).

Our second study (Wachs & Chan, 1985) was done with 48 12-month-old infants. The findings concerning low-affordance parameters of the physical environment show a similar pattern to those in the earlier study of six-month olds and again tend to support either Model B or D.

In contrast to the findings for six-month-olds, however, the data for the 12-month sample indicate many significant relationships between high-affordance physical dimensions and social interactions. Since the two data sets are not longitudinal, it is impossible to tell whether this discrepancy represents a genuine developmental shift in the nature of the infant's environment or whether it is due to sample variation. However, given the similarity in the results for the low-affordance dimensions at 6 and 12 months, I tend to favor the former interpretation. In any event, the results at 12 months suggest that parents who provide their infants with a variety of toys and objects to interact with are also more likely to be highly involved with their infant (either positively or negatively, as in the case of coercion) and are more likely to vocalize and respond to their infant's vocalizations. Given the direction of these relationships, it is not likely that the availability of varied objects in the home leads to greater responsivity and involvement (Model D), but the results could be used to support either Model B (covariance) or Model C (social mediates physical).

Fortunately, it is possible to test these two competing models directly by collapsing the significant social and physical environment predictors into data sets and entering the data sets into a hierarchical multiple regression. Such an analysis does not support the contention that the physical environment must be mediated by the social environment in order to have an impact upon development (Model C). Rather, the physical environment data set added unique predictive variance even after the contribution of the social environment data set had been partialled out.

The nature of the impact of the physical environment, then, seems to depend on what aspect of the physical environment is being considered. Low-affordance parameters seem to covary with social factors (Model B) or mediate social factors (Model D); high-affordance parameters seem to operate independently at six months (Model A) and to covary with social factors at 12 months (Model B). Our data on 12-month-olds also suggest that variation in development occurs not because of the contributions of the physical or social environments per se but rather as a dual function of both parents' characteristics and environmental characteristics. For example, parents who provide their infants with a variety of new play objects are also more likely to name these objects repeatedly for their infants.

Specific Models of Environmental Action

Until very recently, the predominant model of environmental action was what I've called the Guinness model. This title derives from the old British advertising slogan for Guinness stout, "Guinness is good for you." Similarly, researchers and clinicians have tended to assume that good environments (whatever that means) were good for all aspects of development in all children at all ages; similarly, bad environments were bad for all aspects of development in all children at all ages.

Data emerging from our research on the physical environment do not support this global approach. They show a tremendous amount of specificity in environment-development relationships, with specific aspects of the physical environment predicting only specific aspects of development at specific ages for specific individuals. In addition, they suggest that the most appropriate model of environmental effects is one we have dubbed BEAM, for Bifactor Environmental Action Model. As shown in Figure 3, BEAM postulates that a small subset of environmental parameters have global influences upon development while the majority of environmental parameters are highly specific in their effects.

As we contemplated the bifactor model, we began to wonder about individual differences in response to the environment. Is environmental action really organism-environment interaction? This idea is diagrammed in Figure 4.

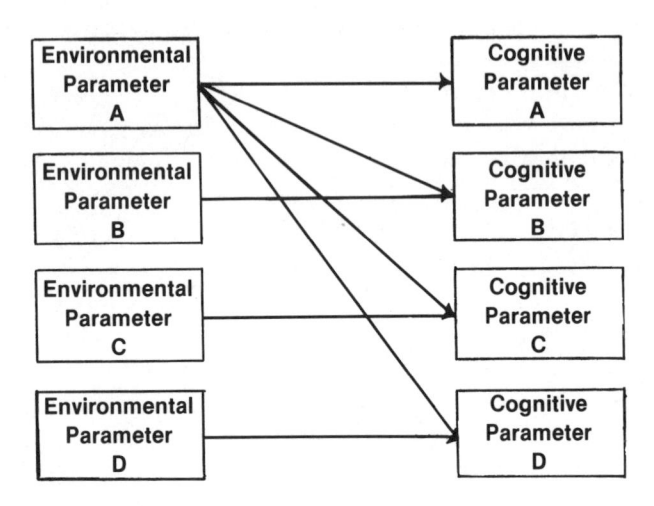

Figure 3. Bifactor Model of Environmental Action (BEAM)

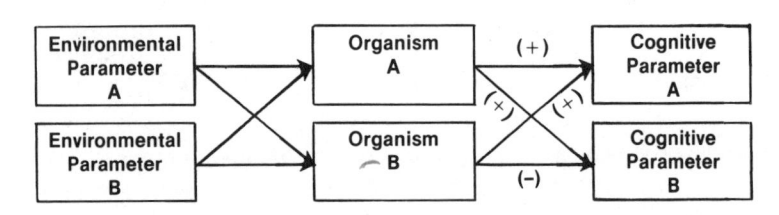

Figure 4. Bifactor Model of Organism-Environment Interaction

Rather than looking at the global question of the relation of environment to child development, I would propose that it is much more productive to ask, What components of environment for which children? For example, a number of studies distinguish between children who are primarily object-oriented and those who are primarily socially oriented (Nelson, 1981; Shotwell, Wolf, & Gardner, 1980; Nakamura & Finck, 1980). Preliminary findings suggest that this distinction holds for mastery behavior (Wachs, 1984).

If a child is primarily object-oriented, optimal development should occur when this child encounters a physically rich environment containing a variety of age-appropriate responsive objects. Similarly, a socially oriented child might do best in an environment emphasizing social interaction. A mismatch between organism and environment could well hinder either child's development. This idea is clearly speculative, but it is congruent with what we know about the nature of environmental action.

Looking at the question of environmental influences more broadly, in terms of theory and public policy, the evidence I have presented here on the physical environment and the bifactor model calls for changes in orientation at both levels. In terms of theory, for the most part we have reified the Law of Parsimony by canonizing main-effects models of environmental action. As McCall has noted (McCall & McGhee, 1977), however, we have no reason to assume that nature has been parsimonious in arranging human development. Environmental models that stress main effects such as "maternal deprivation" or "optimal maternal care" are greatly oversimplified at best. Based on what we now know, it is time to move away from global main-effects theories to more interactive theories that consider the joint contributions of organism and environment (Wachs, 1983).

A similar recommendation can be made concerning intervention programs for children with various cognitive or social deficits. The prevalent intervention approaches have been main effect: Children in a given program are exposed to a heterogeneous mass of so-called enriching experiences. Evaluation studies uniformly show small mean group gains and major variability within groups, indicating individual differences in response to intervention (Wachs & Gruen, 1982; Wachs, in press). It seems likely that some children are receiving environmental inputs that are not appropriate for them.

Simplified main-effects models and interventions do not reflect the reality of the developmental process. If it seems that I have muddied a fairly simple and clearcut question — the relation of environment to development— then I have accomplished my purpose.

DISCUSSION

Inge Bretherton: Are you suggesting, Ted, that an object orientation or a social orientation is something that's in the child and, if we could find it out right from the beginning, we could send them on their optimal pathway?

Ted Wachs: Yes, I've been influenced enough by the behavior genetics people to believe that some traits are in there very early, but how they become manifest depends on what happens to the child. A socially oriented child who lives in a supportive environment is more likely to end up socially oriented than the same child in a nonsupportive environment. The interesting cases are the children who have one initial disposition or the other and get into the wrong kind of environment. I'm not quite sure what to predict there.

Jay Belsky: Your line of reasoning seems accurate for the extreme ends of the sociable/nonobject-oriented and nonsociable/object-oriented ends of the continuum, but I suspect that these extremes combined make up no more than about 15 percent of the distribution. The large majority of children fall in between, and there's probably a lot of plasticity there. I'm not sure we should see a social orientation and an orientation toward objects as alternatives, sort of pit them against each other; that's not quite the same thing as seeing them as the extremes of a range.

Ted Wachs: I'm not going to argue with that, Jay. I think, though, that when you're at an early stage of conceptualization, you have to work with extremes, particularly when there's such resistance to the notion of interaction and individual differences. You have to focus on extremes in order to make your point. Clearly, as you say, there's much more plasticity in the middle of the range.

Lorraine McCune: Denny Wolf has talked about the coming together of these two orientations late in the third year. You may continue to see some dispositional differences, but most children show a development of complex skills in both areas.

I'm somewhat concerned by the tone many of us are taking, which seems to say that we shouldn't or are not able to use the child development information that we have available in support of infants and families. I feel there are lots of ways that our information can be helpful. We shouldn't be prescriptive, which is part of your message and part of the message of others who have said we shouldn't try to do too much. But we can encourage the recognition of individual differences in infants; help people become sensitive to the kinds of signals that babies send, be they weak or strong, at various points in development; help parents respond to those signals; and help daycare centers begin to reproduce some of the better, more sensitive aspects of home life, such as one-on-one care. There's so much we *can* say that it makes me uncomfortable to hear us suggesting that we really don't know enough to help people move forward.

Ted Wachs: I agree we've got a lot to offer, but I think in one sense we've reached a limit. We've got to keep using the information we have until something better comes along. But my own feeling is that what's critically needed is a taxonomy of relevant individual differences, and the integration of this taxonomy with current information, to make our prescriptions, if you will, more precise. Rather than saying, for example, that language stimulation is good for children, we might say that language stimulation may be good for certain children, but there are other children you'll get better results with if you try something else.

Lorraine McCune: I have to say that's the opposite of what I would advise, because I don't think we're ever going to have the precision for that kind of prescription. I think it's more a matter of helping parents and others who work with children to be generative on the basis of the data available than of trying to refine categories sufficiently. I doubt they can be refined sufficiently.

Allen Gottfried: At what point should psychologists become prescriptive? What are we waiting for? We have many longitudinal studies conducted already. We have millions of dollars in grant money invested in environmental studies and lots of fascinating data. What are the criteria that we wait for before we go out there and admit we have relevant data? I think it's more destructive to sit back than it is to say that we *do* have findings about how the environment affects children. We can deal with the theoretical issues in discussions like this.

Robert Bradley: The fact is that other people do take what we say and make prescriptions out of it. I think we have to recognize that is going to happen and has happened historically, and we have to deal with it as a social and political phenomenon.

Allen Gottfried: I've been visiting preschools recently, and I've had directors tell me, "I don't see the purpose of all this environmental stuff. Preschoolers are biological timeclocks. When they're ready, they're ready." I find that astounding in view of the findings we've obtained over twenty years on the impact and power of the environment. So I think we have to try hard to show off the knowledge that we have.

Ted Wachs: I agree with Lorraine's point about trying to teach sensitivity and responsiveness to parents, but I've seen some very insensitive parents, and unfortunately these are the very ones who tend to look for prescriptions. They'll take a "finding" on how to raise your child's IQ some huge number of points and use it as a prescription, stamp it on the child, regardless of whether it fits the child or not.

Allen Gottfried: That's not because of us. That's because of media translations and the like. Very few developmental psychologists convey ion to parents that way.

...achs: The media may be guilty, but for us, would you accept accessory to the crime?

PARENT-CHILD INTERACTION AND SOCIAL-EMOTIONAL DEVELOPMENT

Leila Beckwith, Ph.D.

From the beginning of human history up to the present century, the dominant issue in parenting has been the physical survival of the infant. Only recently has "fun morality" emerged as a significant dimension in parenting and infant care (Wolfenstein, 1955). Play, amusement, enjoying oneself — these are no longer considered potentially wicked, as they were by the Puritans. Now, rather than the fear of being too impulsive, we have lowered self-esteem occasioned by failure to have fun. Play and work, which in the past were more separate, with the danger of sin associated with one and virtue with the other, are now more fused. Infant rearing, for example, which in the past was characterized as serious work, is now increasingly characterized in terms of pleasure. Patience and self-control as psychological requirements for parents have been replaced by a required quality of enjoyment.

The new fun morality has had an increasing influence on developmental research. In this paper, I will discuss findings on what play and pleasure between parents and infants provide the infant, particularly in terms of social development. The focus will be on social play between parents and infants, as distinguished from play with peers or siblings and play with objects, although objects are often used during the play of parents and infants.

Play and Attachment

The essential importance of social experience for infants' development is no longer questioned, but just which aspects of social experience have what developmental consequences is unclear. Attachment theory argues persuasively that the essential function of the primary social relationship between parent and infant is to promote the physical survival of the infant, especially to protect from predators (Ainsworth, 1973; Bowlby, 1969).

Play and attachment overlap greatly, but they exhibit different qualities. Although positive affect is central to Bowlby and Ainsworth's conceptualizations of the attachment system, negative affect tends to be emphasized. The parent in her attachment behavior reassures, consoles, and provides comfort. She reduces stress and anxiety. In contrast, the emphasis in social play is on interest and delight. Social play is characterized by high affective level, mutual pleasure, and shared codes of conduct.

Does play have different consequences for infant development than do other social exchanges between parent and infant? On a practical level, it is difficult to distinguish the influence of social play from the influence of infant-parent social exchanges that occur in other contexts. Parents differ widely in their repertoire of games, the sensitivity with which they play them, and their propensity to do so (Stern, 1974). It is likely that those differences are reflected in the degree to which caregivers are attentive, sensitive, and contingently responsive to infant signals in other contexts.

Research supports this conjecture. In one study, social play was found to load on an optimal maternal factor (Clarke-Stewart, 1973). In our own study (Beckwith et al., 1976), it loaded on a social factor that explained most of the variance in caregiver-infant interaction. In another study it was found to correlate with a high frequency of stimulating with objects, and with generally intense maternal involvement (Pettit & Bates, 1984).

Social Competence

In several very important ways, play between infants and parents promotes social competence. First, social play allows passive experience to be turned into active mastery of social situations. Play selects out one part of the content of the infant's life for the infant to practice with pleasure rather than with the negative feelings that may accompany the real-life event (Sutton-Smith & Sutton Smith, 1974; Sutton-Smith, 1980). For example, in a game of "peek-a-boo" the parent does not really separate from the infant, and the infant does not show separation distress. Such games help the child master tension-arousing experiences and understand the boundary between real and make-believe (Bruner & Sherwood, 1976).

Social play is a cooperative interchange in which infants learn to influence others (Ross & Kay, 1980). In social play, infants' gestures and actions are responded to and acquire meaning. Repetition, a salient aspect of social play, also allows infants to anticipate and thereby control the parents' behavior (Gustafson, Green, & West, 1979).

Most social play involves organized integrated sequences of actions and thus is rule governed. Acquiring game skills amplifies infants' understanding of rules, including rules of language (Lewis & Cherry, 1977; Ross & Kay, 1980).

Finally, to play is not only to learn actions but to practice emotions, such as surprise, anticipation, excitement, and climax. Parents alter their play behavior in accord with infants' affective signals and their signs of attention or inattention (Stern, 1974). The affective systems of infant and parent are the primary means of regulating joint exchanges (Tronick, 1982). An infant signals his or her affective state; the parent responds to those signals; the infant responds to the parent's signals. Prior to verbal communication, the infant's affect is the only reliable representation of the saliency and meaning of events and the primary medium of communication. Social play also preempts attention. One partner becomes the focus of attention of the other, or both share the same focus of attention, promoting joint exchanges (Spitz, 1972).

Emerging Skills

Parents select games to play before their infant has the necessary skills to do so, and the parent enables the infant to play the game. Adult decisions on what to play are finely tuned to the infant's developmental level; to the extent that this is so, it indicates an acute awareness on the adult's part of the infant's emerging skills. The parent provides the scaffold for the infant's emerging skills (Bruner, 1982) in what is done, when it is done, and the affect with which it is done. Initially, minimal participation on the part of the infant is accepted. Young infants are only expected to show attention and amusement. Anything else they do — including nothing—is interpreted as a turn in the game (Kaye, 1982).

Parents use attention-getting behaviors in early rounds of a game. As the game proceeds, the parent models both subroutines and climax, doing so slowly and with conspicuous affect and vocal marking. Repetitive verbalizations and pauses are used to signal the end of the parent's turn and the beginning of the infant's (Bruner, 1977). The parent also offers the child behavioral cues. For example, in the game "roll the ball," the parent holds out a hand to cue the child to return the ball (Hodapp, Goldfield, & Boyatzis, 1984).

As the necessary infant skills to be active in a game emerge, that game becomes more frequent. The height of playing a particular game is when the necessary infant skills converge. Face-to-face interaction is at its maximum at three to four months of age, when the major skills of gaze, externally generated smiling, and cooing become integrated (Stern, 1974). In those early months, tickling, "horsie," and "I'm gonna get you," in which the infant's part is to attend and enjoy but not to be motorically active, are common (Gustafson et al., 1979). From four months on, games become motorically more complex as the infant achieves greater motor skills (Crawley et al., 1978). Peek-a-boo and pat-a-cake, in which infants have an active motoric role, become frequent from 7 to 12 months and then decrease. Only at 12 months do games with toys, such as "give and take," "build and smash," and "point and name" occur (Crawley & Sherrod, 1984).

A particular game goes into a refractory period after the infant achieves competence in it, although the structure of the game may emerge later when the infant invents a new game. For instance, children resist playing peek-a-boo from 11 to 14 months but then begin to play by hiding objects on their own (Bruner, 1982).

Promoting Positive Affect

One of the major goals for the parent in social play is to maintain a level of attention and arousal in which the infant is likely to show positive affect (Stern, 1974). Adults elicit and reinforce positive affect in infants by emitting happy expressions more frequently than negative expressions and by reinforcing positive affect rather than negative affect in the infant. Whereas infants in face-to-face play display a wide range of expressions and a very high rate of change, maternal expressions are limited to positive emotions, especially toward young infants. Mothers respond contingently to only about 25 percent of infant expressive changes and tend not to acknowledge infant negative expressions (Malatesta & Haviland, 1982).

The degree to which games are fun and do interest and delight infants has been studied by ingenious experimental interventions in which the game is interrupted or the parent's affect is altered. The importance of the maternal affective display to the infant's own affect is shown, for example, in studies in which the mother is asked to engage in face-to-face interaction in a "depressed way" or with a "depressed face" (Cohn & Tronick, 1982; Tronick, Ricks, & Cohn, 1982). During the depressed condition, three-month-old infants were more wary, protested more, and hardly played. The differences persisted even after the mothers resumed their normal behavior, indicating that infants pay attention to their partners' affective displays and that the partner's affect regulates the infant's affect.

Fun, Attachment, and Sociability

Several studies indicate that infants are more involved with parents who are more fun. The more playful a mother, and the more positive affect she displays during interaction with the infant, the more socially responsive the infant will be to her, and the more positive affect the infant will show. When mothers were asked to play with their five- and eight-month-old infants in a laboratory situation, infants whose mothers played more games with them engaged in more mutual visual regard with the mothers and, at eight months, smiled more at them (Crawley et al., 1978). For toddlers in the second year of life, Clarke-Stewart (1973) found that mothers who showed more positive emotion had children who were more positively involved with them and who themselves expressed more happiness.

Infants who have had more fun with their mothers tend to become securely attached (Blehar, Lieberman, & Ainsworth, 1977). Infants with mothers who are tense and irritable during early interactions are more likely to become anxiously attached or avoidant (Egeland & Farber, 1984). Securely attached infants later have more fun in tasks and are more persistent (Main, 1973; Matas, Arend, & Sroufe, 1978), more sociable with adult strangers (Thompson & Lamb, 1983), and more sociable with peers (Main, 1973; Lieberman, 1977). At age three, day-campers who at one year were securely attached made more complex and more successful bids to peers. They were also rated as more socially competent with both peers and adults (Kennedy & Bakeman, 1982).

Affect Regulation as a Risk Marker

Parents show less pleasure during interactions with biologically at-risk infants, whether born preterm or postterm, than do parents of healthy full-term infants. This phenomenon was noted in the pioneering research of Leiderman and his associates (1973), which has been replicated in several other studies. Mothers of preterm infants smile less to their infants than do mothers of term infants, regardless of the amount of contact between preterm infant and parent in the hospital. In our own research, we find few differences between parents of preterm and term infants once we equate for conceptional age, except that preterm infant-mother dyads engage in fewer occasions of mutual smiling. Decreased smiling throughout the first year of life in preterm mother-infant dyads has also been noted by other investigators (Crnic et al., 1983).

Microanalytic techniques indicate that the deviation in affect regulation occurs in both the parent and the risk infant (Field, 1979; 1982). Field suggests that at-risk infants may have more difficulty modulating arousal in response to stimulation than do normal infants, creating a more difficult task for their parents in fine-tuning the intensity and amount of stimulation. It is not yet known whether the decreased enjoyment is reflected in later emotional organization, as in the attachment relationship. But preterm infants do continue to show less positive affect when playing with objects. By the second year of life, they also show less pleasure in task mastery, even when equally successful.

Parents as Playmates: Conclusions

My thesis has been that parents have a central role in infants' development, not only as caregivers but as playmates. Social play promotes secure attachment, pleasure in tasks, and sociability with others. Persuasive evidence exists that deviant parent-infant dyads, such as biologically at-risk infants and maltreated infants (Egeland, Sroufe, & Erickson, 1983; Schneider-Rosen & Cicchetti, 1984), differ markedly from normal dyads in their enjoyment and play with each other.

While, in general, parents' choice of games reflects an exquisite fine-tuning to the infant's increasing cognitive and motoric skills, this is not always so. Some parents keep their child passive in a game for extended periods of time, as in tickling or teasing. In addition, infants can become overloaded, and parents differ in their sensitivity and skill in responding to too high a level of arousal in the infant.

Although the data are just beginning to accumulate, it seems that when parents and infants are playful and enjoy their interactions with one another, infants are more likely later to be securely attached, to enjoy problem-solving tasks, and to be sociable with adults and with peers.

DISCUSSION

Inge Bretherton: You've done a wonderful job of pulling all this together, Leila, but there's one thing that puzzles me. The literature on early play seems to show that affective synchrony is very important, so that when the child starts to turn away and show negative affect, the parents should tone things down a little bit. But did you say that parents don't pay very much attention to that?

Leila Beckwith: Not exactly. I was trying to differentiate behavior from affect. Parents need to pause and not talk, perhaps, but they maintain the smiling face rather than shifting into the sad or neutral affect displayed by the infant.

Inge Bretherton: I see. An article by Ainsworth also showed, I think, that pacing is very important. When a child is tired, a sensitive mother shouldn't continue trying to play.

Leila Beckwith: Right. If I make the point that play is fun and fun is good, that doesn't mean these things are always true. Joy is probably a rare occurrence in our lives and a rare occurrence in an infant's life. It's probably better that it not occur all the time.

Kenneth Rubin: I think there's an important relationship between one of your points and the distinction that Ted Wachs made between object-oriented and socially oriented children. You said that the child who feels secure in novel settings, for example, is more likely to explore the environment, to find out what objects do in the environment, and to use those objects creatively and constructively. The important thing that I see here is that a child who spends most of the time with objects in the environment may look object-oriented, but that's been set up by a very positive social relationship that preceded it. In fact, a child who doesn't spend much time with objects in a playroom and seeks a whole lot of attention from the mother might be an insecurely attached baby and yet might appear to be socially oriented.

Leila Beckwith: Exactly. One thing we have overlooked in terms of our data on the securely attached infant exploring the environment is that the infant is very likely, sometime in that play bout, to take a toy back to the parent and show it to her. The social episode may be very brief, but it's important.

Lorraine McCune: I'd like to mention a set of data relating play and language that may not be well known in this country yet. Luigia Camaioni of the University of Rome is now looking at mother-child games as the source of one or more first words in infants. She thinks that one or more of the first words of every infant, if we look very closely, will prove to have its source in a particular social routine that parent and child engage in.

Greta Fein: I may be vastly overextending the theoretical implications of what you've been saying, Leila, but I like your ideas so much that I want to ask whether I'm overextending or just saying what you're saying in my own way. I think you have offered a very powerful and appealing explanatory construct for variations in attachment that are seen at 12 and 18 months. Securely attached babies are actually babies who have acquired a measure of self-regulation in their affective system; they can afford to be securely attached because they're able to handle these urges and surges fairly autonomously. Now, if that's true, it seems to relate to Ken Rubin's data and to some of the other data that attachment research has generated. If you are in control of your own emotional system, it's not hard to go out and do things with peers. You're not threatened; you're not scared. You can handle your feelings fairly well and then acquire the technical skills associated with manipulating and organizing the social environment. You are able to do this because you don't have all this emotional stuff churning all the time and getting in the way, pushing you either into a corner where you don't want to look at anybody or out in the middle where you're hitting and banging.

Jay Belsky: You're more skilled in approaching others, too, so it's less likely you're going to get yourself into a situation in which your arousal is going to become out of control. You're more strategic in the way you go about things.

Greta Fein: The reason I like that is that I have not seen attachment theory, for all the lovely data that's been generated within the construct, come up with a powerful organizing variable that can make sense of all those nice findings. I think you're suggesting one, and it's a very fine model.

Leila Beckwith: I like your interpretation very much.

MOTHERS' INTERACTIVE BEHAVIOR IN PLAY SESSIONS AND CHILDREN'S EDUCATIONAL ACHIEVEMENT

Phyllis Levenstein, Ed.D.

The Mother-Child Home Program and its parent, the Verbal Interaction Project, have been in progress for many years. They provide an unusual opportunity to study the influence of mothers' interactive behavior during play sessions on children's later educational achievement, social-emotional competence, and IQ.

The Mother-Child Home Program was the result of a 1965 pilot study (Levenstein & Sunley, 1968) and was based on some guesses about the kinds of parent behaviors that should be encouraged in children's preschool years in order to prevent the cumulative school disadvantaged too often seen in low-income pupils. We postulated the latent presence in all families of a parent-child network that could be strengthened in low-income families by play-oriented interaction to support the growth of children's competencies in preparation for school. A voluntary, home-based early education/parent education program for low-income two- to four-year-olds evolved (Levenstein, 1976; 1977).

The Verbal Interaction Project used observations made during program home sessions and laboratory videotapes to study verbal and other interactions between low-income mothers and their young children. In follow-up studies, the children's behavior at school was assessed. By relating these data, we hoped to find out whether mothers' early verbal interaction was related to their children's later achievement.

The Mother-Child Home Program

Each mother-child dyad was in the Mother-Child Home Program for two school years, starting when the child was two. Home visitors, called Toy Demonstrators, modeled interactive skills for the mother in home play sessions conducted around gifts of toys and books. Since today's huge literature on play was as yet unwritten, our definition of play followed Webster's: "Recreational activity, especially the spontaneous activity of children."

Each week, a new toy or book, selected on the basis of explicit criteria, was presented to the mother and child. These were the materials around which a fun-oriented curriculum was built. A developmentally appropriate guidesheet was written for each new toy or book around a stable list of concepts (e.g., colors, shapes, numbers) and concept-related activities (e.g., fitting, matching, choosing). Each guidesheet ended with the same reminder: "Have a good time with the (toy or book), the child, and the mother!"

The Toy Demonstrators were paid or volunteer women with a wide range of education and backgrounds. Some were former program participants; some were former teachers. As Toy Demonstrators, they did not teach, preach, or become a close friend of the mother. With the children, too, they kept their relationship light. In home sessions they joined in the children's spontaneity and enjoyment while unobtrusively introducing or reinforcing verbally symbolized concepts. They also followed explicit rules and practiced special techniques to preserve confidentiality and to protect the family against unintended intrusiveness on the part of the program (Levenstein, 1980).

The program's theory was (and still is, after 16 years) that cognitive and social-emotional growth are fostered, and future educational and emotional problems prevented, when a young child and mother exchange language and other positive interactions in mutually enjoyable play around interesting, conceptually rich materials. The interaction must be playful, not didactic, for best effect on the child and the relationship (Clarke-Stewart, 1973), and it must exclude the "experts" as far as possible (Bronfenbrenner, 1974). Our goal was to strengthen the intrinsic motivation for play in both mother and child—that is, to increase their enjoyment of it — in part through extrinsic rewards such as the play materials and, for the child, the mother's praise.

Outcome research from 1967 through 1972 demonstrated the success of the program in preventing educational disadvantage for its child graduates (Lazar & Darlington, 1982; Madden, Levenstein, & Levenstein, 1976). However, a question remained as to whether the program graduates' normal school achievement was linked to their mothers' verbal interaction with them, as was postulated in creating the Mother-Child Home Program.

The Verbal Interaction Project

One way we attempted to answer this question was to measure the verbal interaction in videotaped play sessions of all the mothers in the 1976 cohort, that is, mothers who took part in the Mother-Child Home Program with their preschoolers from 1976 to 1978. We videotaped two play sessions between these mothers and children, one when they finished the program in 1978 and another in 1980, when the children were almost six and were finishing kindergarten. Using an instrument that we developed called the Maternal Interaction Behavior or MIB measure, we rated the mother's verbal and other interactive behaviors during these play sessions. The categories of behavior included in the MIB measure are shown below.

Maternal Interactive Behavior (MIB) Items

1. Gives label information
2. Gives color information
3. Verbalizes actions
4. Gives number and shape information
5. Questions child; solicits information
6. Verbalizes praise
7. Stimulates divergent use of toy
8. Smiles; makes positive gesture
9. Replies to child
10. Does not reply to child

The mothers' 1978 MIB scores were then correlated in multiple regression predictions with three 1980 assessments of their children's kindergarten behavior: reading and mathematics scores on the Wide Range Achievement Test (WRAT); scores on a 20-item measure of social-emotional skills that we developed (Johnson, 1976); and Stanford-Binet IQ. Similar multiple regressions were performed to correlate these mothers' 1980 MIB scores with 1982 school assessments of their children near the end of the second grade.

Both sets of regressions produced some puzzling, even contradictory, results. It is possible that the MIB measure was too crude to tap the specific verbal interaction components that predict children's school success. However, the mothers' general verbal responsiveness (Item 9, Replies to Child) at the end of the program in 1978 predicted the children's self-confidence, social responsibility, and math skills in kindergarten. The same maternal variable, assessed in 1980, predicted the children's 1982 reading scores and IQs as well as social responsibility and self-confidence. Equal in influence was Item 8, Smiles or Makes Positive Gesture. And almost as consistent a predictor of negative outcomes was Item 10, Does Not Reply to Child.

However inexact the MIB measure was for identifying the precise verbal-interaction antecedents of children's school-age competencies, the overall message appears unambiguous. Mothers who show responsiveness by replying verbally to their children and who spontaneously demonstrate their warm feelings toward their youngsters (smiles and hugs) are likely to influence their children toward school success. It appears that mothers' general responsiveness and warmth are much more important to children's school success than attempts to teach specific information.

In an earlier study, mothers who had entered the program in 1972 were rated by their Toy Demonstrators on interactive parenting behavior during their last few home sessions, in 1974. The Toy Demonstrators recorded global ratings of mothers' interactive behavior on an instrument called "Parent and Child Together" or PACT. Five of the 20 PACT items concerned parents' verbal interaction behavior. The same Toy Demonstrators also rated the children's social-emotional behavior during the concluding home sessions. The children's IQs were evaluated independently in the project office by a psychologist who had no connection with the program and knew nothing about the children except their ages.

The children's mean IQ showed a .40 correlation with their mothers' interactive parenting during home sessions and a .56 correlation with their own home session social-emotional behavior, both significant at the .01 level. The concurrent correlations between the PACT scores of the mothers and the social-emotional competence scores of the children were also high, though this is not surprising, since they were scored by the same observer.

All in all, there appeared to be a reliable relationship between children's intellectual development and their mothers' interactive behavior with them by age three-and-one-half, as well as a link between children's IQs and their social-emotional skills at the same age. In other words, the data indicated the presence of a triadic relationship between maternal interactive behavior, children's IQ, and children's social-emotional competence.

In 1977, when this same group of children was six and one-half years old, their first grade teachers rated them on their classroom social-emotional behavior, using the same scale as the Toy Demonstrators had during home sessions three years earlier. The ratings were global, by competent observers (the children's teachers) who had no connection with the Verbal Interaction Project. These first grade ratings, we discovered, were positively correlated with a narrow segment of the mothers' earlier home session behaviors: the five PACT items concerning verbal interactions.

Altogether, there were 27 significant correlations between mothers' early verbal interaction with the children and four categories of social-emotional behavior: Responsible Independence (accepts appropriate help, protects own rights, is self-confident); Task Orientation (enjoys mastering new tasks); Cognitive Orientation (is well organized, expresses ideas in language, understands difference between facts and make-believe, is creative and inventive); and Emotional Stability (is cheerful and content, spontaneous but not explosive).

Five separate correlational studies of relationships between maternal parenting behavior in play situations and children's competencies have been summarized. Three (using simple correlations) followed the 1972 program dyads from 1974 to 1977, that is, from near the end of participation in the Mother-Child Home Program into the children's first grade classrooms. Two (using multiple regression predictions) followed the 1976 cohort of dyads from 1978 to 1982, from the program's end to the children's second grade classrooms.

Whether the dyads' behavior was measured during home sessions, more intrusively by means of laboratory-made videotapes of mother and child together, or by observations of former child subjects in classrooms, a common thread ran through correlations among the behaviors. Mothers' interactions during play with their young children (especially verbal and often nurturing interactions) predicted their children's social-emotional and intellectual (including academic) achievements.

A mother's parenting behavior can be considered to precede her child's intellectual and social-emotional development. The data indicate that these two major aspects of children's personalities are linked, and that each is significantly related, in turn, to the mother's interactive behavior in play with her child.

Reflections

The intercorrelations among mother and child behaviors in every study tend to affirm the existence of a triadic relationship between a mother's parenting and her child's intellectual and social-emotional growth. The three parts of this triad form what perhaps are the main cables of a supportive mother-child network. From them there seem to connect countless strands of specific, reciprocally reinforcing behaviors, not only from mother to child but from child to mother. As Bronfenbrenner (1968) concluded from his analysis of over 150 studies on early environmental deprivation and stimulation,

> In the early years of life, the psychological development of the child is enhanced through his involvement in progressively more complex, enduring patterns of reciprocal contingent interaction with persons with whom he has established a mutual and enduring emotional attachment. (p. 26)

So interwoven are the elements of the mother's interactions, the child's IQ, and the child's classroom attitudes and academic skills as to suggest that the mother's interactive behavior is at the apex of the triad.

But the data also stand as a warning against a flood of didactic instruction. The contradictory aspects of our multiple regression predictions indicate that the supportive parent-child network formed through mothers' play interactions is a delicate one. It can be torn apart by a mother's insisting on the child's learning until it becomes boring and no longer play. The network is formed by the mother's general responsiveness, whether verbal or silently nurturing. The probability is that mothers who approach the young child's learning through play with spontaneous joy will have a child who continues to find joy in learning.

DISCUSSION

Jay Belsky: In the Mother-Child Home Program, did some mothers seem to learn the "play lessons" during home sessions more easily than others? Do you have any idea what might distinguish them from mothers who were less influenced?

Phyllis Levenstein: It took us about 18 years to get to that, Jay, and with your special interests, you're exactly the right person to ask me that question. That's the area in which I wish I had done more thinking and earlier analysis of what was going on in our own data. What I've discovered by statistical analysis in the last couple of years is that among the mothers who entered the program and who were identically low on SES factors— underclass mothers — there is a motivational dichotomy between "Strivers" and "Hesitaters." Strivers were mothers who picked up our ideas so quickly that by the second home session it was obvious that they had not needed the program in the first place. Other mothers were Hesitaters who took longer to catch on; the few who never did catch on were always Hesitaters. The Strivers, in case you're interested in a helpful marker variable, were characterized by high school graduation versus no high school graduation for Hesitaters. Almost all mothers, whether Strivers or Hesitaters, gained significantly in the program.

Jay Belsky: You throw them a lifeline and they can grab onto it.

Phyllis Levenstein: Exactly. However, Strivers grab on right away, and it almost doesn't matter what the lifeline is. Whether it's the Mother-Child Home Program or any other intervention, they'll grab it, and probably do well with it, too. To grab quickly, Hesitaters need a program tailored to their needs.

Ted Wachs: Can we make the same distinction among the children as well? Are there children you would label Strivers and Hesitaters?

Phyllis Levenstein: Probably, but we've never done that. No doubt there were differing motivational and perhaps organic factors influencing the children's development. I have two hats that I wear. As a clinical psychologist, I'm interested almost exclusively in individual differences. But as a developmental research psychologist, I'm interested mainly in group differences. As researchers, we tend to slide too fast over the individual differences.

Robert Bradley: Have you noticed in follow-up studies that the Striver-Hesitater distinction is a stable pattern?

Phyllis Levenstein: Apparently, yes. We've always conducted home interviews along with the follow-ups, and the situation tends to stay stable or improve. For example, we find a trend in the Strivers to go after more education.

Jay Belsky: Do they show higher rates of separation and divorce?

Phyllis Levenstein: Most of the mothers are without husbands when they start the program. We're talking about classic female-headed underclass families.

Vonnie McLoyd: Do you have any insight into the differences in the ways teachers respond to different kinds of children? Teachers typically act differently toward a child who comes into a classroom and is very responsive, speaks a certain kind of language, from the way they act toward a child who is less self-directed and seems to be more dependent.

Phyllis Levenstein: We don't have quantitative data, but mothers' anecdotes supported our hope that the children's school readiness and some of the program materials would serve as a bridge between the preschool home and the classroom the child entered. The books were all very high quality, books that could be read with as much interest by a first grader as listened to by a three-year-old. Teachers noticed children who brought them to school.

Allen Gottfried: In a program run by David Weikert, he found that the teachers were all responding differently to the children, and therefore the children had a different approach and adaptation to the whole school setting.

Phyllis Levenstein: I know we've been told over and over by teachers that they can distinguish a program child from a nonprogram child. I don't mean research subjects, but which children in the classroom have either participated or not participated in the program. So there must have been something that appealed to teachers, but we didn't investigate it systematically.

PARENT-CHILD PLAY: A PLAYFUL EVALUATION

Bettye M. Caldwell, Ph.D.
Discussant

Instead of sticking to my assigned topic, which is "The Significance of Parent-Child Interactions in Children's Development," I'd like to discuss play from the vantage point of a workaholic. I qualify for this job as well as anyone, because I am a true workaholic, or was until two weeks ago when I discovered tennis. If you're coming to a conference on play, discovering tennis certainly helps to orient your thinking as to what play is all about.

Developmental Aspects of Play

I want to start by thinking of play developmentally. We're all developmentalists, and we love to think developmentally—it's one of our favorite occupations and one of our favorite playtime activities. Some years ago, Brian Sutton-Smith wrote about certain basic characteristics of play. I want to think in terms of what you said play should be, Brian. As I recall, you said that children's play, first, should be spontaneous and self-generated, in effect intrinsically motivated. Second, it should not be too serious. Third, it should have no set rules; that is, it should be flexible. Fourth, particularly for young children, it should involve fantasy or the imagination to some extent.

In addition to Brian's characteristics, play is also apparently thought of by children in a couple of other ways. For children, play is something you don't have to do too well. They will say, "Oh, we're just playing." It's rather like being a housewife: "I'm *just* a housewife"; "I'm *just* playing." In other words, don't take me too seriously. Don't expect too much of me. I don't have to do it well because I'm playing. Also, of course, play is fun to children. When you ask them what they want to do, they say, "I want to go play." What's your favorite period in school? "Recess." What do you do in recess? "We play." It's hard to get beyond that point sometimes, but regardless of what they mean by it, most children say that play is fun.

Now then, what happens to play as we develop toward adulthood? Obviously, for adults play is never spontaneous. Adults play because they need exercise, or they play because it's the thing to do. The only playful thing that I'd ever done before taking up tennis two weeks ago — I'm available for a game immediately after this session, incidentally — was run. As all the runners in this group must know, running has to be the most sickeningly difficult task that anybody could ever do. It also has its own rituals—the right shoes, certain kinds of running shorts and tops. These are just some of the things that take all the fun out of it, if ever indeed there could have been any fun in it.

Another type of adult "play" that I'm familiar with is fishing. My husband is a fisherman. This requires, first of all, a $250 graphite rod with a $300 reel. Then you have to go up to northern Quebec in groups of six in a small plane. Each of you can bring home four salmon; that's your allotment from the Canadian government. That salmon costs you maybe $250 a pound. You don't have fun because you cast all the time, you only catch a fish about every hundredth cast, and half of those get away. So the play of adults is never spontaneous.

Second, it's deadly serious. Marriages are broken up over missed shots in doubles. Marriages are broken up when you trump your spouse's ace or refuse to bid when your spouse opens with two no trump because you think that's not a force. Adult play does more to destroy the family than many types of work do. Having a bridge-playing wife can be more destructive to family life than having a working wife.

Third, there is absolutely no flexibility in the way adults play. In tennis, I am pleased to find that you no longer have to play in whites. A number of years ago, I remember reading a quiz given to eight-year-old children who were taking tennis lessons. (You obviously have to start your lessons at eight. If you wait until your fifties, forget it.) I remember seeing the question on this quiz, Why is it important to play in white? All these rules: You had to play in white; you had to stand here to serve; you had to move in just a certain way; and so on. And as we play our little games, of course, we take our blood pressures and check our pulses. We make sure we've gotten sufficiently aerobic before we are ready to play. It's very inflexible, the way grown-ups play.

Brian's fourth characteristic of play was that it is nonliteral. The play of adults is very literal. There is no fantasy. The only fantasy I can think of might be that in a tennis game you say to yourself, "I'll kill him next time." That's a little bit of fantasy, but even so, at the time you say it you probably mean it, so there's no fantasy involved in it at all.

Turning to the points that I added to what Brian said about play, whereas children don't think you have to do it too well—you just get up and play—we adults have to play incredibly well. If we don't, then we aren't allowed to play. You don't go to the Whale River in Quebec unless you fly-fish and know exactly how to do it.

Finally, for children play is fun—what happens to that? I've decided that the way to tell the difference between grown-up play and children's play is, if it's fun, it's for children. If it's not fun, it's adult play—no matter how much it costs, of course.

These developmental trends, if you will, suggest to me that we have *professionalized* play, not just in our society but in our growing up. As we make a profession out of it, it loses its spontaneity, its flexibility.

The Paradox of Play

These differences between child and adult play lead to my second main point, which I've called the paradox of play. At this conference, we're talking about having adults, who don't know how to play, teach children, who know quite well, how to play. In other words, if we want to improve the play of children, we're using the wrong teachers. We're using people whose play is not at all playful, according to the criteria of Sutton-Smith and every child on the block.

What are the implications of this paradox for studies aimed at helping parents know how to play pleasurably, informatively, and educationally with their children? One major implication for the field of parent education is that the adults in charge need a bit of retooling in order to do a decent job. I have four suggestions for parents.

1. They should teach children to play divergently as well as convergently. A lot of adults, because they're so used to playing by rules, playing to kill, playing to do anything but have fun, are oriented only toward play in a convergent way. Most of the developmental tests we use, including intelligence tests, are convergent. On the Bayley, the Cattell, or the Griffiths, give the child eight or ten blocks and a tin cup, and only the child who puts the blocks in the cup gets credit. The child who piles them up, turns the cup upside down on top of them, and pushes it around gets no credit. The only allowable response is to put the blocks in the cup, which is a convergent type of activity.

Many parents get very upset (I speak from sad experience here) when they see their three-year-old son or daughter playing "the wrong way," as by pulling the little train over the couch and up the bookcase, and they say, "Why don't you run the train on the *tracks?*" Convergent play activity only. Play with it right. Have you ever said to one of your children, "Why don't you ever play right with your toys?" It's a clear statement that there is a type of play that is acceptable and that children have to conform to it. One of the educational implications of what happens to play developmentally, then, is that we need to encourage parents to value divergent play, in which doing a large number of things with an object or varying an activity would actually be the more desirable type of response.

2. Parents need to be aware that not all toys are for play as children define play. Puzzles are really not for play. You don't play a puzzle; you work a puzzle. (And you work tennis, really. I don't know why we say you play tennis.) You don't play with a lotto game, either. You learn words from lotto. But with toys that stimulate fantasy and sociodramatic play, you really can play. You can meet all four of Brian's criteria and the one I added, fun. This is very important for parents to realize.

Incidentally, the HOME scale, which Bob Bradley talked about, does include some toys that are just for play. We tried to define the toys in terms of function, and I admit that most of them are functions we think are instrumental in helping children develop, either cognitively or socially. But there are also teddy bears, cuddly toys just to hold, paints or clay that the child can play with, and so on.

3. A third suggestion for parents is that they realize some play will *play out* (I'm still playing on words, if you don't mind) without parental interaction. Parents don't seem to know that intuitively. Mine didn't: The only instruction I remember getting about play from my mother was, "Go outside and play," with the stress on the word *outside.* You understand, I grew up poor. I didn't get to play very much, and when I did, it was not to be done hanging around my mother or inside. My mother, I'm sure, never played anything with me until I learned games with rules, like dominoes. Certainly we never played dolls, and she never acted out dramatic roles with me. So I would say this is something that parents do indeed need to be taught in whatever type of parent education they receive: that children will get bored if there's not some social stimulation somewhere along the way to keep their play going.

4. Children like to play with other children as well as with adults. In the minds of most children (I always assume that I know what most children think), play is eminently social. It's something you do with other children. I'm always telling this to mothers who worry about having their children in childcare programs. The best thing group childcare has going for it is other children. Children love to be around other children, and they love to play with other children.

I should like to reiterate that the reason for these four suggestions was to remind us of a paradox inherent in adult supervision of children's play. Because of the developmental change in the nature of play, we are asking people who no longer play to teach children how to play. We are asking people for whom play is work and effort and maybe stress, a very inflexible procedure, to be the experts on how to be relaxed and spontaneous and flexible.

Means-End Relationships

The third point I want to make is a bit broader. In many of the papers presented here, especially early in the conference, play was treated sometimes as a means and sometimes as an end. Sometimes we use play as an independent variable, and sometimes we use it as a dependent variable. In Brian Sutton-Smith's early writings on this subject, he used to talk about it as a dependent variable. This is what we're interested in. This is something that we want to facilitate in children in and of itself. But in many of the studies cited here, play has been regarded as a means to an end. Does play increase a child's intelligence? Is play associated with more creativity? Does play with tools and objects in an unstructured way lead to better problem solving?

Looking at play as a means is again an adult's view of play. For the young child, play is an end in itself. I'm not saying that there aren't children who also very quickly develop means-end concerns in relation to play, but the reason babies like to play—I've already said I arrogate onto myself certain knowledge of what children are thinking—is that it's a great experience, and the play of preschoolers is often exactly that. It's fun to do it.

Sometimes, then, I think we have so overweighted our research toward play as a means to an end that we have lost the true spark or essence of what play means in the life of the young child. My point is simply that our research on play must not ignore play as an end while investigating play as a means to an end.

The Physical Environment

A lot of Ted Wachs' material has practical implications for the people who care for children. Politically, I grew up as a knee-jerk liberal and I will probably go out that way, and like Bob McCall, I've always thought the Law of Parsimony was fraudulently passed in the first place. We may need a Law of Flamboyance rather than a Law of Parsimony to help us put some of these things to meaningful use in terms of what we do with children. Jerriann Wilson's presentation yesterday was a beautiful example of applying principles in a real setting despite a shortage of research support. It's really a clinical teaching program that she has developed, and that's the way knowledge grows in any area.

Ted, I think that what you said about specificity is very interesting and very important. You mentioned seven things: availability of stimulus materials; variety of stimulus materials; responsivity of the physical environment; ambient background noise; overcrowding; regularity of scheduling; and physical restraints on exploration. These represent dimensions that can be used to design and assess the physical environment of a good childcare program, and they are dimensions that are under the control of people running the program, at least to some extent. For example, availability of stimulus materials is high in most programs. Variety of stimulus materials is reasonably high except that we're stereotyped. The doll corner is always here, and you always eat here, and you work there, and the sandbox is always over there. The same toys are always available. I used to recommend to teachers that they have three full sets, that they never let everything out at once. Every mother knows this, but it's amazing how seldom people do it in a childcare program. They put everything out, and the children habituate to the materials.

After a while they don't see them. This information could be used very constructively in helping people work with young children in groups.

Ambient background noise is very difficult to control when you have a lot of children, though architects can find ways to minimize it. Overcrowding is also hard to deal with. Regularity of scheduling, I think, is a big problem in some of our programs because it leads to monotony.

I think that if we simply were to take these dimensions and say, here are some aspects of the physical environment that don't correlate perfectly with how children do in a variety of things but do correlate to some extent, we'd be offering some handles that childcare workers could grab onto. They could say, even in this totally inadequate building in which I'm expected to operate a program, here is something that perhaps I can do, that I can control.

The key question is whether you can improve quality by slight readjustments of these aspects of the physical environment. There is tremendous stereotyping in the physical environments we create for young children. Here is an area where it might be better to be an adult. We have at least four or five styles of houses: ranch, colonial, Cape Cod, and modern. They really are not all alike. But virtually all early childhood programs look just alike. You could blindfold me in any state of the Union and I could find you the doll corner, the bathrooms, the puzzles, because they were the same way in the last center I visited. I know just where the tires are going to be on the playground, and the rope swings, and all those things that kids never play with but that architecture students think are great for livening up an environment. In many parts of the world, landscape and interior architects are much more creative about trying to design the physical space in ways that children will find useful and interesting. That's an area where we need a real renaissance in this country.

I want to endorse what you said, Ted, about the question of main effects, though I wasn't sure exactly what it had to do with play. I think it's most important in terms of the influence of all aspects of the environment on the development of children. I don't share, as I've already said, your cautiousness about being prescriptive. I think we can feel perfectly free to be reasonably prescriptive right now so long as we admit that we might be wrong; if we're wrong, we will change these things. However, I agree that we need more research that will help us match children—children who vary according to risk factor or come from certain kinds of home environments—to programs. We take children out of all kinds of different settings and put them in the same environment, and it really doesn't make sense to do that. I think we are ready to try some specificity along with some prescriptiveness.

Changes Over Time

My final point relates to Leila Beckwith's question about changes over time in adult play with children. I've already said there are changes in time within ontogeny in the way we play, but I think also there have been changes over time in the attitudes of parents toward play. I mentioned my own mother, who would have to be considered an excellent mother in anybody's book. For her, a child at play was a child out from under foot. Today, there is an orientation on the part of many parents to impose downward an adult concept of play. You've got to play with the toy just right; you use it the way it was meant to be used. This is related, I think, to the tremendous recent stress on cognitive development in children. Many parents, particularly middle-class parents, have been sold on what we have preached for the last twenty years. People have listened, and now we have baby gyms and ways to build super babies, and this is why our mothers are deadly serious about play. They play with their babies the same way they play tennis and bridge—and that's no way to play with a baby.

These patterns do change. In my own years as an adult professional, I have seen a swing from an extremely social and emotional emphasis to this cognitive stress. Furthermore, I remember that when the stress was on social and emotional development we used to say we really are also concerned about intellectual development, but nobody paid attention. Now we continually say that though we want to help children cognitively, we are just as concerned about their social and emotional development, and nobody is hearing that.

In considering the public information aspect of developmental research, we have to get across the fact that playful play is related to all the things that we want children to learn to do. The data from Leila's study and the others that she cited show that early playfulness in the relationship between parent and child is associated with secure attachment, which, in itself, is associated with creative use of play materials, enjoyment of peers, and so on. This is the kind of thing that we have to get into the public consciousness.

Allison Clarke-Stewart has reported that fathers are more playful with their children than mothers, which doesn't surprise me. Mothers work all the time with their children. (They work all the time without their children.) It's very nice that some children have a father figure who can play with them, but think of all those children growing up without fathers and all those mothers growing old, if you will, without the enjoyment of this beautiful, mutually pleasurable, reciprocal play with their babies and young children. I really feel that mutually enjoyable play between parent and child is one of the most important foundations for social development, as well as cognitive development. I also consider it one of life's most pleasurable experiences for both parent and child. I think those are very important points to stress.

As Leila said, the game is difficult to play with some infants, and this returns us to my point about the paradox of play. I just tried to make it sound as though it's always fun to play with a child. But it isn't fun to hold a baby in the air and be wet upon, if the game turns into that. It's not fun to play something that a child wants to do 130 times. Most adults play out after about ten times, but there are some children who want to go on and on. And there are other children who won't play. They look away, or they have a bland expression and won't smile when they're supposed to. We need to keep in mind that it is difficult to play with some infants.

But if we can help parents keep it light, this should help keep them from feeling bad if their child doesn't want to play or wants to play the same game forever and ever. Here again, we need to help parents learn about the paradox of play, the developmental paradox that children's play is sometimes different from our own. Sometimes we will both enjoy the game for the same length of time, and that's when you've really got it made. But sometimes the child won't enjoy it at all, and sometimes the child will enjoy it on and on when you are bored sick with it. You have to be aware that these things happen. Still, we can encourage parents in our parent education literature and contacts to see that much play with young children should have Brian's four characteristics. It ought to be spontaneous. It shouldn't all be bound by rules and patterns. It should be flexible. It should involve some fantasy. It should not be a deadly serious business and, most of all, it should be fun for both.

DISCUSSION

Jay Belsky: I agree that we have been pushing cognition and not emotion, except in one domain, which you started to talk about: daycare. Daycare is the only place where we want to think first and only about socioemotional development.

There is a paradox right there. We generally don't focus on it, but when it comes to that area, we almost fixate on it. We don't consider specificity at all. It's all main effect, when there is no main effect.

Bettye Caldwell: That's a good point. I think that we do that because of the history of daycare as having come from the field of social service and having been offered for children from families with social pathology. Those are the main professional roots of the field of daycare. It has only been during the last twenty years that daycare was ever conceptualized as the type of service that could offer cognitive benefits.

But that is changing. I met with some parents from Ned O'Gorman's storefront project in Harlem last week. Many of these parents are on drugs. They're the dispossessed; they don't have hope. Twenty years ago, no parent in such a group would have asked me some of the questions these parents asked. They've converted the program into a Montessori program, and these mothers were saying, Well now, when my kid leaves here and goes to public school, if he has this Montessori stuff, will he be able to read and so on? I mean, even a group of mothers most likely to be behind whatever kind of screen we have up between our communications and their receivers had gotten the cognitive message. So I do think there's been a change. Daycare operators want to make sure there's cognitive stimulation for the children, which is certainly right. But, I hope we don't allow daycare to be flip-flopped totally to the other side.

Judy Dunn: It's an interesting point. When Jerry Bruner came to England and set up a large-scale study of new schools, collaborating with preschool practitioners, he was very keen to collaborate rather than to instruct practitioners and do an intervention study. But he really had to think twice because the practitioners did *not* want to know about cognitive experience. What they saw as appropriate was the social and emotional factors. In the end everybody involved in the research had to think about the other side, which was a very salutary experience.

Bettye Caldwell: To some extent, Judy, that is the difference between the British tradition and the American tradition. All our original ideas and all our early childhood heroines were from Europe, Margaret and Rachael McMillan being the two main ones from Great Britain. They stressed good nutrition, fresh air, and a wholesome environment. Cognitive objectives were just barely considered. But when the nursery school movement hit America, it almost immediately began to change. The interest in social and emotional development was very strong, and it is still strong. I hope that it doesn't go out. But it has been amazing to see the extent to which cognitive concerns have become paramount in the minds of many parents and program designers.

This is one of the reasons so many parents want their young children in group childcare settings rather than family daycare or individual care. They are convinced that the children have more opportunities to learn, to get ready for school, because of all the play materials available in group childcare. Home daycare mothers do not have such variety of materials and don't have the training in that orientation.

Allen Gottfried: Do we have data on the differences between family daycare and center-based daycare?

Bettye Caldwell: There are quite a few studies that deal with the effects of family daycare. Rarely are they in comparison with group daycare. Cochran's study in Sweden, which is about ten years old now, showed that toddlers up to age three in family daycare had slight superiority in language development. They were also a little bolder. (This study ran counter to some others.) The New York City infant daycare study done by Mark Golden and others suggested that family daycare might be better for children up to about 18 to 24 months, but that certainly by age three, the children in group daycare had slight cognitive advantages.

Jay Belsky: That's what Sandra Scarr found in her Bermuda study. I think it's still fair to say, though, that the variability within the milieus is ultimately going to be much more important than the social address, center or family. In the right center at the wrong age you're better off than in the wrong family daycare arrangement at the right age.

Phyllis Levenstein: That's a very important point. Also, there is more instability in family daycare than in group daycare, unfortunately. I'm in favor of family daycare, but it changes. Daycare homes disappear.

Bettye Caldwell: Yes, there really are more risks in family daycare, though not many people will say that. It is an underground service in America. There is licensing or registration in most states, but many of the providers as well as the parents object to this. However, some sort of public regulation is essential. Until any service is out in the open, it's a risky service. Any service that we turn our children over to has to be monitored.

Jay Belsky: It's a supply-demand equation. One can increase the supply and breed competition, it gets visible, and then the consumer has a choice. The trick is to create circumstances that will increase the supply.

Bettye Caldwell: Right, it's very difficult.

Lorraine McCune: Going back to the more upbeat aspects of your presentation, I've noticed while running on beaches—an adult play activity—that you pass lots of parents and children of different ages, doing things along the beach. On one vacation I ran several days in a row, and I gradually developed a concept that kept going through my mind, child-as-toy, child-as-toy. You know, when you're running you sometimes say things like that to yourself.

Bettye Caldwell: It's the only thing that saves you, Lorraine.

Lorraine McCune: I started thinking about how many parents see the play potential of their child as a partner. But they also see the child as a kind of vehicle—a toy, you could almost say—that lets them engage in activities that otherwise are not sanctioned as appropriate for adults.

Bettye Caldwell: Yes, like building sandcastles.

Lorraine McCune: There are so many little things like that, but most of the time we don't call them to parents' attention because we don't know that they're good for the child. Sure they are, but the main thing is what fun they are for parents.

Bettye Caldwell: Right. That's a great point, another one to build on as an implication for parent education. These things are fun for you, too, and you're lucky if you have a child you can play with.

SUMMARY

THE RELATIONSHIPS OF PLAY MATERIALS AND PARENTAL INVOLVEMENT TO YOUNG CHILDREN'S DEVELOPMENT

Allen W. Gottfried, Ph.D.

I would like to present data from five contemporary longitudinal studies in North America dealing specifically with the contribution of play materials and parental involvement to cognitive development in infants and preschoolers (see Gottfried, 1984a). The data are based on the studies by Bradley and Caldwell, 1984; Gottfried and Gottfried, 1984; Barnard, Bee, and Hammond, 1984; Johnson, Breckenridge, and McGowan, 1984; and Siegel, 1984. These studies are selected because the researchers have chosen similar home and developmental assessments and ages at which to conduct assessments. This provides a unique opportunity to compare findings across studies as well as to conduct integrative analyses. Furthermore, there is considerable variation among the studies in sample demographics.

The Bradley and Caldwell study is based on a predominantly black lower-class population in Little Rock, Arkansas. The Gottfried and Gottfried study is being conducted in Southern California with a middle-class, predominantly white population. The population in the study by Barnard and colleagues is predominantly white and middle-class; all subjects are firstborns and reside in the Seattle, Washington, area. Johnson and colleagues conducted their study with a lower-class population of Mexican-Americans in Houston, Texas. Siegel's study was done in Ontario, Canada, with premature and full-term children from a white, blue-collar working population.

These studies have all used the infant version of the HOME scale developed by Caldwell and Bradley (1979). The HOME scale was designed to measure the socioemotional and cognitive supports in the home. It contains 45 items forming six subscales and yields a total score based on all items. Higher scores indicate a greater quality and quantity of home stimulation. The six subscales are:

1. Emotional and Verbal Responsivity of Mother
2. Avoidance of Restriction and Punishment (sometimes referred to as Acceptance of the Family)
3. Organization of the Physical and Temporal Environment
4. Provisions of Appropriate Play Materials
5. Maternal Involvement with the Child
6. Opportunities for Variety in Daily Stimulation

Play Materials and Maternal Involvement (subscales 4 and 5) are the focus of this Round Table and this paper. The Play Materials scale include such items as a child having toys that involve pulling or pushing, eye-hand coordination, fitting together, building, role-playing, music, or literature. It is important that the toys be readily available to the child. The Maternal Involvement scale includes such items as parent-structured play periods, provides toys that challenge a child to develop new skills, invests maturing toys with value via her attention, and encourages developmental advances.

It is an empirical fact that home environment correlates with developmental status (Gottfried, 1984a; Wachs & Gruen, 1982). Recently, psychologists have begun to pursue this issue in greater depth. In particular, they have (1) investigated the relationship between demographic factors and home environmental variables, and (2) tried to determine the specific home environmental variables that are most highly and pervasively correlated with young children's cognitive development.

One of the most consistent findings concerning the relationship between demographic factors and home environment involves the covariation of socioeconomic status (SES) and home environmental variables. All five found a significant positive correlation between SES and home environment. The relationship emerges as early as four months of age (Barnard et al., 1984; also see Beckwith & Cohen, 1984). Hence, children from higher SES families receive an intellectually advantageous home environment. This holds for white, black, and Hispanic children; for children within lower- and middle-class families; and for children born preterm and full-term.

The association of play materials and maternal involvement with SES across studies is presented in Table 5. The studies are arranged in order by population SES, with the lowest SES population at the left (Johnson et al.) and the highest (the equivalent populations of Barnard et al. and Gottfried and Gottfried) at the right. The mean scores for play materials and maternal involvement (along with the other HOME scales) at one year of age show that middle-class parents, in contrast to parents of lower SES, make available a greater amount of play materials and are more involved with their children, particularly in play oriented activities.

Table 5. Means on 1-Year HOME Scales Across Studies

1-Year HOME	Johnson, Breckenridge, & McGowan N = 367	Bradley & Caldwell N = 67	Siegel N = 170	Barnard, Bee, & Hammond N = 169	Gottfried & Gottfried N = 129
1. Responsivity	8.5	8.0	9.0	9.7	8.7
2. Restriction and punishment	5.4	5.3	6.2	5.4	6.4
3. Organization	4.5	4.9	5.1	4.8	5.2
4. Play materials	4.6	6.4	7.2	7.9	8.6
5. Involvement	3.4	3.3	3.8	5.0	4.0
6. Variety	2.6	3.0	3.1	3.4	3.4
Total	28.9	31.9	34.4	36.3	36.4

From: A.W. Gottfried, *Home Environment and Early Cognitive Development: Longitudinal Research,* Academic Press, 1984. Reprinted by permission of Academic Press.

Determining the home environmental variables that are most highly and pervasively correlated with young children's cognitive development is an issue of both theoretical and applied significance. Conceptually, it is important to ascertain the specific environmental factors that possibly regulate developmental status. Practically, having knowledge of the specific home environmental variables that correlate with developmental status is useful in the design of early childhood intervention programs.

To determine which environmental variables correlated most highly and pervasively with cognitive development from infancy through the preschool years, a meta-analysis was conducted. The purpose of the meta-analysis is not to alter the integrity of the findings from the individual studies but to provide a statistical integration of findings across studies. It serves to establish the magnitude of the relationships that can be anticipated collapsing across diverse populations.

The meta-analysis focused on the correlations between the one-year HOME and cognitive development measured at one, two, three, and three and one-half to five years of age. Bayley scales were used to assess development at ages one and two. At age one, the HOME subscales that correlated most highly with the Bayley scores were Maternal Responsivity, Play Materials, and Maternal Involvement. At age two, Play Materials, Maternal Involvement, and Variety correlated most highly with Bayley scores. At three years and three and one-half to five years, standard intelligence tests (usually the Stanford-Binet) were used to assess cognitive development. At both ages, Play Materials, Maternal Involvement, and Variety correlated most highly. A grand mean based on 17 size effects was computed to provide an overview of the relationships between home environment assessed at age one year and cognitive development between one and five years. The grand mean correlations ranged from .12 to .30, with the correlation of the greatest strength found with Play Materials, Maternal Involvement, and Variety.

In Table 6 are the correlations for each study contributing data on the relationship between the two-year HOME and preschool cognitive development (36-54 months). The average correlations ranged from .21 to .50. Maternal Responsivity, Play Materials, and Maternal Involvement yield the highest relationships.

Table 6. Correlations Between 2-Year HOME and Preschool Cognitive Development

2-Year HOME	Bradley & Caldwell[a] N = 77	Bradley & Caldwell[b] N = 77	Barnard, Bee, & Hammond[c] N = 133	Johnson, Breckenridge, & McGowan[d] N = 47	Mean *r*
1. Responsivity	.49*	.50*	.42*	.01	.38
2. Restriction and punishment	.41*	.28*	.56*	-.21	.29
3. Organization	.41*	.33*	.05	.04	.21
4. Play materials	.64*	.56*	.21*	.04	.37
5. Involvement	.55*	.55*	.37*	-.01	.38
6. Variety	.50*	.39*	.20*	-.01	.28
Total	.71*	.57	.60*	-.04	.50

[a]36-Month Stanford-Binet IQ
[b]54-Month Stanford-Binet IQ
[c]48-Month Stanford-Binet IQ
[d]36-Month Stanford-Binet IQ on control group
*Correlation reached statistical significance in study.

From: A.W. Gottfried, *Home Environment and Early Cognitive Development: Longitudinal Research,* Academic Press, 1984. Reprinted by permission of Academic Press.

Two major conclusions can be drawn from the meta-analyses of these longitudinal studies. First, the most potent and pervasive early home environment variables that correlate with cognitive development during infancy and the preschool years are Play Materials and Maternal (parental) Involvement. Second, with advancement in age, the relationship between Play Materials, Maternal Involvement, and cognitive development become increasingly strong.

References

Aber, J. L., & Cicchetti, D. 1984. The socio-emotional development of maltreated children: An empirical and theoretical analysis. In H. Fitzgerald, B. Lester & M. Yogman (Eds.), *Theory and Research in Behavioral Pediatrics.* New York: Plenum Press.

Adler, L. 1982. Quality of mother-child interaction in relation to play and cognitive development. Unpublished doctoral dissertation, Rutgers University.

Ainsworth, M. D. S. 1973. The development of infant-mother attachment. In B. M. Caldwell & H. N. Ricciuti (Eds.), *Review of Child Development Research* (Vol. 3). Chicago: University of Chicago Press.

Ainsworth, M. D. S., Blehar, M. C., Waters, E., & Wall, S. 1978. *Patterns of attachment: A psychological study of the strange situation.* Hillsdale, NJ: Erlbaum.

Ainsworth, M. D. S., & Wittig, B. A. 1969. Attachment and exploratory behavior of one-year olds in a strange situation. In B. M. Foss (Ed.), *Determinants of Infant Behavior* (Vol. 4). New York: Wiley.

Akbar, N. 1974. *Racial differences and the black child.* Paper presented at the American Psychological Association Headstart Regional Consultants Meeting, Atlanta, GA.

Amsterdam, B. K. 1972. Mirror self-image reactions before age two. *Developmental Psychology* 5:297-305.

Arnold, H. J. 1976. Effects of performance feedback and extrinsic reward upon high intrinsic motivation. *Organizational Behavior and Human Performance* 17:275-288.

Azarnoff, P., & Flegal, S. 1975. *A pediatric play program.* Springfield, IL: Charles C. Thomas.

Bakhtin, M. 1981. *The dialogic imagination.* Austin: University of Texas Press.

Barnard, K. E., Bee, H. L., & Hammond, M. A. 1984. Home environment and cognitive development in a healthy, low-risk sample: The Seattle study. In A. W. Gottfried (Ed.), *Home Environment and Early Cognitive Development: Longitudinal Research.* New York: Academic Press.

Barthes, R. 1972. *Mythologies.* New York: Hill & Wang. (Orig. 1957.)

Bateman, S. 1984. The digital palette: Fundamentals of computer graphics. *Compute,* May:20-32.

Bates, E. 1979. On the evolution and development of symbols. In E. Bates, L. Benvigni, I. Bretherton, L. Camaioni, & V. Volterra, (Eds.), *The Emergence of Symbols: Cognition and Communication in Infancy.* New York: Academic Press.

Bates, E., Benvigni, L., Bretherton, I., Camaioni, L., & Volterra, V. 1977. From gesture to the first word: On cognitive and social prerequisites. In M. Linus & L. Rosenblum (Eds.), *Interaction, Conversation, and the Development of Language.* New York: Wiley.

Bateson, G. 1955. A theory of play and fantasy. *American Psychiatric Association Research Reports* II:39-51. Reprinted 1972 in G. Bateson (Ed.), *Steps to an Ecology of Mind.* New York: Chandler.

Bateson, G. 1956. The message "This is play." In B. Schaffner (Ed.), *Group Processes: Transactions of the Second Conference.* New York: Josiah Macy, Jr. Foundation. Reprinted 1971 in R. E. Herron & B. Sutton-Smith (Eds.), *Child's Play.* New York: Wiley.

Bateson, G. 1972. *Steps to an ecology of mind.* New York: Chandler.

Baughman, S. S., & Clagett, P. D. (Eds.). 1983. Video games and human development: A research agenda for the '80s. Cambridge: Gutman Library, Harvard Graduate School of Education.

Beckwith, L., & Cohen, S. E. 1984. Home environment and cognitive competence in preterm children during the first five years. In A. W. Gottfried (Ed.), *Home Environment and Early Cognitive Development: Longitudinal Research.* New York: Academic Press.

Beckwith, L., Cohen, S. E., Kopp, C. B., Parmelee, A. H., & Marcy, T. 1976. Caregiver-infant interaction and early cognitive development in preterm infants. *Child Development* 47:579-587.

Belsky, J. 1980. Child maltreatment: An ecological integration. *American Psychologist* 35:320-335.

Berlyne, D. E. 1960. *Conflict, arousal, and curiosity.* New York: McGraw-Hill.

Berlyne, D. E. 1965. Curiosity and education. In J. D. Krumboltz (Ed.), *Learning and the Educational Process.* Chicago: Rand McNally.

Billingsley, A. 1968. *Black families in white America.* Englewood Cliffs, NJ: Prentice-Hall.

Blehar, M. C., Lieberman, A. F., & Ainsworth, M. D. S. 1977. Early face-to-face interaction and its relation to later infant-mother attachment. *Child Development* 48:182-194.

Bolig, R. 1984. Play in hospital settings. In T.P. Yawkey & A.D. Pellegrini (Eds.), *Child's Play: Developmental and Applied.* Hillsdale, NJ: Erlbaum.

Bowers, K. S. 1976. *Hypnosis for the seriously curious.* New York: Norton.

Bowlby, J. 1969. *Attachment and loss* (Vol. 1). New York: Basic Books.

Bradley, R., & Caldwell, B. 1984. The relation of infants' home environments to achievement test performance in first grade: A follow-up study. *Child Development* 55:803-809.

Bradley, R. H., & Caldwell, B. M. 1984. 174 children: A study of the relationship between home environment and cognitive development during the first 5 years. In A. W. Gottfried (Ed.), *Home Environment and Early Cognitive Development: Longitudinal Research.* New York: Academic Press.

Bretherton, I. 1984. Event representation in symbolic play: Reality and fantasy. In I. Bretherton (Ed.), *Symbolic Play: The Development of Social Understanding.* New York: Academic Press.

Bretherton, I. (Ed.), 1984. *Symbolic play: The development of social understanding.* New York: Academic Press.

Bronfenbrenner, U. 1968. Early deprivation: A cross-species analysis. In G. Newton & S. Levine (Eds.), *Early Experience and Behavior.* Springfield, IL: Charles C. Thomas.

Bronfenbrenner, U. 1974. *Is early intervention effective? A report on longitudinal evaluations of preschool programs* (Vol. 2). Washington, DC: U. S. DHEW, OHD 74-25.

Bronfenbrenner, U. 1977. Toward an experimental ecology of human development. *American Psychologist* 72:513-521.

Bruner, J. S. 1972. The nature and uses of immaturity. *American Psycologist* 27:687-708.

Bruner, J. S. 1973. Organization of early skilled action. *Child Development* 44:1-11.

Bruner, J. S. 1977. Early social interaction and language acquisition. In H. R. Schaffer (Ed.), *Studies in Mother-Infant Interaction.* London: Academic Press.

Bruner, J. S. 1982. The organization of action and the nature of the adult-infant transaction. In E. Z. Tronick (Ed.), *Social Interchange in Infancy: Affect, Cognition, and Communication.* Baltimore: University Park Press.

Bruner, J. S. 1984. Narrative and paradigmatic modes of thought. Paper presented at the annual meeting of the American Psychological Association, Toronto.

Bruner, J., & Sherwood, V. 1976. Peekaboo and the learning of role structures. In J. Bruner, A. Jolly & K. Sylva (Eds.), *Play: Its Role in Development and Evolution.* New York: Basic Books.

Caldwell, B. M., & Bradley, R. H. 1979. *Home observation for measurement of the environment.* Little Rock: University of Arkansas Press.

Caldwell, B., Elardo, P., & Elardo, R. 1972. The longitudinal observation and intervention study. Paper presented at the Southeastern Conference on Human Development, Williamsburg, VA.

Campbell, P. F., & Schwartz, S. S. 1984. Microcomputers in the preschool: Children, parents and teachers. In P. F. Campbell & G. G. Fein (Eds.), *Young Children and Microcomputers: Conceptualizing the Issues.* Reston, VA: Reston.

Cazden, C. B. 1970. The situation: A neglected source of social class differences in language use. *Journal of Social Issues* 26:35-60.

Chan, J. M. 1980. Preparation for procedures and surgery through play. *Paediatrician* 9:210-219.

Chance, P. 1979. *Learning through play.* Piscataway, NJ: Johnson & Johnson Baby Products Company.

Cicchetti, D., & Rizley, R. 1981. Developmental perspectives on the etiology, intergenerational transmission, and sequelae of child maltreatment. *New Directions for Child Development* 11:31-55.

Cicchetti, D., & Schneider-Rosen, K. In press. An organizational approach to childhood depression. In M. Rutter, C. Izard & P. Read (Eds.), *Depression in Children: Developmental Perspectives.* New York: Guilford.

Cicchetti, D., Taraldson, G., & Egeland, B. 1978. Perspectives in the treatment and understanding of child abuse. In A. Goldstein (Ed.), *Prescriptions for Child Mental Health and Education.* Elmsford, NY: Pergamon Press.

Clarke-Stewart, K. A. 1973. Interactions between mothers and their young children: Characteristics and consequences. *Monographs of the Society for Research in Child Development* 38, Nos. 6 and 7.

Cohn, J. F., & Tronick, E. Z. 1982. Communicative rules and the sequential structuring of infant behavior during normal and depressed interaction. In E. Z. Tronick (Ed.), *Social Interchange in Infancy: Affect, Cognition, and Communication.* Baltimore: University Park Press.

Coie, J. D., & Kupersmidt, J. B. 1983. A behavioral analysis of emerging social status in boys' groups. *Child Development* 54:1400-1416.

Corrigan, R. 1982. The control of animate and inanimate components in pretend play and language. *Child Development* 53:1343-1353.

Cowen, E. L., Pederson, A., Babigian, H., Isso, L. D., & Trost, M. A. 1973. Long-term follow-up of early detected vulnerable children. *Journal of Consulting and Clinical Psychology* 41:438-446.

Crawley, S. B., Rogers, P. P., Friedman, S., Iacobbo, M., Criticos, A., Richardson, L., & Thompson, M. A. 1978. Developmental changes in the structure of mother-infant play. *Developmental Psychology* 14:30-36.

Crawley, S. B., & Sherrod, K. B. 1984. Parent-infant play during the first year of life. *Infant Behavior and Development* 7:65-75.

Crittenden, P. M. In press. Relationships at risk. In J. Belsky & T. Nezworski (Eds.), *Clinical Implication of Attachment Theory*. New York: Plenum Press.

Crnic, K. A., Ragozin, A. S., Greenberg, M. T., Robinson, N. M., & Bashaw, R. B. 1983. Social interaction and developmental competence of preterm and full-term infants during the first year of life. *Child Development* 54:1199-1210.

Crocker, E. 1981. Play programs in pediatric settings. In E. Gellert (Ed.), *Psychological Aspects of Pediatric Care*. New York: Grune & Stratton.

Csikszentmihalyi, M. 1975. *Beyond boredom and anxiety*. San Francisco: Jossey-Bass.

Dale, N. 1983. Early pretend play within the family. Unpublished doctoral dissertation, University of Cambridge, Cambridge, England.

Deci, E. L. 1975. *Intrinsic motivation*. New York: Plenum Press.

Deci, E. L., & Ryan, R. M. 1980. The empirical exploration of intrinsic motivational processes. In L. Berkowitz (Ed.), *Advances in Experimental Social Psychology* (Vol. 13). New York: Academic Press.

Dodge, K. A. 1983. Behavioral antecedents of peer social status. *Child Development* 54:1386-1399.

DuBois, C. 1944. *Peoples of Alor*. Minneapolis: University of Minnesota Press.

Dunn, J. 1980. Playing in speech. In C. Ricks & L. Michaels (Eds.), *The State of the Language*. Berkeley: University of California Press.

Dunn, J., & Dale, N. 1984. "I a daddy": 2-year-old's collaboration in joint pretend with sibling and with mother. In I. Bretherton (Ed.), *Symbolic Play: The Development of Social Understanding*. New York: Academic Press.

Dunn, J., & Kendrick, C. 1982. In press. *Siblings: love, envy, and understanding*. Cambridge: Harvard University Press.

Dunn, J., & Wooding, C. 1977. Play in the home and its implications for learning. In B. Tizard & D. Harvey (Eds.), *Biology of Play*. Philadelphia: Lippincott.

Egeland, B., & Farber, E. A. 1984. Infant-mother attachment: Factors related to its development and changes over time. *Child Development* 55:753-771.

Egeland, B., & Sroufe, L. A. 1981a. Attachment and early maltreatment. *Child Development* 52:44-52.

Egeland, B., & Sroufe, L. A. 1981b. Developmental sequelae of maltreatment in infancy. *New Directions for Child Development* 11:77-92.

Egeland, B., Sroufe, L. A., & Erickson, M. 1983. The developmental consequence of different patterns of maltreatment. *Child Abuse and Neglect* 7:459-469.

Eiferman, R. R. 1971. Social play in childhood. In R. E. Herron & B. Sutton-Smith (Eds.), *Child's Play*. New York: Wiley.

Eiferman, R. R. 1972. It's child's play. In L. M. Shears & E. M. Bower (Eds.), *Games in Education and Development*. Springfield, IL: Charles C. Thomas.

Elder, J. L., & Pederson, D. R. 1978. Preschool children's use of objects in symbolic play. *Child Development* 49:500-504.

Ellis, M. J. 1984. Play, novelty, and stimulus seeking. In T. D. Yawkey & A. D. Pellegrini (Eds.), *Child's Play: Developmental and Applied*. Hillsdale, NJ: Erlbaum.

Epstein, G., Weitz, L., Roback, H., & McKee, E. 1975. Research in bereavement: A selection and critical review. *Comprehensive Psychiatry* 16:537-546.

Erikson, E. H. 1963. *Childhood and society*. New York: Norton.

Erikson, E. H. 1977. *Toys and reasons*. New York: Norton.

Fagen, R. 1981. *Animal play behavior*. New York: Oxford University Press.

Fein, G. 1975. A transformational analysis of pretending. *Developmental Psychology* 11:291-296.

Fein, G. G. 1979. In P. Chance, *Learning through Play*. Piscataway, NJ: Johnson & Johnson Baby Products Company.

Fein, G. G. 1981. Pretend play: An integrative review. *Child Development* 52:1095-1118.

Fein, G. G. 1984. The self-building potential of pretend play or "I got a fish, all by myself." In T. D. Yawkey & A. D. Pellegrini (Eds.), *Child's Play: Developmental and Applied.* Hillsdale, NJ: Erlbaum.

Fein, G. G. 1985. Pretend play: Creativity and consciousness. In D. Gorlitz & J. Wohlwill (Eds.), *Curiosity, Imagination, and Play: On the Development of Spontaneous Motivational and Cognitive Processes.* Hillsdale, NJ: Erlbaum.

Fein, G. G., & Robertson, A. R. 1975. Cognitive and social dimensions of pretending in two-year olds. ERIC No. ED 119806.

Fein, G., & Stork, L. 1981. Sociodramatic play in a socially integrated setting. *Journal of Applied Developmental Psychology* 2:267-279.

Feitelson, D. 1954. Patterns of early education in the Kurdish community. *Megamot* 5:95-109.

Feitelson, D. 1977. Cross-cultural studies of representational play. In B. Tizard & D. Harvey (Eds.), *Biology of Play.* Philadelphia: Lippincott.

Feitelson, D., & Ross, G. S. 1973. The neglected factor—play. *Human Development* 16:202-223.

Fenson, L. 1984. Developmental trends for action and speech in pretend play. In I. Bretherton (Ed.), *Symbolic Play: The Development of Social Understanding.* New York: Academic Press.

Fenson, L., Kagan, J., Kearsley, R. B., & Zelazo, P. R. 1976. The developmental progression of manipulative play in the first two years. *Child Development* 47:232-236.

Fenson, L., & Ramsay, D.S. 1980. Decentration and integration of play in the second year of life. *Child Development* 51:171-178.

Field, T. 1979. Games parents play with normal and high-risk infants. *Child Psychiatry and Human Development* 10:41-48.

Field, T. 1982. Affective displays of high-risk infants during early interactions. In T. Field & A. Fogel (Eds.), *Emotion and Early Interaction.* Hillsdale, NJ: Erlbaum.

Fischer, K. 1980. A theory of cognitive development: The control and construction of hierarchies of skills. *Psychological Review* 87:477-531.

Frankl, V. E. 1959. *Man's search for meaning.* New York: Pocket Books.

Friedrich, O. 1983. The computer moves in. *Time,* Jan.:14-24.

Frodi, A., & Lamb, M. 1980. Child abuser's responses to infant smiles and cries. *Child Development* 51:238-241.

Gaensbauer, T., Mrazek, D., & Harmon, R. 1980. Affective behavior patterns in abused and/or neglected infants. In N. Frude (Ed.), *The Understanding and Prevention of Child Abuse: Psychological Approaches.* London: Concord Press.

Gardner, G. G., & Olness, K. 1981. *Hypnosis and hypnotherapy with children.* New York: Grune & Stratton.

Garvey, C. 1977. *Play.* Cambridge: Harvard University Press.

Garvey, C., & Berndt, R. 1977. Organization of pretend play. *JSAS Catalogue of Selected Documents in Psychology* 7, Manuscript 1589.

Genishi, C. 1983. Role initiation in the discourse of Mexican-American children's play. Paper presented at the American Educational Research Association, Montreal.

Gibson, J. 1979. *The ecological approach to visual perception.* Boston: Houghton Mifflin.

Gilmore, J. B. 1966. The role of anxiety and cognitive factors in children's play behavior. *Child Development* 37:397-416.

Giovannoni, J., & Becerra, R. 1979. *Defining child abuse.* New York: Free Press.

Golden, D. B. 1983. Play therapy for hospitalized children. In C.E. Schaeffer & K. J. O'Connor (Eds.), *Handbook of Play Therapy.* New York: Wiley.

Golomb, C. 1979. Pretense play: A cognitive perspective. In N. Smith & M. Franklin (Eds.), *Symbolic Functioning in Childhood.* New York: Wiley.

Goodman, F. L., 1984. The computer as plaything. *Simulation and Games* 15:65-73.

Gottfried, A. W. (Ed.), 1984a. *Home environment and early cognitive development: Longitudinal research.* New York: Academic Press.

Gottfried, A. W. 1984b. Home environment and early cognitive development: Integration, meta-analyses, and conclusions. In A. W. Gottfried (Ed.), *Home Environment and Early Cognitive Development: Longitudinal Research.* New York: Academic Press.

Gottfried, A. W., & Gottfried, A. E. 1984. Home environment and cognitive development in young children of middle-socioeconomic-status families. In A. W. Gottfried (Ed.), *Home Environment and Early Cognitive Development: Longitudinal Research.* New York: Academic Press.

Greenfield, P. M. 1984. *Mind and media.* Cambridge: Harvard University Press.

Griffing, P. 1980. The relationship between socioeconomic status and sociodramatic play among black kindergarten children. *Genetic Psychology Monographs* 101:3-34.

Gustafson, G. E., Green, J. A., & West, M. J. 1979. The infant's changing role in mother-infant games: The growth of social skills. *Infant Behavior and Development* 2:301-308.

Guttentag, D. N. & Kettner, R. B. 1983. Closed circuit television: A unique tool. *Children's Health Care* 12:25-28.

Hannerz, U. 1969. *Soulside: Inquiries into ghetto culture and community.* New York: Columbia University Press.

Harkness, S., & Super, C. M. 1983. The cultural structuring of children's play in a rural African community. Presented at the annual meeting of the Association for the Anthropological Study of Play, Baton Rouge, Louisiana.

Harter, S. 1978. Effectance motivation reconsidered: Toward a developmental model. *Human Development* 21:34-64.

Henderson, B., & Moore, S. 1979. Measuring exploratory behavior in young children: A factor analytic study. *Developmental Psychology* 15:113-119.

Higgins, E. T. 1976. Social class differences in verbal communication accuracy. A question of "which question?". *Psychological Bulletin* 83:695-714.

Hodapp, R. M., Goldfield, E. C., & Boyatzis, C. J. 1984. The use and effectiveness of maternal scaffolding in mother-infant games. *Child Development* 55:772-781.

Hostadter, D. R. 1979. *Godel, Escher, Bach: An eternal golden braid.* New York: Basic Books.

Hughes, M. 1978. Sequential analysis of exploration and play. *International Journal of Behavioral Development* 1:83-97.

Hunt, J. McV. 1981. Experimental roots of intention, initiative, and trust. In H. I. Day (Ed.), *Advances in Intrinsic and Aesthetics.* New York: Plenum Press.

Hutt, C. 1970. Specific and diverse exploration. In H. Reese & L. Lipsett (Eds.), *Advances in Child Development and Behavior* (Vol. 5). New York: Academic Press.

Hutt, C. 1981. Toward a taxonomy and conceptual model of play. In H. I. Day (Ed.), *Advances in Intrinsic Motivation and Aesthetics.* New York: Plenum Press.

Huttenlocher, J., & Higgins, E.T. 1978. Issues in the study of symbolic development. In W. A. Collins (Ed.), *Minnesota Symposia on Child Psychology* (Vol. 11). Hillsdale, NJ: Erlbaum.

Jackowitz, E. R., & Watson, M. W. 1980. The development of object transformation in early pretend play. *Developmental Psychology* 16:543-549.

Jennings, K. D., Harmon, R. J., Morgan, G. A., Gaiter, J. L., & Yarrow, L. J. 1979. Exploratory play as an index of mastery motivation: Relationships to persistence, cognitive functioning, and environmental measures. *Developmental Psychology* 15:386-394.

John, R., Mednick, S., & Schulsinger, F. 1982. Teacher reports as a predictor of schizophrenia and borderline schizophrenia: A Bayesian decision analysis. *Journal of Abnormal Psychology* 91:399-413.

Johnson, D. L., Breckenridge, J. N., & McGowan, R. J. 1984. Home environment and early cognitive development in Mexican-American children. In A. W. Gottfried (Ed.), *Home Environment and Early Cognitive Development: Longitudinal Research*. New York: Academic Press.

Johnson, O. G. (Ed.), 1976. *Tests and measurements in child development, handbook*. II. San Francisco: Jossey-Bass.

Kagan, J. 1981. *The second year: The emergence of self awareness*. Cambridge: Harvard University Press.

Kagan, J., Kearsley, R. B., & Zelazo, P. R. 1978. *Infancy: Its place in human development*. Cambridge: Harvard University Press.

Kaye, K. 1982. Organism, apprentice, and person. In E.Z. Tronick (Ed.), *Social Interchange in Infancy: Affect, Cognition, and Communication*. Baltimore: University Park Press.

Kee, D. W. 1981. Implications of hand held electronic games and microcomputers for informal learning. Paper presented at the National Institute of Education Conference, Washington, DC.

Kee, D. W., Beauvais, C., & Whittaker, A. 1983. Motivational and learning aspects of a microelectric learning aid. Paper presented at the annual meeting of the American Psychological Association, Anaheim, CA.

Kee, D. W., & Worden, P. E. In press. Personal computers in language and reading research: Three vignettes. In B. A. Hutson (Ed.), *Advances in Reading/Language Research*. Greenwich, CT: JAI Press.

Kennedy, J. H., & Bakeman, R. 1982. The early mother-infant relationship and social competence with peers and adults at three years. *Journal of Child Psychology and Psychiatry* 23:185-190.

Kluckhohn, C. 1949. *Mirror for man.* New York: McGraw-Hill.

Kochman, T. 1972. *Rappin' and stylin' out: Communication in urban black America.* Chicago: University of Illinois Press.

Konner, M. 1975. Relations among infants and juveniles in comparative perspective. In M. Lewis & L. A. Rosenblum (Eds.), *Friendship and Peer Relations.* New York: Wiley.

Kreitler, S., Zigler, E., & Kreitler, H. 1975. The nature of curiosity in children. *Journal of School Psychology* 13:185-200.

Kubler-Ross, E. 1969. *On death and dying.* New York: Macmillan.

Labov, W. 1972. *Language in the inner city: Studies in the black English vernacular.* Philadelphia: University of Pennsylvania Press.

Lawler, R. W. 1982. Designing computer-based microworlds. *Byte* 7:138-160.

Lazar, I., & Darlington, R. 1982. Lasting effects of early education: A report from the consortium for longitudinal studies. *Monographs of the Society for Research in Child Development* 47, No. 195:2-3.

Leiderman, P. H., Leifer, A. D., Seashore, M. J., & Barnett, C. R. 1973. Mother-infant interaction: Effects of early deprivation, prior experience and sex of infant. In J. N. Nurnberger (Ed.), *Biological and Environmental Determinants of Early Behavior.* Baltimore: Williams & Wilkins.

Lepper, M. R. 1983. Extrinsic reward and intrinsic motivation: Implications for the classroom. In J. M. Levine & M. C. Wang (Eds.), *Teacher and Student Perceptions: Implications for Learning.* Hillsdale, NJ: Erlbaum.

Lepper, M. R., & Greene, D. 1979. *The hidden costs of reward.* Hillsdale, NJ: Erlbaum.

Lepper, M. R., Greene, D., & Nisbett, R. E. 1973. Undermining children's intrinsic interest with extrinsic rewards: A test of the "overjustification" hypothesis. *Journal of Personality and Social Psychology* 28:129-137.

Levenstein, P. 1976. Cognitive development through verbalized play: The mother-child home program. In J. S. Bruner, A. Jolly & K. Sylva (Eds.), *Play: Its Role in Development and Evolution.* New York: Basic Books.

Levenstein, P. 1977. The Mother-Child Home Program. In M. C. Day & R. K. Parker (Eds.), *The Preschool in Action,* 2nd ed. Boston: Allyn and Bacon.

Levenstein, P. 1980. Ethical considerations in home-based programs. In M. Bryce & J. C. Lloyd (Eds.), *Treating Families in the Home.* Springfield, IL: Charles C. Thomas.

Levenstein, P., & Sunley, R. 1968. Stimulation of verbal interaction between disadvantaged mothers and children. *American Journal of Orthopsychiatry* 38:116-121.

Levin, J. A., & Kareev, Y. 1980. Personal computers and education: The challenge to schools (Technical Report No. 98). LaJolla, CA: University of California, San Diego, Center for Human Information Processing.

Lewis, M., & Cherry, L. 1977. Social behavior and language acquisition. In M. Lewis & L. A. Rosenblum (Eds.), *Interaction, Conversation, and the Development of Language.* New York: Wiley.

Lewis, M., Feiring, C., McGuffog, C., & Jaskir, J. 1984. Predicting psycopathology in six-year-olds from early social relations. *Child Development* 55:123-136.

Lieberman, A. F. 1977. Preschoolers' competence with a peer: Relations with attachment and peer experiences. *Child Development* 48:1277-1287.

Lindsay, K. E. 1981. The value of music for hospitalized infants. *Children's Health Care* 9:104-107.

Loftus, G. R., & Loftus, E. F. 1983. *Mind at play.* New York: Basic Books.

Looff, D. H. 1971. *Appalachia's children.* Lexington: University Press of Kentucky.

Lowe, M. 1975. Trends in the development of representational play in infants from one to three years: An observational study. *Journal of Child Psychology and Psychiatry* 16:33-47.

MacPhee, D., Ramey, C., & Yates, K. 1984. The home environment and early mental development. In A. W. Gottfried (Ed.), *Home Environment and Early Cognitive Development: Longitudinal Research.* New York: Academic Press.

Madden, J., Levenstein, P., & Levenstein, S. 1976. Longitudinal IQ outcomes of the Mother-Child Home Program. *Child Development* 47:1015-1025.

Main, M. 1973. Exploration, play, and level of cognitive functioning as related to child-mother attachment. Unpublished doctoral dissertation, Johns Hopkins University, Baltimore, MD.

Malatesta, C. Z., & Haviland, J. M. 1982. Learning display rules: The socialization of emotion expression in infancy. *Child Development* 53:991-1003.

Malone, T. W. 1980. What makes things fun to learn? A study of intrinsically motivating computer games. Xerox, Palo Alto Research Center, Palo Alto, CA.

Malone, T. W., & Lepper, M. R. In press. Making learning fun: A taxonomy of intrinsic motivation for learning. In R. E. Snow & M. J. Farr (Eds.), *Aptitude, Learning, and Instruction. III. Cognitive and Affective Process Analyses.* Hillsdale, NJ: Erlbaum.

Mandler, M. 1983. Representation. In P. H. Mussen (Ed.), *Handbook of Child Psychology* (Vol. 3), 4th ed. New York: Wiley.

Maretzki, T., & Maretzki, H. 1963. Taira: An Okinawan village. In B. Whiting (Ed.), *Six Cultures: Studies of Child Rearing.* New York: Wiley.

Mason, E. A. 1965. The hospitalized child — his emotional needs. *New England Journal of Medicine* 272:406-414.

Matas, L., Arend, R. A., & Sroufe, L. A. 1978. Continuing of adaptation in the second year of life: The relationship between quality of attachment and later competence. *Child Development* 49:547-556.

Matthews, W. S. 1977. Modes of transformation in the initiation of fantasy play. *Developmental Psychology* 13:211-216.

McCain, G. C. 1982. Parent created recordings for hospitalized children. *Children's Health Care* 10:104-105.

McCall, R. B. 1974. Exploratory manipulation and play in the human infant. *Monographs of the Society for Research in Child Development* 39, No. 155:2.

McCall, R., & McGhee, P. 1977. The discrepancy hypothesis of attention and affect in infants. In I. Uzgiris & F. Weizman (Eds.), *The Structuring of Experience.* New York: Plenum Press.

McCune, L. In press. *Symbolic play: Development in the first three years.*

McCune-Nicolich, L. 1981. Toward symbolic functioning: Structure of early pretend games and potential parallels with language. *Child Development* 52:785-797.

McCune-Nicolich, L., & Bruskin, C. 1981. Combinatorial competency in play and language. In K. Rubin (Ed.), *The Play of Children: Current Theory and Research.* Basel, Switzerland: Karger.

McLoyd, V. C. 1980. Verbally expressed modes of transformation in the fantasy play of black preschool children. *Child Development* 51:1133-1139.

McLoyd, V. C. 1982. Social class differences in sociodramatic play. A critical review. *Developmental Review* 2:1-30.

McLoyd, V. C. 1983. Class, culture, and pretend play: A reply to Sutton-Smith and Smith. *Developmental Review* 3:11-17.

McLoyd, V. C. 1983. The effects of the structure of play objects on the pretend play of low-income preschool children. *Child Development* 54:626-635.

Mead, G. H. 1934. *Mind, self, and society.* Chicago: University of Chicago Press.

Melamed, B. G., & Siegel, L. J. 1975. Reduction of anxiety in children facing hospitalization and surgery by use of filmed modeling. *Journal of Consulting and Clinical Psychology* 43:511-521.

Mendel, G. 1965. Children's preferences for differing degrees of novelty. *Child Development* 36:453-465.

Mergen, B. 1980. Playgrounds and playground equipment, 1885-1925: Defining play in urban America. In H. B. Schwartzman (Ed.), *Play and Culture.* Cornwall, NY: Leisure Press.

Miller, P., & Garvey, C. 1984. Mother-baby role play: Its origins in social support. In I. Bretherton (Ed.), *Symbolic Play: The Development of Social Understanding.* New York: Academic Press.

Mitchell, E. 1984. Home video games: Children and parents learn to play and play to learn. Paper presented at the annual meeting of the American Educational Research Association, New Orleans, LA.

Mueller, C. W., & Parcel, T. L. 1981. Measures of socioeconomic status: Alternatives and recommendations. *Child Development* 52:13-30.

Nakamura, C., & Finck, D. 1980. Relative effectiveness of socially oriented and task oriented children and predictability of their behaviors. *Monographs of the Society for Research in Child Development, 45.*

National Center on Child Abuse and Neglect. 1981. *Study findings: National study of incidence and severity of child abuse and neglect.* Washington, DC: DHHS Publication No. (OHDS) 81-3125, September.

Nelson, K. 1981. Individual differences in language development. *Developmental Psychology* 17:170-187.

Nelson, K., & Gruendel, J. 1981. Generalized event representations: Basic building blocks of cognitive development. In A. Brown & M. Lamb (Eds.), *Advances in Developmental Psychology* (Vol. 1). Hillsdale, NJ: Erlbaum.

Nelson, K., & Seidman, S. 1984. Playing with scripts. In I. Bretherton (Ed.), *Symbolic Play: The Development of Social Understanding.* New York: Academic Press.

Neumann, E. A. 1971. *The elements of play.* New York: MSS Information Corporation.

Newson, J., & Newson, E. 1970. *Four years old in an urban community.* Harmondsworth, England: Pelican Books.

Newson, J., & Newson, E. 1978. *Seven years old in the home environment.* Harmondsworth, England: Pelican Books.

Nicolich, L. M. 1977. Beyond sensorimotor intelligence: Assessment of symbolic maturity through analysis of pretend play. *Merrill-Palmer Quarterly* 2:88-99.

Nihira, K., Meyers, E., & Mink, I. 1980. Home environment, family adjustment and development of mentally retarded children. *Applied Research in Mental Retardation* 1:5-24.

Nihira, K., Meyers, E., & Mink, I. 1983. Reciprocal relationship between home environment and development of TMR adolescents. *American Journal of Mental Deficiency* 88:139-149.

Nunnally, J. C., & Lemond, L. C. 1973. Exploratory behavior and human development. In H. Reese (Ed.), *Advances in Child Development and Behavior* (Vol. 8). New York: Academic Press.

Nuttin, J. R. 1973. Pleasure and reward in human motivation. In D. E. Berlyne & K. B. Madsen (Eds.), *Pleasure, Reward, Preferences.* New York: Academic Press.

O'Connell, B., & Bretherton, I. 1984. Toddler's play, alone and with mother. In I. Bretherton (Ed.), *Symbolic Play: The Development of Social Understanding.* New York: Academic Press.

O'Connell, B., & Gerard, A. In press. Scripts and scraps: The development of sequential understanding. *Developmental Psychology.*

O'Connell, S. R. 1984. Recreation therapy: Reducing the effects of isolation for the patient in a protected environment. Children's Health Care 12:118-121.

Opie, I., & Opie, P. 1959. *The lore and language of school children.* Oxford University Press.

Opie, I., & Opie, P., 1969. *Children's games in street and playground.* Oxford: Oxford University Press.

Papert, S. 1980. *Mindstorms.* New York: Basic Books.

Parke, R. 1978. Children's home environment: Social and cognitive affects. In L. Altman & J. Wohlwill (Eds.), *Children and the Environment.* New York: Plenum Press.

Parten, M. B. 1932. Social participation among preschool children. *Journal of Abnormal and Social Psychology* 27:243-269.

Pearson, J. E. R., Cataldo, M., Tureman, A., Bessman, C., & Rogers, M. C. 1980. Pediatric intensive care unit patients — effects of play intervention on behavior. *Critical Care Medicine* 8:64-67.

Pederson, D. R., Rook-Green, A., & Elder, J. L. 1981. The role of action in the development of pretend play in young children. *Developmental Psychology* 17:756-759.

Pediatric News, October 1982. Video games may ease chemotherapy sessions in young.

Peller, L. 1954. Libidinal phases, ego development, and play. *Psychoanalytic Study of the Child* 9:178-198.

Pettit, G. S., & Bates, J. E. 1984. Continuity of individual differences in the mother-infant relationship from six to thirteen months. *Child Development* 55:729-739.

Piaget, J. 1932. *The moral judgment of the child.* Glencoe: Free Press.

Piaget, J. 1952. *The origins of intelligence in children.* New York: International Universities Press.

Piaget, J. 1962. *Play, dreams, and imitation in childhood.* New York: Norton.

Piserchia, E. A., Bragg, C. F., & Alvarez, M. M. 1982. Play and play areas for hospitalized children. *Children's Health Care* 10:135-138.

Pittman, T. S., Boggiano, A. K., & Ruble, D. N. 1983. Intrinsic and extrinsic motivational orientations: Limiting conditions on the undermining and enhancing effects of reward on intrinsic motivation. In J. M. Levine & M. C. Wang (Eds.), *Teacher and Student Perceptions: Implications for Learning.* Hillsdale, NJ: Erlbaum.

Provence, S., & Lipton, R. 1962. *Infants in institutions.* New York: International Universities Press.

Pulaski, M.A. 1970. Play as a function of toy structure and fantasy predisposition. *Child Development* 41:531-537.

Rae, W. A. 1981. Hospitalized latency-age children: Implications for psychosocial care. *Children's Health Care* 9:59-63.

Revelle, G., Honey, M., Ansel, E., Schauble, L., & Levine, G. 1984. Sex differences in the use of computers. Paper presented at the annual meeting of the American Educational Research Association, New Orleans, LA.

Richter, P. 1984. This year's computer trends: Higher-priced models, cartoon characters. *Los Angeles Times,* June 10, V:2.

Roff, M., Sells, S. B., & Golden, M. M. 1972. *Social adjustment and personality development in children.* Minneapolis: University of Minnesota Press.

Rosen, C. E. 1974. The effects of sociodramatic play on problem-solving behavior among culturally disadvantaged preschool children. *Child Development* 45:920-927.

Ross, H. S., & Kay, D. A. 1980. The origins of social games. In K. Rubin (Ed.), *New Directions for Child Development*. San Francisco: Jossey-Bass.

Rubenstein, J. L. 1976. Concordance of visual and manipulative responsiveness to novel and familiar stimuli: A function of test procedures or of prior experience? *Child Development* 47:1197-1199.

Rubin, K. H. 1982. Non-social play in preschoolers: Necessarily evil? *Child Development* 53:651-657.

Rubin, K. H., & Clark, L. 1983. Preschool teachers' ratings of behavioral problems. *Journal of Abnormal Child Psychology* 11:273-285.

Rubin, K. H., Fein, G. G., & Vandenberg, B. 1983. Play. In P. H. Mussen (Ed.), *Handbook of Child Psychology* (Vol. 4), 4th ed. New York: Wiley.

Rubin, K. H., & Krasnor, R. In press. Social-cognitive and behavioral perspectives on problem solving. In M. Perlmutter (Ed.), *Minnesota Symposia on Child Psychology* (Vol. 18). Hillside, NJ: Erlbaum.

Rubin, K. H., & Maioni, T. L. 1975. Play preference and its relationship to egocentrism, popularity, and classification skills in preschoolers. *Merrill-Palmer Quarterly* 21:171-179.

Rubin, K. H., Maioni, T. L., & Hornung, M. 1976. Free play behaviors in middle- and lower-class preschoolers: Parten and Piaget revisited. *Child Development* 47:414-419.

Sameroff, A., & Chandler, M. 1975. Reproductive risk and the continuum of caretaking casualty. In F. Horowitz (Ed.), *Review of Child Development Research* (Vol. 4). Chicago: University of Chicago Press.

Scarlett, W. G., & Wolf, D. 1979. When it's only make-believe: The construction of a boundary between fantasy and reality. *New Directions for Child Development*. 3:29-40.

Schank, R., & Abelson, R. 1977. Scripts, plans and knowledge. In P. Johnson-Laird & P. Wason (Eds.), *Thinking: Readings in Cognitive Science*. New York: Cambridge University Press.

Schneider-Rosen, K., Braunwald, K. G., Carlson, V., & Cicchetti, D. In press. Current perspectives in attachment theory: Illustration from the study of maltreated infants. *Monographs of the Society for Research in Child Development*.

Schneider-Rosen, K., & Cicchetti, D. 1984. The relationship between affect and cognition in maltreated infants: Quality of attachment and the development of visual self-recognition. *Child Development* 55:648-658.

Schwartzman, H. B. 1976. Children's play: A sideways glance at make-believe. In D. F. Lancy & B. Allan Tindall (Eds.), *The Anthropological Study of Play: Problems and Prospects.* Cornwall, NY: Leisure Press.

Schwartzman, H. B. 1978. *Transformations: The anthropology of children's play.* New York: Plenum Press.

Schwartzman, H. B. 1984. Imaginative play: Deficit or difference? In T. D. Yawkey & A. D. Pellegrini (Eds.), *Child's Play: Developmental and Applied.* Hillsdale, NJ: Erlbaum.

Schwarz, J. C. 1972. Effects of peer familiarity on the behavior of preschoolers in a novel situation. *Journal of Personality and Social Psychology* 24:276-284.

Sears, R. R. 1947. Influence of methodological factors on doll play performance. *Child Development* 18:190-197.

Shore, C., O'Connell, B., & Bates, E. 1984. First sentences in language and symbolic play. *Developmental Psychology* 20:872-880.

Shotwell, J., Wolf, D., & Gardner, H. 1980. Styles of achievement in early symbol use. In M. Foster & S. Brandes (Eds.), *Symbol as Sense.* New York: Academic Press.

Siegel, L. S. 1984. Home environmental influences on cognitive development in preterm and full-term children during the first 5 years. In A. W. Gottfried (Ed.), *Home Environment and Early Cognitive Development: Longitudinal Research.* New York: Academic Press.

Silvern, S. B., Countermine, T. M., & Williamson, P. A. 1982. Young children's interaction with a microcomputer. Paper presented at the meeting of the American Educational Research Association, New York.

Silvern, S. B., Williamson, P. A., & Countermine, T. A. 1983. Video-game playing and aggression in young children. Paper presented at the meeting of the American Educational Research Association, Montreal.

Silvern, S. B., Williamson, P. A., & Countermine, T. A. In press. Video-game play and social behavior. In J. L. Frost & F. Rhodes (Eds.), *Play and Play Environments.* Washington, DC: Association for Childhood Education.

Singer, J. L. 1973. *The child's world of make-believe: Experimental studies of imaginative play.* New York: Academic Press.

Skipper, J. K., & Leonard, R. C. 1968. Children, stress, and hospitalization: A field experiment. *Journal of Health and Social Behavior* 9:275-287.

Smilansky, S. 1968. *The effects of sociodramatic play on disadvantaged preschool children.* New York: Wiley.

Smith, P. K. 1982. Does play matter? Functional and evolutionary aspects of animal and human play. *Behavioral and Brain Sciences* 5:139-184.

Smith, P. K. 1983. Differences or deficits? The significance of pretend and sociodramatic play. *Developmental Review* 3:6-10.

Smith, P. K., & Dodsworth, C. 1978. Social class differences in the fantasy play of preschool children. *Journal of Genetic Psychology* 133:183-190.

Spitz, R. A. 1972, Fundamental education. In M. W. Piers (Ed.), *Play and Development.* New York: Norton.

Sroufe, L. A. 1979. Socioemotional development. In J. Osofsky (Ed.), *Handbook of Infant Development.* New York: Wiley.

Sroufe, L. A. 1983. Infant-caregiver attachment and patterns of adaptation in preschool: The roots of maladaptation and competence. In M. Perlmutter (Ed.), *Minnesota Symposium in Child Psychology* (Vol. 16).

Sroufe, L. A., Fox, N. E., & Pancake, V. R. 1983. Attachment and dependency in developmental perspective. *Child Development* 54:1615-1627.

Sroufe, L. A., & Waters, E. 1977. Attachment as an organizational construct. *Child Development* 48:1184-1199.

Stern, D. N. 1974. The goal and structure of mother-infant play. *Journal of the American Academy of Child Psychiatry* 13:402-421.

Stern, V., Bragdon, N., & Gordon, A. 1976. *Cognitive aspects of young children's symbolic play.* Unpublished paper, Bank Street College of Education, New York.

Stern, W. 1924. *Psychology of early childhood.* New York: Holt.

Sutton-Smith, B. 1979. Play as a meta-performance. In B. Sutton-Smith (Ed.), *Play and Learning.* New York: Gardner Press.

Sutton-Smith, B. 1980. Children's play: Some sources of play theorizing. In K. Rubin (Ed.), *New Directions for Child Development.* San Francisco: Jossey-Bass.

Sutton-Smith, B. 1984. Recreation as folly's parody. *TAASP Newsletter* 10:4-13.

Sutton-Smith, B., 1985. *Toys as culture.* New York: Gardner Press.

Sutton-Smith, B., & Heath, S. B. 1981. Paradigms of pretense. *The Quarterly Newsletter of the Laboratory of Comparative Human Cognition* 3:41-45.

Sutton-Smith, B., & Sutton-Smith, S. 1974. *How to play with your children (and when not to)*. New York: Hawthorn/Dutton.

Thompson, R. A., & Lamb, M. E. 1983. Security of attachment and stranger sociability in infancy. *Developmental Psychology* 19:184-191.

Trilling, L. 1971. *Sincerity and authenticity*. Cambridge: Harvard University Press.

Tronick, E. Z. 1982. Affectivity and sharing. In E. Z. Tronick (Ed.), *Social Interchange in Infancy: Affect, Cognition, and Communication*. Baltimore: University Park Press.

Tronick, E. Z., Ricks, M., & Cohn, J. F. 1982. Maternal and infant affective exchange: Patterns of adaptation. In T. Field & A. Fogel (Eds.), *Emotion and Early Interaction*. Hillsdale, NJ: Erlbaum.

Turkle, S. 1984. *The second self: Computers and the human spirit*. New York: Simon and Schuster.

Udwin, O., & Shmukler, D. 1981. The influence of sociocultural, economic and home background factors on children's ability to engage in imaginative play. *Developmental Psychology* 17:66-72.

Ulvund, S. E. 1980. Cognition and motivation in early infancy: An interactionist approach. *Human Development* 23:17-32.

UNESCO. 1980. *The child and play. Theoretical approaches and teaching application*. Paris.

Valentine, C. W. 1937. A study of the beginnings and significance of play in infancy. II. *British Journal of Educational Psychology*. 8:285.

Vandenberg, B. 1978. Play and development from an ethological perspective. *American Psychologist* 33:724-738.

Vandenberg, B. 1980. Play, problem solving and creativity. In K. H. Rubin (Ed.), *New Directions for Child Development: Children's Play*. San Francisco: Jossey-Bass.

Vernon, D. T. A., Foley, J. M., Sipowicz, R. R., & Schulman, J. L. 1965. *The psychological responses of children to hospitalization and illness*. Springfield, IL: Charles C. Thomas.

Vidler, D. C. 1977. Curiosity. In S. Ball (Ed.), *Motivation in Education*. New York: Academic Press.

Vygotsky, L. S. 1966. Play and its role in the mental development of the child. *Voprosy psikhologii* 12:62-76.

Vygotsky, L. S. 1967. Play and its role in the mental development of the child. *Soviet Psychology* 5:6-18.

Wachs, T. 1976. Utilization of a Piagetian approach in the investigation of early experience effects: A research strategy and some illustrative data. *Merrill-Palmer Quarterly* 22:11-29.

Wachs, T. D. 1983. The use and abuse of environment in behavior genetics research. *Child Development* 54:396-408.

Wachs, T. D. 1984. *Mastery motivation as a potential individual differences parameter.* Paper presented at NICHD workshop on measurement and conceptualization of mastery motivation, Bethesda, MD.

Wachs, T. D. In press. Environment and the development of competence in children. *Monographs of the World Health Organization.*

Wachs, T. D., & Chan, A. 1985. *Physical and social environment correlates of three aspects of 12 month language functioning.* Paper presented at the biennial meeting of the Society for Research in Child Development, Toronto.

Wachs, T. D., & Gandour, M. 1983. Temperament, environment and 6 months cognitive intellectual development. *International Journal of Behavioral Development* 6:135-152.

Wachs, T. D., & Gruen, G. E. 1982. *Early experience and human development.* New York: Plenum Press.

Wachs, T., Uzgiris, I., & Hunt, J. 1971. Cognitive development in infants from different age levels and different environmental backgrounds: An explanatory investigation. *Merrill-Palmer Quarterly* 17:283-317.

Waedler, R. 1933. The psychoanalytic theory of play. *Psychoanalytic Quarterly* 2:208-224.

Waters, E., & Sroufe, L. A. 1983. Competence as a developmental construct. *Developmental Review* 3:79-97.

Watson, J. S. 1971. Cognitive-perceptual development in infancy: Setting for the seventies. *Merrill-Palmer Quarterly* 17:139-152.

Watson, M. W., & Fischer, K. W. 1977. A developmental sequence of agent use in late infancy. *Child Development* 48:828-836.

Watson, M. W., & Fischer, K. W. 1980. Development of social roles in elicited and spontaneous behavior during the preschool years. *Child Development* 18:483-494.

Watt, D. 1983. Computers and creativity. *Popular Computing,* Nov.: 75-78.

Watt, D. 1984. Musical microworlds. *Popular Computing,* Aug.:91-94.

Weisler, A., & McCall, R. 1976. Exploration and play. *American Psychologist* 31:492-508.

Werner, H., & Kaplan, B. 1963. *Symbol formation: An organismic-developmental approach to language and the expression of thought.* New York: Wiley.

White, B. 1975. *The first three years of life.* New York: Prentice-Hall.

White, B. 1978. *Experience and environment* (Vol. 2). Englewood Cliffs, NJ: Prentice-Hall.

White, B. L. 1980. *A parent's guide to the first three years.* Englewood Cliffs, NJ: Prentice-Hall.

White, R. W. 1959. Motivation reconsidered: The concept of competence. *Psychological Review* 66:297-333.

Williams, F., Coulombe, J., & Lievrouw, L. 1983. Children's attitudes toward small computers: A preliminary study. *Educational Communication Technology Journal* 31:3-7.

Williams, Y. B., & Powell, M. 1980. Documenting the value of supervised play in a pediatric ambulatory care clinic. *Journal of the Association for the Care of Children's Health* 9:15-22.

Wilson, J. M. 1979a. Child life. In P. J. Valletutti & F. Christoplos (Eds.), *Preventing Physical and Mental Disabilities - Multidisciplinary Approaches.* Baltimore: University Park Press.

Wilson, J. M. 1979b. School as part of a child life program. *Australasian Nurses Journal* 8:4-8.

Wohlwill, J. F. 1983. Physical and social environment as factors in development. In D. Magnusson, & V. Allen (Eds.), *Human Development: An Interactional Perspective.* New York: Academic Press.

Wohlwill, J. F. 1984. Relationships between exploration and play. In T. D. Yawkey & A. D. Pellegrini (Eds.), *Child's Play: Developmental and Applied.* Hillsdale, NJ: Erlbaum.

Wolf, D. 1982. Understanding others: A longitudinal case study of the concept of independent agency. In G. Forman (Ed.), *Action and Thought: From Sensorimotor Schemes to Symbol Use.* New York: Academic Press.

Wolf, D., & Grollman, S. 1982. Ways of playing: Individual differences in imaginative play. In K. Rubin & D. Pepler (Eds.), *The Play of Children: Current Theory and Research.* New York: Karger.

Wolfenstein, M. 1955. Fun morality: An analysis of recent American child-training literature. In M. Mead & M. Wolfenstein (Eds.), *Childhood in Contemporary Cultures.* Chicago: University of Chicago Press.

Wood, P. F., & Kee, D. W. In press. Effects of extrinsic reward on intrinsic interest and task performance in elementary school classrooms.

Worden, P. E., & Kee, D. W. 1984. Parent-child interaction and computer learning: An alphabet game for preschoolers. Paper presented at the annual meeting of the American Educational Research Association, New Orleans, LA.

Yarrow, L., Rubenstein, J., & Pederson, F. 1975. *Infant and environment.* Washington, DC: Hemisphere Publishing Corp.

Yarrow, L. J., Morgan, G. A., Jennings, K. D., Harmon, R. J., & Gaiter, J. 1982. Infants' persistence at tasks: Relationships to cognitive functioning and early experience. *Infant Behavior and Development* 5:131-141.

Zilliacus, K., & Enberg, S. 1980. Play therapy in the pediatric out-patient department. *Paediatrician* 9:224-230.